Bernhard Rammerstorfer
Taking the Stand: We Have More to Say

D1104226

I dedicate this book to the nine Holocaust survivors whose interviews it contains, as well as to their families, who were also victims of the Nazi regime.

Bernhard Rammerstorfer

Taking the Stand
We Have More to Say

100 Questions—900 Answers
Interviews with Holocaust Survivors and Victims of Nazi Tyranny

Published with the support of

Austrian Federal Ministry of Science and Research

BM.W_Fª

Austrian Federal Ministry for Education, the Arts and Culture

bm:uk

Salzburg Provincial Government	Upper Austrian Provincial Government	Carinthian Provincial Government

Arnold-Liebster Foundation

Library of Congress Control Number: 2013902596
ISBN: Hardcover   978-1-4797-9419-5
                 Softcover   978-1-4797-9418-8
                 eBook   978-1-4797-9420-1

Bernhard Rammerstorfer, Schickerstrasse 3, 4175 Herzogsdorf, Austria, Europe
E-mail: office@rammerstorfer.cc
Web sites: www.rammerstorfer.cc
            www.TakingTheStand.net
            www.unbrokenwill.com

Original title: Im Zeugenstand: Was wir noch sagen sollten, 100 Fragen—900 Antworten, Interviews mit Holocaust-Überlebenden und NS-Opfern
Published by Bernhard Rammerstorfer
Copyright © 2012 by Bernhard Rammerstorfer
Bernhard Rammerstorfer, Schickerstrasse 3, 4175 Herzogsdorf, Austria, Europe
E-mail: office@rammerstorfer.cc
Web sites: www.rammerstorfer.cc
            www.TakingTheStand.net
            www.unbrokenwill.com

Taking the Stand: We Have More to Say, 100 Questions—900 Answers, Interviews with Holocaust Survivors and Victims of Nazi Tyranny
Translated from the German by Neil Perkins / WORDWORKS

Cover design by Christian Höllinger

Printed in the United States of America by BookMasters, Inc
Ashland OH
January 2015

To order additional copies of this book, contact:
Xlibris
1-888-795-4274
www.Xlibris.com
Orders@Xlibris.com
548865

Contents

Foreword

by Walter Manoschek

Those who witnessed the era of National Socialism[1] are dying out. For years, strenuous efforts have been undertaken to develop concepts for preserving the memory of the murderous Nazi regime once the last witness to this period of history has died. In particular, various Holocaust museums and memorial sites have used video interviews with victims of National Socialism in an effort to find ways of keeping the memory of that time alive.

This book also fits into the context of "preserving the memory." But Bernhard Rammerstorfer has chosen a different and novel approach. The 100 questions he asks the interviewees were selected from a catalog of 1,400 questions posed by schoolchildren and students from all over the world. The questions were collected and chosen by Rammerstorfer. It took several years just to complete the worldwide search for questions, which was supported by leading Holocaust institutions such as the *United States Holocaust Memorial Museum* in Washington, D.C., and *Yad Vashem*[2] in Jerusalem.

Like the questions, the nine interviewees are also from widely differing backgrounds: they are from Austria, the Czech Republic, France, Germany, and the United States. What they have in common is the fact that they were persecuted for reasons of ethnicity, politics/ideology, or religion during the era of National Socialism. This great diversity highlights the different ways in which persecution was experienced, while

---

[1] *National Socialism* is commonly known by the term *Nazism*.
[2] Memorial to the martyrs and heroes of the state of Israel during the Holocaust.

the "systematic" catalog of questions makes it possible to compare the various stories.

The catalog of questions compiled from questions posed by schoolchildren and students at over sixty schools and universities in thirty countries is representative of the knowledge of National Socialist[3] tyranny that young people all over the world seek to acquire. Here, young people ask questions that they probably never asked before, or to which they never received authentic answers before, and to which, in a few years' time, they will no longer receive any answers for biological reasons.

This book is anything but a superficial account; Bernhard Rammerstorfer meticulously checked the historical accuracy of the interviewees' statements, discussed the answers several times with those concerned, and made additions where necessary. As a result, the book has value as a scientific work. But it is by no means tedious to read; on the contrary, it is engrossing, not just because of the individual stories, but also because one is always aware in the back of one's mind that these questions were asked by young people from all over the world. In this respect, Bernhard Rammerstorfer has, with this innovative approach, succeeded in making another important contribution to the documentation of the National Socialist era for the time following the demise of the generation that lived through it.

Prof. Walter Manoschek is a political scientist at the Department of Government, University of Vienna, and a filmmaker. He has written numerous papers and articles about National Socialism and the Holocaust. He was one of the organizers of the exhibition "War of Annihilation: Crimes of the Wehrmacht 1941-1944." Among his most important publications on the subject are the following: Opfer der NS-Militärjustiz: Urteilspraxis—Strafvollzug—Entschädigungspolitik in Österreich *(ed., Vienna 2003, with others)*; The Discursive Construction of Memory: Reliving the Wehrmacht's War of Annihilation *(Basingstoke 2008);* Der Fall Rechnitz: Das Massaker an Juden im März 1945 *(ed., Vienna 2009);* If That's So, Then I'm a Murderer *(documentary, Vienna 2012).*

---

[3]   The term *National Socialist* is better known by its abbreviation *Nazi*.

Letter of Endorsement of the Austrian Federal Ministry for Education, the Arts and Culture

Recommendation of the book *Taking the Stand: We Have More to Say*

The Department of Political Education at the Federal Ministry for Education, Arts and Culture is pleased that, with the publication in 2012 of the book and DVD by Bernhard Rammerstorfer entitled *Taking the Stand: We Have More to Say*[4], a highly recommended resource has become available for use in educational institutions and schools for the purposes of raising awareness of, providing proof of, and vividly invoking the human suffering that the National Socialist state apparatus caused.

The strategy employed in the project is particularly noteworthy: questions were sent from educational institutions all over the world, and 100 of these were selected and put to nine people, also from different countries, who were victimized by the National Socialists' totalitarian system of rule for various reasons. Selected answers from the survivors are included on a DVD as an audiovisual document, together with accompanying educational material.

This approach means that the accounts and memories related by the witnesses of history in the interviews can be compared, and they also represent irrefutable testimony of the consequences of a policy of marginalization, segregation, dehumanization, and even murder of those

---

[4]   The German edition entitled *Im Zeugenstand: Was wir noch sagen solten* was released in 2012.

9

groups specifically identified by the National Socialists as a result of their obsession with race.

The Department of Political Education at the Federal Ministry for Education, the Arts and Culture wishes to express its sincere gratitude to Mr. Bernhard Rammerstorfer for the years he has spent accompanying the witness of history Leopold Engleitner, and for the commitment he showed that led to the publication of this book.

Vienna, February 29, 2012
Manfred Wirtitsch
On behalf of the Ministry
1014 Wien Minoritenplatz 5
T 01 531 20-0
F 01 531 20-3099
ministerium@bmukk.gv.at
www.bmukk.gv.at

Introduction

by Bernhard Rammerstorfer

Since 1999, I have visited over 170 schools, universities, concentration camp memorials, and Holocaust museums with Leopold Engleitner, from Austria, now the world's oldest active witness of history, to speak about his experiences of persecution and the era of National Socialism. We held talks in Europe and the United States in institutions such as the *United States Holocaust Memorial Museum* in Washington, D.C., and the universities *Columbia, Harvard,* and *Stanford.*

The enthusiastic reaction of the young people there showed me how precious personal encounters and dialogue between those persecuted under the Nazi regime and the young generation are—for both sides. The youngsters have the unique opportunity to discover firsthand what these witnesses of history went through, and they have the means to receive authentic answers to their questions. They can learn valuable lessons for their own lives from the suffering endured by the survivors, whose lives were characterized by inconceivable hardship, and from their wealth of experience. These young people find role models and will carry the legacy of the witnesses of history with them for the rest of their lives and be able to pass it on to future generations. They will become "witnesses to witnesses of history." For the survivors, these encounters provide unexpected moments of joy; the genuine interest shown by the young people gives them a new lease on life and renewed strength.

Realistically, the great age of these last surviving victims of Nazi tyranny means that face-to-face encounters of this kind will sadly soon be a thing of the past. It is for this reason that I decided to embark on this ambitious project to produce a book and a DVD, which aims to shed light on the following questions:

> What would today's young people like to know from the last surviving victims of the Holocaust and Nazism?
>
> What message would the victims like to pass on to young people?

Above all, the aim was to adopt an innovative approach to the subject of Nazi rule that would involve young people. My experiences at schools and universities have shown me that interviews are one of the best ways of presenting survivors' stories in an interesting, personal, and authentic manner. However, the number of interviews that deal with this topic is legion. I knew that it would be necessary to adopt a different approach. What is truly innovative about this book is that all the Holocaust survivors were asked the same questions. As a result, a point-for-point comparison of their answers is possible. Because the whole world was involved in this horrific war, people from all over the world should be given the chance to ask questions.

So in 2006 I started collecting questions for Holocaust survivors and victims of National Socialism posed by schoolchildren and students. I was supported in this task by Holocaust institutions and memorials such as the *United States Holocaust Memorial Museum* in Washington, D.C., the *Yad Vashem* memorial in Israel, *The South African Holocaust and Genocide Foundation*, the *Sydney Jewish Museum* in Australia, and the *Center for Jewish Studies Shanghai* in China.

The result, after years of research, was a list of 1,400 questions from 61 schools and universities in 30 countries on 6 continents, as well as from the *United States Holocaust Memorial Museum* in Washington, D.C. Together with the political scientist Walter Manoschek from the University of Vienna, who acted as my scientific adviser on the project, I selected 100 questions. This unique catalog represents the questions asked by the young people of the world. The questions are listed in detail on one of the following pages, together with the countries that participated.

The questions covered the following topics:

-   Childhood, teenage years, and family background
-   Details from the years of persecution
-   Differences in conditions that prevailed in the camps

Introduction

- The most frightening moment
- Survival strategies
- The role played by religion or an ideology
- Liberation, postwar life, and social reintegration
- Physical and mental scars
- Personal strategy for coming to terms with the past
- Memories of historically significant events
- Personal lessons and maxims
- Awareness-raising activities and personal legacy
- Current life and worldview
- Future plans
- Advice and a message for future generations

Just as the questions are of international origin, the interviewees also come from several different countries. They belong to a number of different groups of victims and were held in various camps or "corrective institutions." In addition, their persecution began at different stages of their lives: some were children, some had already reached adulthood. Those whose voices are heard here not only include witnesses of history who have devoted their lives to raising awareness of the Holocaust, but also people who have never told their stories in public before. They range from an average housewife and an unskilled laborer to a fashion designer, from those who have been relatively silent to active "Holocaust teachers" and to survivors who have already been widely featured in the media and whose life stories have even been the subject of Oscar-winning films. Readers are thus offered a broad cross section of former victims.

I am delighted that nine Holocaust survivors and victims of the Nazi regime agreed to take part: Josef Jakubowicz and Richard Rudolph, from Germany; Simone Liebster, from France; Ernst Blajs, Leopold Engleitner, Frieda Horvath, and Hermine Liska, from Austria; Adolf Burger, from the Czech Republic; and Renée Firestone, from the United States. They were persecuted for reasons of race, politics/ideology, or religion.

All in all, the interviewees were held in a total of 31 different concentration camps or other camps, 20 prisons, and 3 homes [reformatories]. The total time they spent in internment is 528 months: that is 44 years. The combined age of the 9 witnesses of history is 806, and over the course of those years, they have amassed an enormous wealth of experience.

Leopold Engleitner (born 1905) and Richard Rudolph (born 1911) have already passed their 100th birthdays. In addition, Richard Rudolph is one of the last surviving victims of "double persecution" under two German dictatorships and had to spend almost 19 years in imprisonment.

I owe the nine witnesses of history a very special debt of gratitude for telling me their moving stories in film interviews and conversations that went on for hours—and in some cases, for days—despite the fact that their traumatic experiences cause them great emotional distress and that old wounds were reopened. They "took the stand" to "testify" to historical events and to leave a legacy for future generations. Every single one of their answers was checked for historical accuracy and edited, and subsequently discussed and revised several times with the survivor in question.

Every one of these remarkable personalities has gained a place in my heart, and I have tremendous respect for them. For me, they set examples to be followed, and I am grateful that I was able to make their acquaintance.

The accompanying DVD contains not only a short film biography of each of the nine survivors, but also a selection of their most interesting answers lasting approximately ten to twenty minutes each. Also included is material for educational projects and exercises about the Holocaust and the films. This makes the DVD eminently suitable for use in schools.

The years spent accompanying Leopold Engleitner, and the activities we participated in during that time, have led to a very special friendship and have given me as a young person many valuable lessons for my own life. For this reason, I would like to make the following recommendation to every young person: "Try to spend as much time as you can with people of the older generation, listen closely to what they have to say, learn from their experiences, and find true friends!"

List of Countries

The 1,400 questions sent in during the course of the project came from the following 30 countries:

- Argentina
- Australia
- Austria
- Bosnia and Herzegovina
- Brazil
- Canada
- China
- Czech Republic
- Finland
- France
- Germany
- India
- Iran
- Israel
- Italy
- Japan
- Mexico
- Montenegro
- Namibia
- Paraguay
- Peru
- Romania
- Russian Federation
- Slovakia
- South Africa
- Spain
- Switzerland
- Thailand
- United Kingdom
- USA

List of Questions

A total of 1,400 questions for Holocaust survivors and victims of Nazi persecution were collected at 61 schools and universities in 30 countries on 6 continents, and at the *United States Holocaust Memorial Museum*. From these questions, the following 100 were selected:

1. **When were you born? What was your father like? What was your mother like?**
Hauptschule der Kreuzschwestern Linz, Austria, Europe

2. **What is your earliest childhood memory?**
Universität Linz, Austria, Europe

3. **What kind of childhood did you have?**
Hauptschule der Kreuzschwestern Linz, Austria, Europe

4. **How long did you go to school, and what schools did you attend?**
Behram-begova medresa u Tuzli, Bosnia and Herzegovina, Europe

5. **What was your adolescence like? What trade did you learn, and what did you do for a living?**
Harvard University, Massachusetts, USA, North America

6. **What can you tell us about your family?**
Universität Salzburg, Austria, Europe

7. **Did you use the Nazi greeting "Heil Hitler!" and/or the Nazi salute?**
Sir-Karl-Popper-Schule am Wiedner Gymnasium, Austria, Europe

8. **Why were you persecuted by the National Socialists?**
The American School Foundations of Guadalajara, A.C., Mexico, North America

9. **When were you arrested?**
Namibian College of Open Learning (NAMCOL), Namibia, Africa

10. **Why were you imprisoned?**
Scuola Secondaria di Primo Grado "Carlo Viali," Italy, Europe

11. What exactly happened when you were arrested?
Palmetto High School, Florida, USA, North America

12. Did people know right from the start what was happening in the camps? Before you were taken away, did you know what would happen to you?
Deutsche Schule London, United Kingdom, Europe

13. How many different camps were you in? How many years did you spend in each camp?
Manchester Middle School, Virginia, USA, North America
Instituto Superior de Educación "Dr. Raul Peña," Paraguay, South America

14. Were you the only member of your family in the concentration camp, or were family members or friends there as well? If so, did you have any contact with them?
Gymnázium UDT Poprad, Slovakia, Europe

15. What were the first things that happened immediately following your arrival at the concentration camp?
German International School Sydney, New South Wales, Australia

16. Why did they shave the heads of the prisoners?
Instituto de Enseñanza Secundaria Juan del Enzina, Spain, Europe

17. What prisoner category were you put in?
Städtisches Gymnasium Steinheim, Germany, Europe

18. Can you describe the daily routine in the concentration camp?
Sekundarschule Hungerbühl, Switzerland, Europe

19. What was the worst thing about the daily routine?
Fenton High School, Illinois, USA, North America

20. Did everyday life lead more to solidarity, or did the prisoners try to cope on their own?
Deutsche Schule Shanghai, China, Asia

21. **Was there anything that helped you take your mind off the horror of daily life for a while (such as music)? What gave you strength?**
Deutsche Schule Shanghai, China, Asia

22. **What were living conditions like in the barracks (prisoner allocation, food supplies, hygiene, clothing, etc.)?**
Collège Rabelais de Meudon, France, Europe

23. **What jobs did you have to do? How many hours a day did you have to work?**
Deutsche Botschaftsschule Tehran, Iran, Asia
Gymnázium UDT Poprad, Slovakia, Europe

24. **What effect did the slogan "Work liberates" have on you?**
Gymnázium UDT Poprad, Slovakia, Europe

25. **What were the guards like in the camp?**
Gymnázium UDT Poprad, Slovakia, Europe

26. **Was there any contact between the prisoners and the local population?**
Deutsche Schule London, United Kingdom, Europe

27. **Were you aware of how the war was proceeding in the outside world?**
Wildwood School, California, USA, North America

28. **In the concentration camp, were you allowed to receive letters, food parcels, etc.?**
Hauptschule der Kreuzschwestern Linz, Austria, Europe

29. **What forms of torture did you suffer?**
Escuela Italiana de Mar del Plata, Argentina, South America

30. **What was the most frightening moment for you?**
Yeshiva High School Jerusalem, Israel, Asia
Cedar House School, South Africa, Africa
Hiroshima Municipal Eba Junior High School, Japan, Asia
Notre Dame Seishin Junior High School, Japan, Asia
Hobart High School, Indiana, USA, North America

31. Were there any entertaining or lighthearted incidents that enabled you to forget all the suffering for a moment? Can you describe them?
Deutsche Schule Shanghai, China, Asia

32. What were your day-to-day thoughts while you were in the concentration camp?
Moorpark College, California, USA, North America
Hiroshima Municipal Asakita Junior High School, Japan, Asia

33. Was it possible for children to be born in a concentration camp? If so, what happened to these babies?
Hauptschule der Kreuzschwestern Linz, Austria, Europe

34. Was it possible to make friends with prisoners?
Střední odborná škola waldorfská v Ostravě, Czech Republic, Europe

35. Who was your best friend during this dreadful time, and how did he or she help you?
Erundu Senior Secondary School, Namibia, Africa

36. What did you do to relieve the suffering of other inmates?
German International School Sydney, New South Wales, Australia

37. Were there particular hierarchies among the inmates?
German International School Sydney, New South Wales, Australia

38. Were there any differences in the way the various groups of prisoners (religious, political groups) were treated?
Deutschsprachige Schule Bangkok, Thailand, Asia

39. What diseases and illnesses were prevalent in the concentration camp?
EDV-Hauptschule Pressbaum, Austria, Europe

40. Did you receive a physical injury?
Hauptschule der Kreuzschwestern Linz, Austria, Europe

41. How much did you weigh when you were in the concentration camp?
Hauptschule der Kreuzschwestern Linz, Austria, Europe

42. What did death mean to you?
Institución Educativa Francisco Bolognesi del A.H. Las Lomas, Peru, South America

43. What was the closest you came to death?
Woonona High School, New South Wales, Australia

44. Did you ever build a kind of "wall" to shield yourself from the terrible things that were being done so that the death of a fellow prisoner no longer affected you?
Deutsche Schule Shanghai, China, Asia

45. What happened to the dead bodies in the concentration camp?
Escuela Italiana de Mar del Plata, Argentina, South America

46. Was there ever a possibility for you to be released from the concentration camp?
Univerzitet u Tuzli, Bosnia and Herzegovina, Europe

47. Were there any escape attempts or opportunities to escape? Did you try to escape?
Gymnázium UDT Poprad, Slovakia, Europe
Institución Educativa Francisco Bolognesi del A.H. Las Lomas, Peru, South America

48. Were there any inmates in the concentration camp who dared to stage a revolt against the camp authorities?
Städtisches Gymnasium Steinheim, Germany, Europe

49. Did you think you would ever make it out alive?
West Bay High School, California, USA, North America
Gardens Commercial High School, South Africa, Africa

50. Were there any times when you gave up all hope? If so, why?
Pädagogische Hochschule Zentralschweiz Luzern, Switzerland, Europe
Stanford University, California, USA, North America

51. Did anyone commit suicide?
Stonefountain College, South Africa, Africa

52. During the Holocaust, did you ever consider committing suicide out of sheer despair?
Deutsche Schule New Delhi, India, Asia

53. What thoughts, ideas, hopes, wishes, or religious convictions did you cling to?
Deutschsprachige Schule Bangkok, Thailand, Asia
Hiroshima Municipal Ushita Junior High School, Japan, Asia

54. Did you lose your faith in God while you were in the camp?
Wildwood School, California, USA, North America

55. What role did your religion play in how you felt about what was going on? Why?
Thomas Jefferson High School, Virginia, USA, North America

56. Did you pray during your internment?
Städtisches Gymnasium Steinheim, Germany, Europe

57. Did you ever consider changing your religion (or ideology)? Why?
Instituto Superior de Educación "Dr. Raul Peña," Paraguay, South America

58. What was the date of your liberation from the camp?
Instituto Superior de Educación "Dr. Raul Peña," Paraguay, South America

59. How were you liberated from the camp, or how did you manage to get out of it?
Städtisches Gymnasium Steinheim, Germany, Europe
United States Holocaust Memorial Museum, Washington, D.C., USA, North America

60. How were you treated by the people who liberated you?
Deutsche Schule London, United Kingdom, Europe

61. What was the first thing you did after you were liberated?
Deutsche Schule Moskau, Russian Federation, Europe

62. Did you have any problems when you returned home? How did people in your home environment react to you?
Gymnázium UDT Poprad, Slovakia, Europe

63. Were you able to rejoin your family?
Escuela Secundaria Básica Numero 33 de Mar del Plata, Argentina, South America

64. Did you have any acquaintances, friends, or relatives in the camps? Did they survive their internment?
Städtisches Gymnasium Steinheim, Germany, Europe

65. What happened to your possessions?
Instituto Superior de Educación "Dr. Raul Peña," Paraguay, South America

66. To what extent have you received compensation for your internment?
German International School Sydney, New South Wales, Australia

67. How did you set about rebuilding your life?
Escola Alemã Corcovado—Deutsche Schule Rio de Janeiro, Brazil, South America

68. How long did it take you to return to a "normal" life after the Holocaust?
Manchester Middle School, Virginia, USA, North America

69. What was your life like after the war?
Escola Alemã Corcovado—Deutsche Schule Rio de Janeiro, Brazil, South America

70. What is your life like today? Do you still often think back to those days?
Osnovna škola "Bratstvo—jedinstvo" Skarepača, Montenegro, Europe
Pädagogische Hochschule Zentralschweiz Luzern, Switzerland, Europe

71. What physical and mental scars do you carry from that time?
Woonona High School, New South Wales, Australia

72. Did you have any moral support to help your emotional and social recovery?
Instituto Superior de Educación "Dr. Raul Peña," Paraguay, South America

73. Has your view of the world changed since that time?
Deutsche Schule Shanghai, China, Asia

74. Can you think of anything positive that you have gained from your experiences?
Manchester Middle School, Virginia, USA, North America

75. Have you ever been back to visit the concentration camp you were held in, and if so, what were your feelings?
Waldorfschule Klagenfurt, Austria, Europe

76. Are you still in touch with your fellow internees from the concentration camps?
Deutsche Schule New Delhi, India, Asia

77. What did you tell your family about your internment in the concentration camp? How did your relatives react to what you told them?
Hauptschule der Kreuzschwestern Linz, Austria, Europe

78. Do you find it difficult to talk about those days?
Deutsche Schule London, United Kingdom, Europe

79. Which moment from those days has remained most firmly etched in your memory?
Thomas Jefferson High School, Virginia, USA, North America

80. Did you ever see or meet Hitler?
Hauptschule der Kreuzschwestern Linz, Austria, Europe

81. What was your opinion of Hitler in those days, and what is your opinion of him now?

Hauptschule der Kreuzschwestern Linz, Austria, Europe

82. Hypothetically, if Adolf Hitler were still alive and you could have five minutes alone with him, what would you say or do?

Palmetto High School, Florida, USA, North America

83. After the war, did you ever meet any of the people who had tormented you?

Harvard University, Massachusetts, USA, North America

84. What do you think of the punishments the Nazis received after the war, in the Nuremberg trials, for example?

Tampereen Rudolf Steiner-koulu, Finland, Europe

85. Have you forgiven your persecutors?

Manchester Middle School, Virginia, USA, North America
Cedar House School, South Africa, Africa
Columbia University, New York, USA, North America
Chilliwack Senior Secondary School, Canada, North America

86. What is your opinion of neo-Nazis?

Waldorfschule Klagenfurt, Austria, Europe

87. What do you do to explain to people what exactly happened in the Holocaust?

Rustenburg High School for Girls, South Africa, Africa

88. From today's perspective, how can you explain that "normal people" were capable of such atrocities?

Deutschsprachige Schule Bangkok, Thailand, Asia

89. What exactly do you feel when you hear that there are still people who claim that the Holocaust never took place?

Internationale Deutsche Schule Paris, France, Europe
Georgetown University, Washington, D.C., USA, North America

90. What consequences did the proclamation of the "Nuremberg Laws" on September 15, 1935, have for you?
Harvard University, Massachusetts, USA, North America

91. What are your personal memories of the "Night of Broken Glass" on November 9/10, 1938?
Sir-Karl-Popper-Schule am Wiedner Gymnasium, Austria, Europe

92. What are your personal memories of the beginning of the war in 1939?
Deutsche Schule London, United Kingdom, Europe

93. Did you hear that the National Socialists had decided to implement the "final solution to the Jewish question"—the systematic extermination of Jews in Europe—at the Wannsee Conference on January 20, 1942? If so, when and how?
Sir-Karl-Popper-Schule am Wiedner Gymnasium, Austria, Europe

94. When you heard that World War II was over, what feelings did you have?
Qiqihar University, China, Asia
Liceul Teoretic "Adam Müller Guttenbrunn" Arad, Romania, Europe

95. Do you think that humankind has learned something from the Holocaust?
Deutsche Schule Shanghai, China, Asia

96. Should the atrocities be forgotten and no longer talked about, as some people wish?
Bundesoberstufenrealgymnasium Bad Radkersburg, Austria, Europe

97. What plans do you still have for the future?
EDV-Hauptschule Pressbaum, Austria, Europe

98. How would you like to be remembered?
Sir-Karl-Popper-Schule am Wiedner Gymnasium, Austria, Europe

99. What else would you like to say to us? Which question was not asked?
Universität Wien, Austria, Europe

100. After all you have been through, what advice can you give us young people?
Erundu Senior Secondary School, Namibia, Africa

Ernst Blajs:
"All I Did Was Bring Food"

Ernst Blajs, born January 3, 1928
Grounds for persecution: Political prisoner (Carinthian Slovene)
Length of imprisonment: 1 year, 6 months
Country: Austria

1. Ernst Blajs, 1941　　　　　*2. Ernst Blajs, 2008*

Ernst Blajs was born on January 3, 1928, in Bad Eisenkappel, Austria. As a Carinthian Slovene, he came into contact with Tito's partisans. His stepmother instructed him to take food regularly to the partisans in the mountain woods. On October 13, 1943, at the age of fifteen, he was arrested and held in the Gestapo prison in Klagenfurt until November 8, 1943. Following this, he and his brother Franz Blajs were sent to the Moringen *Jugendschutzlager* (youth protection camp) for young male prisoners. This camp was later renamed a juvenile concentration camp. Every day, he had to work underground (to a depth of around three thousand feet) at the munitions factory in Volpriehausen. Toward the end of the war, he was sent on a death march before being liberated on April 11, 1945.

For a short time, he worked on a farm and was placed in a collection camp. On August 27, 1945, he was able to return home. After the war, he worked first on his parents' farm, then in forestry and as a clog maker. He retired in 1987. Ernst Blajs lives in Austria.

The interviews took place on October 27, 2008; January 12, 2009; August 12, 2011; and August 25, 2011.

1. When were you born? What was your father like? What was your mother like?

BLAJS: I was born on January 3, 1928, at Leppen 15 in Bad Eisenkappel in Carinthia [Austria]. My father Franz Blajs was a good man. I never knew my mother. Her name was Albine Blajs, and she died when I was only thirteen months old. She committed suicide by poisoning herself. She had married at sixteen when our father was twenty-three. We were three boys: my brother Franz and our half-brother Stanislav. Two sisters died in infancy, a few weeks after they were born, and the third one, a half-sister, was about three years old when she died. My father died during World War II in Latvia in 1941.

2. What is your earliest childhood memory?

BLAJS: My brother Franz, who was thirteen months older than me, and I stripping a tree on the way home from school. The tree was right by the road. We were talking in front of the tree and stripped off the bark while we talked. Our father was strict about things like that and punished us for it afterward. I was about eight years old at the time.

3. What kind of childhood did you have?

BLAJS: The housekeeper was the first person who was chiefly responsible for my upbringing. After my mother's death, my godmother [Katharina Kogoj] looked after me for a year, then gave me back. I was two when I came home again, and then it was my aunt [Maria Blajs] who took charge of raising me. We—by which I mean me, my brother, and a cousin—had to lie on three benches in the living room for two or three hours after our midday meal, especially in winter. Whenever a stranger came to the house, we weren't even allowed to move our heads and look at him. If you did, it was enough to earn you a punishment.

The toilet was outside. If we needed to use it, our uncle [Johann Blajs] often came to check that we really were on it. You could see through the side of the toilet whether we really needed to go or not. We hardly ever asked to go out without a reason, but they were so strict. They thought we only wanted to go out to get some fresh air.

We had to eat what we were given, no matter if it was too little or too much. If it was too little, we never got a second helping. That was your portion and you had to eat it up. Even if it was not enough, you would not get a second helping.

In 1933, my father remarried. Our stepmother, Amalia Blajs, was kind to us, at least as long as she had no children of her own. But once she had her own children, she did not treat us as well as she treated them. We were somewhat neglected.

Our upbringing as children meant that later on the camp didn't seem as bad to us as it did to others.

4. How long did you go to school, and what schools did you attend?
BLAJS: Only primary school; and I didn't even finish that. In 1941, when I was thirteen, I had to leave school because there was no one to do the work on the farm. My brother and I had to take on a lot more work. Our father died in the war in Latvia in 1941.

3. *Left to right: Franz, Amalia, Stanislav, and Ernst Blajs, 1941*

Our uncle Josef Blajs was drafted. He was an invalid. He was only in the army for about three weeks, and then they sent him home again. That was the end of my schooling, and I had no further education afterward.

5. What was your adolescence like? What trade did you learn, and what did you do for a living?

BLAJS: I never learned a trade. I always worked on the farm. I did get a place as an apprentice salesman at a general store in Eisenkappel where I could have started work in 1944, but the war prevented that. When my father went to war, I left school and worked on the farm until my arrest. It was all work, work, and more work. Sunday was a day off, but even then, we had to feed the animals.

6. What can you tell us about your family?

BLAJS: My wife, Maria, née Verdel, was from Slovenia. We met on the farm where we were both working and married on June 20, 1955. The children came one after the other, eight in all. One son was killed in an accident at work. First came a son, then a daughter, Caroline, then Konrad, then the boy who was killed—Andreas—next came Maria, then Ernst, Toni, and Brigitte. The first boy's name was Josef. We had eight children in twenty years. Now I have sixteen grandchildren and one great-grandchild. My wife died on January 6, 2001, of lung cancer. She never smoked and never drank.

7. Did you use the Nazi greeting "Heil Hitler!" and/or the Nazi salute?

BLAJS: Yes, at school. During the war, when the second teacher arrived, we had to use that greeting. He was very strict on this point. Speaking Slovene was forbidden, and we had to say "Heil Hitler." Apart from that, at home and so on, we never used it at all.

8. Why were you persecuted by the National Socialists?[5]

BLAJS: I'm a Carinthian Slovene. We had connections to Tito's partisans who were hiding in the woods in the mountains. Some of them were Carinthians, but most of them came from Yugoslavia.

---

[5]   A *National Socialist* is commonly known by the abbreviated term *Nazi*.

9. When were you arrested?
BLAJS: I was arrested on October 12, 1943.

10. Why were you imprisoned?
BLAJS: One of the partisans told the police about us. That same day, several families from here were arrested and imprisoned. The partisans often came to our farm and got something to eat from us, and one of them betrayed us. We had no choice but to take food to the partisans on many occasions. "Take the food with you because you're going that way!" My brother Franz and I used to transport brushwood on a horse-drawn wagon. Where the horse was hitched to the wagon, we fixed a covered bucket of food such as potato soup. That was less obvious than if we had carried the bucket in full view. That way it was partly concealed. I thought to myself, "If the police catch us now . . . !" We drove to a cross set in concrete; and nearby, a little further down, the partisans had their bunker. One of them always came out to collect the food because we weren't allowed in the bunker.

11. What exactly happened when you were arrested?
BLAJS: We were in the field harvesting potatoes. My brother Franz was still at home when the police came. He went out to the field and told our uncle Josef to come home. Our uncle fled into the woods to the partisans. Our stepmother was just bringing the partisans something to eat and saw the police arrive from up in the woods. So she stayed in the woods, fled to the partisans, and never came back to the farm. My brother came home one more time. I don't know why. Then the policemen beat him and took him away. In the evening, they came back again and took my aunt Paula Maloveršnik and me away too. The room my brother and I slept in was in a cellar that you entered from outside. I ran around the corner, the policeman ran after me. Right in front of the door, he gave me a shove from behind so that I fell right on the bed. He whipped me with a switch. The whole way from the farm down to Eisenkappel, a good three and a half miles, my mouth was bleeding.

They detained me for about one and a half hours in Eisenkappel, and that evening I was taken to the Gestapo prison in Klagenfurt, where my brother Franz was too. At the prison, I was given a severe beating. The Gestapo questioned me, asking me how often and when the partisans had come to our farm. I resolutely denied everything. "I never saw them, I never heard anything about them," I said. My brother didn't say anything either, but they told me he had made a confession. I replied, "Well, if my brother said something, it means he knew about it. I know nothing about it," even though I did know something. One of them had a lovely red apple and he tempted me with it, saying, "Look, if you say something, you can have this apple." "I'm afraid I have nothing to say," I replied. Apart from that, I had great difficulty understanding him, and he could hardly understand me. In those days, my German was even worse than it is today.

12. Did people know right from the start what was happening in the camps? Before you were taken away, did you know what would happen to you?
BLAJS: No, they didn't know that. How could they?

13. How many different camps were you in? How many years did you spend in each camp?
BLAJS: From October 12 to November 8, 1943, I was in the Gestapo prison in Klagenfurt. Then I was put on a transport to Moringen *Jugendschutzlager* (youth protection camp) for young male prisoners. This camp was later renamed a juvenile concentration camp. I was there from November 8, 1943, to April 11, 1945. But before April 11, they sent us on a death march because they had to get us out of the camp.

14. Were you the only member of your family in the concentration camp, or were family members or friends there as well? If so, did you have any contact with them?
BLAJS: I was there with my brother Franz, my friend Johann Kogoj, and Michael Sadonik. We were always together, also when we were working. I was always in contact with them. When we were under supervision, we were only allowed to speak German. But we could hardly speak it at all. That's why we found out so little. We understood so little and could barely talk to anyone. As a result, we remained very isolated. I didn't know anything about what was going on in the camp.

15. What were the first things that happened immediately following your arrival at the concentration camp?
BLAJS: When we were registered, we were asked everything: where we were from, why we were there, etc. We were given a blue triangle and a white stripe to go over it. I was given a number as well. The number

wasn't displayed anywhere on your clothing, you had to remember it. Mine was 1089, and I was put in ST Block in camp 2. That's where the political prisoners were. In camp 2, there were only barracks and the blocks ST, E, D, F, G, and S. In camp 1, there were the clothing room, the kitchen, the sickbay, and the saddlery. The commandant's office was at the beginning of the long road. There was a U Block as well, for so-called "unfit" inmates who could not do full shifts of work.

16. Why did they shave the heads of the prisoners?
BLAJS: As a punishment or to prevent the spread of lice. I don't know for sure, but I can imagine those were the reasons. Nobody said why it was done. Our heads were shaved at the beginning and after that our hair was cut at a normal length. We had our hair again, then. Runaways always had their heads shaved bald as a punishment. They also sewed strips of red cloth on their chests, sleeves, backs, pants, and caps.

17. What prisoner category were you put in?
BLAJS: The politicals. I was a Carinthian Slovene.

18. Can you describe the daily routine in the concentration camp?
BLAJS: First thing in the morning, after getting up, we had to go to the washroom outside the barrack. Then we had breakfast: a piece of bread and some coffee. At least they called it coffee. It was a soupy brown liquid. There was plenty of coffee, but it was very hot. I even got an upset stomach in the camp from the hot coffee. We just gulped it down. They were always shouting, "Hurry! Hurry! Hurry!" so we wouldn't be late for roll call.

Roll call was in camp 2. Some of the prisoners had to work in the quarry. Others worked for the Piller Company. Before starting work, we had to report to camp 1. There was another roll call there, and we were counted again. Then came the trucks that we had to get on. There were thirty or forty of us on one truck, and one or two *Sicherheitsdienst* (Security Service) guards always escorted us. Then we were driven to work in the munitions factory. We worked there all day. Lunch was brought to us. Normally we worked almost 1,800 feet underground every day, though sometimes we went down to 3,000 feet. The air was full of gas, "Azin gas." We could only work wearing gas masks.

In the evening, we were driven back to the camp. Roll call was held again and we were counted. Then we had a wash or a shower and our evening meal. At eight or half past eight, we went to bed.

In the morning, we only washed our faces; in the evening, we could take a shower. Often there was no hot water if you got there too late. But most of the time there was hot water.

19. What was the worst thing about the daily routine?
BLAJS: The roll calls that were held as a punishment. Then we had to crawl, do knee bends or push-ups. For the knee bends, we always had to hold a four-legged stool in our hands and do fifteen, twenty, or even fifty knee bends with it. To do fifty was real hard. Often they canceled mealtimes, and that was tough because we were so hungry anyway. If there was anything they didn't like, such as a bed not properly made or not done the way they wanted it, they didn't give you any food. Those are things I remember very well. [Imagine!] Denying food to a young person who was already so thin . . .

20. Did everyday life lead more to solidarity, or did the prisoners try to cope on their own?
BLAJS: Most of the inmates were seventeen or eighteen years old. The youngest one wasn't in our block: that was a thirteen-year-old. The oldest were twenty-one or twenty-two. There were very few twenty-two-year-olds. Because we didn't speak much German, we kept more or less to ourselves. I did talk with the people I mentioned earlier to try to get along better. I didn't have much contact with the others, because of the language. My mother tongue is Slovene.

21. Was there anything that helped you take your mind off the horror of daily life for a while (such as music)? What gave you strength?
BLAJS: Nothing, really. I don't know . . . the work, maybe. We seldom sang. When we were ordered to, we did. On the morning march from camp 2 to camp 1, they always said, "Sing a song!" So then we sang, sure. I bawled along a little too. We didn't know any German songs, except those we learned there. But that wasn't really any kind of distraction. It was an order; we had to do it.

22. What were living conditions like in the barracks (prisoner allocation, food supplies, hygiene, clothing, etc.)?

BLAJS: In the barrack, there was a block senior, room senior, and the table seniors. There were two rooms for eating in. The food was served to the block seniors first, then the room seniors, then the table seniors, and finally to the individual prisoners.

The block senior took the best potatoes or the biggest pieces of bread for himself. Then it was the turn of the room seniors, followed by the table seniors. The food was a mixture of vegetables twice a week, something like a stew. Now and then there were beans and potatoes. Sometimes it was only bread with a little bit of butter or jam and potatoes boiled in their skins. On Sundays it was a little better, initially. There was a meatball, as it was called in the camp, consisting of a small amount of meat and leftover pieces of bread. That was the best thing we got there. In the evening, we pressed the potato peelings together and ate them too. You had to make sure that no one saw you. The boiled potatoes were served in their skins and we had to peel them before we ate them. The peelings were taken back to the kitchen.

There were two dormitories with bunk beds. Iron frames with pallets and wood wool. That's where we slept, and it was very hard. When we made our beds in the morning, everything had to be just so and perfect down to the last detail. If you didn't do it properly, you would find all your bedclothes outside when you came back from work in the evening. Then you had to go out into the yard for a punishment drill, and when you came back, you had to make your bed according to the rules. In the dormitory, the bunk beds lined the walls, and down the middle there were three bunk beds end to end. These were where the bedwetters slept. If a prisoner had to use the bathroom during the night, he had to use a bucket in the dayroom. In the morning, the two buckets had to be taken away and breakfast fetched. It was the job of the new arrivals to bring the food. For taking away the buckets, there was a roster. First it was the turn of these two, then another two. Everyone had to do it maybe three or four times a year. An iron bar was put through the handles of the buckets. If a tall prisoner carried one end of the bar and a small one the other, and if the buckets were full, urine would spill out over the small guy.

23. What jobs did you have to do? How many hours a day did you have to work?

BLAJS: I had to work in the munitions factory in Volpriehausen, about seven and a half miles from Moringen. The grounds were huge. If someone had taken me to the far end of the eastern or southern field when I first started, I would never have found my way out. There were enormous sheds there, all full of weapons and ammunition that the Nazis had taken from the occupied territories.

Every day we were sent down a shaft. The elevator went down so fast that for a moment our feet were off the floor. When we first started there and weren't used to it yet, it turned our stomachs. Later we got used to it, so it wasn't so bad anymore. The elevator had three levels, each with enough room for ten prisoners. So, thirty prisoners could go down at once. They used this elevator to transport everything else as well. At the bottom, there were small trains with ten to fifteen cars for transportation.

Flak grenades were made in workroom 1. But I was only in there three or four times. The rest of the time I was always part of the gang [of workers, prisoners]. We had to load various grenades and various types of powder [gunpowder] that were going out, or unload and store what came in. There were crates that weighed 165 pounds. We had to drag them in pairs. That was hard work!

Now and then we also had to work in workroom 1 where a particular group was permanently detailed. But if one of them was absent because he was sick or couldn't work, they recruited a replacement. In that room, they assembled the flak grenades from individual components, packed them up, and in the beginning, stored them. Toward the end of the war, everything was sent out on a daily basis. When we had to go down to a depth of three thousand feet, there was this "Azin [gas]," and we could only work wearing gas masks. It stung the eyes and mouth really bad. It was impossible to work without the masks.

We started work at seven o'clock in the morning and finished at six in the evening. By the time we arrived back in the camp, it was seven o'clock, even later if there was an air-raid warning because we couldn't leave the factory then.

24. What effect did the slogan "Work liberates" have on you?
BLAJS: At that time, I had never heard it. It was mounted over the entrances to other camps, but not in the juvenile camp. During my time as a prisoner, I never heard that work liberated.

25. What were the guards like in the camp?
BLAJS: One block leader was almost unbearable. He just beat prisoners the whole time. He would punish you for even the slightest misdemeanor. He would make you do knee bends or push-ups, or even beat you with a stick. Another of the block leaders, who wore the SS insignia, was the best. Though he was an SS man, he was very friendly toward the prisoners. All the others were only SD men, from the *Sicherheitsdienst* (Security Service), or Hungarians and *Volksdeutsche* (ethnic Germans). Some of them were comparatively friendly. They changed the block leader in our block once, and the one we got was Zimmermann. That was the bad one. The previous one had been nice. We didn't have much contact with the guards when we were working, even though they were always there. Our foremen were civilians. They gave us the orders. They weren't SS.

26. Was there any contact between the prisoners and the local population?
BLAJS: Russians doing labor service worked in the munitions factory. Several prisoners had contact with them, but not us, and I in particular never did. The whole time we never had contact with a civilian worker or civilians, except occasionally with the foremen on the gang. But with no one else, apart from them.

27. Were you aware of how the war was proceeding in the outside world?
BLAJS: No, I wasn't. How could I have been? Certainly not.

28. In the concentration camp, were you allowed to receive letters, food parcels, etc.?
BLAJS: Yes, but everything was censored. All letters had to be written in German. Every month we were allowed to write a few words: "Hello everyone! I'm doing fine, and am healthy." All the time I was there, I received only three or four letters. My relatives were hiding in the woods or had been put in a concentration camp, and as a fifteen-year-old, I didn't have any acquaintances. The people I knew from school had forgotten that I wasn't there anymore.

We received food too; I think two parcels came for my brother and me to share. That was permitted. One parcel was sent by our grandmother, the other by an aunt, a sister of our stepmother. The bread, the most important item, was moldy. It took fourteen days to reach us by mail. What they didn't take away from us we ate because we were so hungry. If it was too moldy, they told us, "No, that's no longer edible!"

29. What forms of torture did you suffer?

BLAJS: One time I was beaten with a stick, even though I was innocent: my spoon had been stolen. At the evening meal, I was unable to eat. I waited until my brother had finished, and then ate with his spoon. The block leader was there and he asked me why I wasn't eating. I told him that I couldn't eat, because my spoon had been stolen. He made a note of that and said, "Get a new spoon from the clothing store tomorrow evening." But next day we were late because there had been an air-raid warning. We couldn't leave the factory. We stayed in the munitions factory and got back to the camp too late. The clothing store was already shut. I still wanted to go up there, but I couldn't. The block leader was there again, and I was unable to eat again. Although I explained to him that we had gotten back too late for me to go to the clothing store, he gave me ten blows with his stick for refusing to obey an order.

That was the only time I was beaten with a stick. For that, you had to bend over a stool and drop your pants. Then you were beaten. Afterward you had to stand up again quickly, stand to attention, and say, "Prisoner such and such has received ten blows for refusing to obey an order." That was one punishment. Apart from that, there were other less-severe ones, such as knee bends and push-ups. Some prisoners were not so obedient and were punished more often.

30. What was the most frightening moment for you?

BLAJS: Fear of death. One time, the prisoners in the munitions factory committed sabotage. They wanted to blow up a room that was full of explosives; there were thousands of pounds of explosives in there. If that had gone up, the whole factory would have gone up with it. That would have been the end of all of us. The fuse was already burning, and one of the guards or civilian workers saw it in time and pulled it out or cut it off. That was at the end of 1944, on the gang that was working in the eastern field. But they never found out for sure who the culprit was.

Then one Sunday, the camp commandant said to us, "You all deserve to be shot!" I kept thinking, "Will it really happen one day?" It never did, but those words shocked us. It still sends a shiver down my spine today whenever I think of it.

31. Were there any entertaining or lighthearted incidents that enabled you to forget all the suffering for a moment? Can you describe them?

BLAJS: No. Well, Sunday afternoons in the barracks, there was wrestling among the prisoners, just for fun. We sometimes watched it. They were two guys from Luxembourg. The smaller one wasn't strong but was quicker. We laughed at it a few times, although it wasn't really anything to laugh about. Apart from that, we had nothing to laugh about.

32. What were your day-to-day thoughts while you were in the concentration camp?

BLAJS: Whether we would ever go home again! We certainly thought about that. Otherwise, we just saw to it that we did everything properly to avoid being punished.

33. Was it possible for children to be born in a concentration camp? If so, what happened to these babies?

BLAJS: That wasn't the case with us, since only male juveniles were there. Children were born in other camps. A lady who now lives in Eisenkappel was born in Ravensbrück concentration camp. She came home; they didn't kill her in the camp. In *Frauenaurach* "resettlement camp," a distant relative of mine, Jakob Jerlich, was born. His mother was pregnant when she was interned there.

34. Was it possible to make friends with prisoners?

BLAJS: Well, among the people I knew, yes, but I didn't have any real friends among the others. I had more friends among the Slovenes than among the rest of them. The Slovenes were my brother, Johann Kogoj, and Richard Potočnik, from Bleiburg, who has since died.

35. Who was your best friend during this dreadful time, and how did he or she help you?

BLAJS: My brother Franz. We stuck together.

36. What did you do to relieve the suffering of other inmates?
BLAJS: I can't think of anything in particular, except that we had to help the weaker ones with their work.

37. Were there particular hierarchies among the inmates?
BLAJS: The block senior and room seniors had a higher status. There were some prisoners who had more contact with the block senior in order to gain some advantage. When the food was handed out, they were given the soup from the bottom of the pot where it was a little thicker.

38. Were there any differences in the way the various groups of prisoners (religious, political groups) were treated?
BLAJS: Yes. The Bible Students, as we called Jehovah's Witnesses in the camp, were treated somewhat more roughly. They didn't want to work in the munitions factory at all, because it's against their religion, so it was said. Two newcomers were assigned to the munitions factory, and they absolutely refused to do the work. The Bible Students said they wouldn't work on the manufacture of weapons or ammunition, because it was contrary to their convictions. They were punished and assigned to office duties. We Carinthian Slovenes were treated no worse than others.

39. What diseases and illnesses were prevalent in the concentration camp?
BLAJS: I had mumps once, which put me in sickbay. Visits weren't allowed in cases like that, because it's infectious. But my brother came to see me one day after work, and he got mumps too. I don't know whether he really caught it there or someplace else. That was the only illness I had. Because he came to visit me and got infected, meaning he had to spend a few days in sickbay, my brother was later given a beating as a punishment. Whenever there was an air-raid warning, we had to go into the trenches. A few people, especially in rainy weather, caught such bad colds there that they died.

40. Did you receive a physical injury?
BLAJS: No.

41. How much did you weigh when you were in the concentration camp?
BLAJS: About eighty-eight pounds.

42. What did death mean to you?

BLAJS: Fear. I thank God that I didn't see anyone die in the camp, although several people did die. The fear was always there. We want to live, after all.

43. What was the closest you came to death?

BLAJS: When the prisoners sabotaged the munitions factory and wanted to blow it up. The fuse had been laid and was already burning, so there would have been an explosion. A guard or civilian worker saw it in time and pulled it out or cut it off so that it stopped burning. Every single one of us who worked there could have died. It still sends shivers down my spine today.

44. Did you ever build a kind of "wall" to shield yourself from the terrible things that were being done so that the death of a fellow prisoner no longer affected you?

BLAJS: I don't know. We had to work, work, and work some more. We just didn't think about much of anything else.

45. What happened to the dead bodies in the concentration camp?

BLAJS: We didn't see at the time what happened to the bodies. I never saw any bodies. They were buried in the burial ground in Moringen, outside the camp. I went there after the war and saw about sixty little stones marking where the prisoners were buried. Their names and ages were written on them. There was no crematorium or anything like that in our camp. We were about 1,400 prisoners.

46. Was there ever a possibility for you to be released from the concentration camp?

BLAJS: Yes, but not from our block. Some people were released from other blocks, but they were sent to join the Wehrmacht. So they got out of the camp, but had to join the army. That was never offered to me. I was still too young. Friedrich Tomasin, from Slovenia, who was in the camp with his brother like I was, was once asked whether he wanted to join the army. He was two years older than me. He told them he would join up if they let his parents go home too, since they were also locked up. If they didn't release his parents, he wouldn't go. They didn't let his parents go, so he didn't join the army.

47. Were there any escape attempts or opportunities to escape? Did you try to escape?

BLAJS: There were opportunities to escape, but I never tried it. Some prisoners broke out, but they were all caught again. There was only one prisoner who really managed to escape, and he somehow made it to England.

One time, seven prisoners who worked for the Piller Company staged a breakout. They made a copy of the key to the camp gate and escaped. Of course, they didn't get far.

When the SS caught an escaping prisoner, he was given a beating, sometimes three or four times in succession or fifteen times a week. His hair was shaved off, and for several months, he had to wear red stripes on his prisoner's clothing, one on the left side of his chest and one on the right, one on his pants and on his left and right sleeves, one on his back, and one on his cap. That was for the "runaways" as we called them.

48. Were there any inmates in the concentration camp who dared to stage a revolt against the camp authorities?

BLAJS: I myself was never aware that anybody tried it.

49. Did you think you would ever make it out alive?

BLAJS: Yes, I always had that hope and always believed that we would go home one day. I don't think they [the Nazis] intended to kill the young people. They needed them to work. And in the end, we thought, "Well, there's no way they'll win the war, so that means we'll go home one day."

50. Were there any times when you gave up all hope? If so, why?

BLAJS: No, there weren't, because I was always convinced that things would get better again one day.

51. Did anyone commit suicide?

BLAJS: Not that I'm aware of.

52. During the Holocaust, did you ever consider committing suicide out of sheer despair?

BLAJS: No, I didn't.

53. What thoughts, ideas, hopes, wishes, or religious convictions did you cling to?
BLAJS: My hope was that the war would end quickly so that we would be able to go home again soon. Apart from that, there were no religious thoughts or anything.

54. Did you lose your faith in God while you were in the camp?
BLAJS: I neither lost it nor did it get stronger.

55. What role did your religion play in how you felt about what was going on? Why?
BLAJS: I was too young to think about things like that. I'm Catholic, but religion didn't play any role.

56. Did you pray during your internment?
BLAJS: No. Farmers used to have the custom of midday prayers, but in the camp, I stopped praying. We just lived one day at a time, like cattle, so to speak, without faith and without reflecting on anything. We just tried to survive each day so we would be able to come back, and we worked.

57. Did you ever consider changing your religion (or ideology)? Why?
BLAJS: No. At that time I wasn't very interested in politics. But I knew that Hitler would bring no good.

58. What was the date of your liberation from the camp?
BLAJS: April 11, 1945. Before that, there was the death march. We marched for three nights, away from the camp.

59. How were you liberated from the camp, or how did you manage to get out of it?
BLAJS: There was the death march. Where it would have taken us, I don't know. At the time we didn't know it was intended to be a death march. We marched for three nights. We only moved at night. In the daytime, the guards found somewhere for us to take shelter, either in an abandoned school or some other building. During the march, some prisoners collapsed. When that happened, a piece of paper—I think it was a release certificate—was placed in their hands, and they were simply left lying at the roadside. On the third day, after the SS and SD ["*Sicherheitsdienst*"] men had let us go, we were in a barn out in a field. The prisoners had

already removed some of the wood slats in the afternoon, and a lot of them had escaped. The guards did nothing to stop them. They saw them, but they didn't do anything. In the evening, we were supposed to be given something to eat. We had a field kitchen with us. But there was nothing left. All of a sudden, all the guards were just gone. They just left us there without saying a word.

We prisoners didn't know where to go and set off in little groups. My brother and I went along a path with about ten others. Then we came to a village. It was completely deserted. I thought, "Where is everybody?" Then two men came running after us, shouting, "What are you doing here? Where did you come from?" We told them we had been in the concentration camp. One of them said, "You can't stay here. A factory is about to be blown up, and all civilians must leave the village." We decided to follow these men because we didn't know where the factory was and we didn't want to get too close to it. So we went into some woods and spent the night there at a little distance from the civilians. That night was another occasion when death seemed close. From ten at night till four in the morning, there was one explosion after another. There was a munitions factory there too, and the Germans blew it up before they fled. It gave us all an almighty shock.

In the morning, we thought about where we should go next. We carried on along a track between some fields and reached the village of Schauen. We went to a farm there. The farmer asked us where we came from and who we were. We told him and begged him to give us some breakfast. And he actually did give us a thick soup and some bread to go with it. So we stayed there awhile. In the late afternoon, the Americans suddenly appeared. That was on April 11, 1945. They came in, and one of them wanted to know where we were from. He asked, "Are you Germans?" "No," we replied, "we're prisoners from a camp." Since we weren't Germans, he was well-disposed toward us right away. He climbed up a ladder into the hayloft, and one of the rungs snapped under his foot. He looked around to see if any German soldiers were hiding up there. Then they went away again.

We stayed at the farm. On the second day, we helped plant potatoes, and the farmer said, "I can't keep all ten of you on, two at the most." My brother and I volunteered at once. Because we were brothers, we were allowed to stay. The others had to go, unfortunately. Among them was Johann Kogoj, who got back home in mid-June. We didn't get home until August 27, 1945. In fact, only my brother stayed with that farmer; I was sent to the neighboring farm. We stayed there until May 22, 1945, working for our food.

On May 22, 1945, the prisoners and people who weren't from the area were sent to various resettlement camps. In mid-August, we were taken away with the Yugoslavian prisoners of war. We were taken to Yugoslavia as well and spent three days in Jesenice and seven days in Ljubljana. Then we were taken back to Rosental and Villach, arriving home on August 27, 1945.

60. How were you treated by the people who liberated you?
BLAJS: Okay, no sooner had we seen them than the Americans were gone again. We didn't see them anymore after that. Then we were working on the farms where we were treated well, I mean at least we had something to eat. We had to work for it, mind you.

61. What was the first thing you did after you were liberated?
BLAJS: I worked for the farmer in Schauen, and then on the farm at home.

62. Did you have any problems when you returned home? How did people in your home environment react to you?
BLAJS: We had no problems really, though my uncle [Anton Blajs], who was on the farm, would have preferred it if we hadn't come back. That's what a Croatian who worked on the farm told us. My uncle would have liked to inherit the farm, since he was my father's brother. But even if we hadn't come back, my half-brother would have been next in line to inherit it. My uncle lived in Lobnig, and when we were arrested on the farm, he went to live there with his family. He kept the farm running while we weren't there. It was my brother Franz who next took it over.

63. Were you able to rejoin your family?
BLAJS: Only my stepmother and half-brother were still there. Uncle Anton left the farm after the war. A handicapped woman was there too; she just lived there and didn't really do anything. She had a crippled hand and foot. Another uncle [Josef Blajs], who had fled to the partisans, was killed in the war fighting for them. My aunt Paula Maloveršnik, who

was arrested with me, was in Ravensbrück and Auschwitz concentration camps. She was released early, in 1944, because her husband, who was in the army, kept applying for her release until she was finally freed.

64. Did you have any acquaintances, friends, or relatives in the camps? Did they survive their internment?

BLAJS: Yes, all the people we knew in our camp survived, as did my brother Franz. Other family members were in other camps, for instance, my stepmother who had initially escaped to the partisans. She was taken prisoner in 1944 and interned in Ravensbrück. She came home too. And a cousin, who was in Dachau and Mauthausen, came home as well. He died only recently.

Some distant relations died in camps. Three of my father's cousins died in concentration camps, one of them in Dachau. And there's another one whose place of death we still don't know to this day.

65. What happened to your possessions?

BLAJS: As a fifteen-year-old, I didn't have much to begin with. But my father's personal possessions, such as hunting rifles, field glasses—he was a hunter—which by rights should have passed to me and my brother, disappeared. When I was thirteen months old, I inherited a small gold pocket watch from my mother. It was set in leather so I could wear it as a wristwatch. That was gone too.

66. To what extent have you received compensation for your internment?

BLAJS: First of all, I received compensation for wrongful detention from the Republic of Austria. Later I was awarded compensation from the state fund of the Republic of Austria for my father's possessions and for the watch I had from my mother.

Because I had [performed] an apprenticeship at a general store before my arrest, they worked out what I could have earned as a trained retail salesman and what I actually earned as a forestry worker. For that, I was awarded twenty-three thousand dollars by an international organization, but I only actually received a little over three thousand dollars. I was told that if there were still some money left over when all the applications had been dealt with, there was a chance that I might get some more.

67. How did you set about rebuilding your life?
BLAJS: By working. That's it, pure and simple.

68. How long did it take you to return to a "normal" life after the Holocaust?
BLAJS: In reality, I had to return to a normal life immediately after the Holocaust. I didn't want to think too much about what had happened in the camp anymore.

69. What was your life like after the war?
BLAJS: After the war, I worked on the farm for a few more years. In 1955, I got married and started a family. After that, we lived another five years on the farm in a single room that served as both living room and bedroom. Following that, we lived in an apartment and built our own house here in Leppen in Eisenkappel, moving in in 1967.

From 1955 on, I worked in the woods as a forestry worker. When the forestry work got too strenuous for me and I couldn't manage it any longer, I applied for retirement. But it was refused, so I worked for a shoemaker for another three years and retired in 1987.

70. What is your life like today? Do you still often think back to those days?
BLAJS: I live with my daughter, son-in-law, and grandchildren in the house I built with my wife. I help them out when they need me, and I enjoy knitting socks for my grandchildren. Nowadays I don't have so much work to do, and as a result, I often think back to those days. Especially at night when I can't sleep. The events in the camp come back to me more and more often. The older I get, the more often I think about dying. If my wife were still alive, it would be nice.

71. What physical and mental scars do you carry from that time?
BLAJS: No physical ones, but increasingly often I feel nervous and restless. At night especially, the thought keeps coming back more and more often that we would all have been dead and buried in one fell swoop if the munitions factory had gone up and taken us with it. The memory of those events constantly weighs on me.

72. Did you have any moral support to help your emotional and social recovery?
BLAJS: No, after the war, these things were hardly ever mentioned. They were swept under the carpet more than anything.

73. Has your view of the world changed since that time?
BLAJS: I don't think so. Nothing has changed.

74. Can you think of anything positive that you have gained from your experiences?
BLAJS: Did I gain anything positive? No.

75. Have you ever been back to visit the concentration camp you were held in, and if so, what were your feelings?
BLAJS: Yes, I've visited the camp four times: twice in 2005, once in 2007, and most recently in 2010. The first visit was entirely private, with my daughter. The second was for the meeting of survivors in 2005. That time I went with my son. Of course, I experienced some unpleasant feelings. We even went to the site of the munitions factory we worked at. The elevator shaft has been concreted over and you can't go down there now. The sheds are still there, but they're all empty. There's nothing at all left of camp 2, where we were. All the barracks were demolished and houses have been built there. There's only one small space left where the barracks used to stand, and that's wilderness now. Most of the site has been built on. There's a psychiatric clinic where camp 1 used to be.

76. Are you still in touch with your fellow internees from the concentration camps?
BLAJS: Yes, sometimes. On September 13, 2008, there was a meeting in Marburg of former prisoners who had survived Moringen. There were eight of us in all, with two from Austria, Timotej Malli and I. All the rest have died. I always maintained close contact with Johann Kogoj, but he died too.

My brother Franz died much earlier, in 1972. He committed suicide. A lot of people on my mother's side of the family did the same: two of my mother's cousins, my mother, grandmother, and my brother.

77. What did you tell your family about your internment in the concentration camp? How did your relatives react to what you told them?

BLAJS: I didn't talk about it to many of them. My stepmother seldom told me anything about what she had experienced in the camps. If other relatives came, she used to say more. I didn't talk about it much with my wife, either.

It wasn't until the children had grown up a bit that I told them something about it. It interested them, and they felt sorry for me. My oldest son especially was very interested. That was in the early 1970s. It wasn't until then that I began to talk about it. Before then, everyone was glad to have some peace and quiet and to be home.

78. Do you find it difficult to talk about those days?

BLAJS: It's not hard to talk about them now. In the first years after the war, I couldn't do it at all. Nowadays I often speak with people who were in a concentration camp too, and we swap experiences.

In other camps, it was far worse than in ours, especially for those who were in Auschwitz, Dachau, or Mauthausen. Especially in Auschwitz. What happened there is inconceivable.

79. Which moment from those days has remained most firmly etched in your memory?

BLAJS: There were several. For one, being arrested right by the house and being interrogated in the Gestapo prison. Those guys really gave us a beating, and that has somehow remained the clearest in my mind. During interrogation, they kept telling me my brother said this, my brother said that. But I said nothing, and then they whipped me like a dog.

This questioning has remained a very vivid memory, as has the speech delivered by the camp commandant after the attempted sabotage when he said we all deserved to be shot.

80. Did you ever see or meet Hitler?

BLAJS: No.

81. What was your opinion of Hitler in those days, and what is your opinion of him now?

BLAJS: At the time, as a child, I didn't connect everything to Hitler, because I didn't know who was behind it all. There were enough people in this area who joined in. Hitler didn't put us in prison himself, did he? But he gave the orders, and it was his fault that we were in the camp. Today I think he was a criminal.

82. Hypothetically, if Adolf Hitler were still alive and you could have five minutes alone with him, what would you say or do?

BLAJS: I don't know that I wouldn't kill him. It goes without saying that I would like to kill him, but maybe I would also like to talk to him about everything he did. Killing off all the Slavonic people, as was his plan. If he had won the war, that would likely have happened too. All the Slavonic people, the gypsies, and all those he didn't like.

83. After the war, did you ever meet any of the people who had tormented you?

BLAJS: No. I never again met the policeman who arrested us and took us to the Gestapo, even though he lived somewhere in Western Carinthia. After the war, I never saw him again.

84. What do you think of the punishments the Nazis received after the war, in the Nuremberg trials, for example?

BLAJS: I never knew much about them. Many Nazis got off scot-free anyway. I know the trials were held there, but what punishments the others received, I don't know. At any rate, the main culprits deserve a life sentence. Many of them were just opportunists, but I would lock them all up for the rest of their lives.

85. Have you forgiven your persecutors?

BLAJS: You have to forget, but you cannot forgive. So I would say, no.

86. What is your opinion of neo-Nazis?

BLAJS: I can't understand at all how anyone can be like that. A lot of them deny that it happened and say, "Things like that never existed!" I don't know what I should say in answer to that. I cannot understand that there are still people like that around these days.

87. What do you do to explain to people what exactly happened in the Holocaust?
BLAJS: If anyone asks me, I tell them about my experiences.

88. From today's perspective, how can you explain that "normal people" were capable of such atrocities?
BLAJS: I don't know how they came to do such things. They must have been crazy about the regime to have been capable of things like that and of torturing people. There were farmers' sons among them and people from all walks of life. The regime suited them, so they just went along with it. People from this area were in the SS too. Today it's just impossible to imagine it.

89. What exactly do you feel when you hear that there are still people who claim that the Holocaust never took place?
BLAJS: I don't know what you can say to people like that. I think, deep down, they know it's true, but they don't want to know it. It's impossible that they don't know it. Either they are not normal, or they are so cunning that they deny it just to humiliate the people who went through it, saying, "It's not true. It never happened." All of that, the camps and the crematoria where thousands of people were burned to a cinder—They deny all that, saying it never happened.

I see it in Mauthausen, which I visited a couple of times. Even there, the farmers whose farms were closest to the camp and who actually saw it denied it had been there: "There was nothing there." How can that be? Probably they have repressed all memory of it. The same is true of our camp. It was slap in the middle of the little town of Moringen and many people say, "It never existed." Unbelievable. Unbelievable.

90. What consequences did the proclamation of the "Nuremberg Laws" on September 15, 1935, have for you?
BLAJS: None, I never even heard about it.

91. What are your personal memories of the "Night of Broken Glass" on November 9/10, 1938?
BLAJS: There was only one Jewish store in Eisenkappel, and that wasn't destroyed. The Jewish family managed to escape in time. Here, nothing happened during the "Night of Broken Glass." Afterward, a German took over the store. In Klagenfurt, on the other hand, quite a lot happened.

92. What are your personal memories of the beginning of the war in 1939?

BLAJS: We first heard that war had broken out on the radio. But we saw no signs of it where we were, and conscription didn't start right away. My father didn't have to join up till later on. One thing was sure: no one thought that the war would last so long.

93. Did you hear that the National Socialists had decided to implement the "final solution to the Jewish question"—the systematic extermination of Jews in Europe—at the Wannsee Conference on January 20, 1942. If so, when and how?

BLAJS: No.

94. When you heard that World War II was over, what feelings did you have?

BLAJS: Good feelings—because we thought we would be going home again at last. We were already feeling good when we left the camp and went on the death march because we already knew that the front was no longer very far away. The Allies would be here soon, and we were more hopeful of returning home.

95. Do you think that humankind has learned something from the Holocaust?

BLAJS: Some have, but not all. There are still people who you can tell have learned nothing from it.

96. Should the atrocities be forgotten and no longer talked about, as some people wish?

BLAJS: No. Why should they be forgotten? So many years have already gone by without any of it finding its way into our schools and with nothing being taught about it. It took decades for some of it to start appearing, for recent history to be taught and explained.

97. What plans do you still have for the future?

BLAJS: I must leave that in the hands of fate. I hope to stay healthy yet awhile. If my wife were still here, it would be even better. My main wish is to stay healthy.

98. How would you like to be remembered?

BLAJS: My children will remember me. And the others, the outside world, will remember me maybe as a war victim. If they remember me as a victim, a prisoner, that might be nice, sure. And as a working man, a man who did nothing but work from childhood to the present day.

99. What else would you like to say to us? Which question was not asked?

BLAJS: I can't think of any question that wasn't asked.

100. After all you have been through, what advice can you give us young people?

BLAJS: Be good, work hard, and be obedient. Nowadays it's not like it used to be. And always take care to live a decent life. Always be sure to have something to do.

I would advise young people always to fight against neo-Nazism so that this movement never again comes to power like it did several decades ago.

Adolf Burger:
The Counterfeiter

Adolf Burger, born August 12, 1917
Grounds for persecution: Jew (political prisoner, Slovak)
Length of imprisonment: 2 years, 9 months
Country: Czech Republic

4. *Adolf Burger, 1945*   5. *Adolf Burger, 2009*

Adolf Burger was born on August 12, 1917, in Grosslomnitz,
Austria-Hungary [now Vel'ka Lomnica, Slovakia] to a Jewish family.
Although a Jew, he was initially spared arrest due to his profession
as a printer, but on August 11, 1942, he was taken into custody
for printing [forged] Catholic certificates of baptism for Jews and
having them legalized by a civil law notary. Following three weeks
in prison in Bratislava, he was sent to the camp in Žilina and, from

September 19, 1942, to the concentration camps Auschwitz, Birkenau, Sachsenhausen, Mauthausen, Redl-Zipf, and Ebensee, from which he was liberated on May 6, 1945. As a printer, he was a member of the special detail known as "Operation Bernhard" in Sachsenhausen concentration camp and had to work in the "counterfeiters' workshop," printing millions of forged English pound notes. English postage stamps were also counterfeited. Liberation by American forces thwarted the plan to print fake US dollar bills. The counterfeit money was sunk in Lake Toplitz.

His wife, Gisela, was gassed in 1942 in Birkenau concentration camp. His mother and stepfather were also killed in a concentration camp. His brother and sisters were able to escape to Israel. After the war, he held talks about his experiences in numerous schools in Germany, Austria, and the Czech Republic. In all, he spoke to over a hundred thousand young people. Soon after the war, in October 1945, Burger wrote about his experiences in the book *Číslo 64401 mluví* (*Number 64401 Speaks*), and later in the book *The Devil's Workshop*. This book formed the basis of the movie *The Counterfeiters*. Burger acted as adviser during the making of the film, which was an Oscar winner in 2008. Adolf Burger lives in the Czech Republic.

The interviews took place on September 4, 2009; August 10, 2011; August 23, 2011; and September 14, 2011.

1. When were you born? What was your father like? What was your mother like?

BURGER: I was born on August 12, 1917, in Grosslomnitz [Austro-Hungary] to Jewish parents. My father, Moritz Burger, died when I was four years old. My mother, Gisela, née Schäfer, had to work to support the whole family. She made skirts for lady customers who came to her. I had my grandparents, one brother, Jitzhak, and two sisters, Malka and Jaffa. My mother later married a Christian. So he was my stepfather, and his name was Kočis.

2. What is your earliest childhood memory?

BURGER: I can only remember that we lived in Poprad. At first, we lived in Grosslomnitz, and after my father died, we moved to a small town called Poprad. We lived in a single room, which also contained the kitchen. There was no running water: we had to go fetch it. My mother, my grandparents, and four children lived there. I was about five or six years old.

3. What kind of childhood did you have?

BURGER: My childhood was the same as all the other children's. I went to school in Poprad, where we lived. As a child, I learned to speak a lot of different languages because I grew up with children from other countries. At home we spoke Slovak, and there were Germans, Hungarians, and Slovaks living in Poprad. So I learned to speak Hungarian and German as well.

4. How long did you go to school, and what schools did you attend?

BURGER: I had five years of primary school and three years of secondary school.

5. What was your adolescence like? What trade did you learn, and what did you do for a living?

BURGER: I spent my adolescence as a member of Hashomer Hatzair. This was a Zionist organization because its aim was to go to Palestine. In reality, I spent my entire youth in this organization. I just loved to read, but we had no money for books. So I thought to myself, "If I work as a printer, I'll have free books." That was the biggest mistake of my life because when I started as an apprentice, we didn't print any books at all.

It was just a small printer's workshop with a staff of four. Nonetheless, I trained as a typesetter, completing the training four years later.

6. What can you tell us about your family?
BURGER: I've been married twice. Seven months before I was deported to Auschwitz concentration camp, I married Gisela, née Markstein. She was gassed in December 1942. In 1947, I married my second wife Anna. She died in 2004. I have three daughters, Eva, Vera, and Jana. I have grandchildren and great-grandchildren.

7. Did you use the Nazi greeting "Heil Hitler!" and/or the Nazi salute?
BURGER: No, why should I have greeted with "Heil Hitler!"? There was no reason at all to do so. People were free to use whatever greeting they chose.

8. Why were you persecuted by the National Socialists?
BURGER: Because I was Jewish and was active in the underground.

9. When were you arrested?
BURGER: August 11, 1942. I'll never forget it because August 12 is my birthday.

10. Why were you imprisoned?
BURGER: It was this way: I was a typesetter, and in Slovakia, typesetters were rare at that time, so, as a Jew, I was granted special exemption by the government. I didn't have to wear the yellow badge, because if I had worn it, I wouldn't have been able to enter an Aryan factory. That's why I wasn't sent to Auschwitz.

One day, three people came into the workshop and said, "We must save lives. You could help us." They were Jews from Nitra and they said, "Print Catholic certificates of baptism for us. Every certificate will save one person's life." I said, "All right." So I printed the baptismal certificates. But I didn't only print them; I took them to a civil law notary and had them authenticated. I went to the notary some two hundred or three hundred times. And then the Slovakian Gestapo discovered it.

11. What exactly happened when you were arrested?
BURGER: I was printing in the workshop. Three Slovakian Gestapo [men] came in and arrested me—I was still at the machine—without even letting me wash my hands first. They took me home, but my wife wasn't there. Next day, my wife was arrested, and I was taken to Žilina. They interned a whole crowd [of Jews] there. In Žilina, there were already a thousand of us Jews who had been arrested all over Slovakia. Then we were put on a train and taken to Auschwitz.

12. Did people know right from the start what was happening in the camps? Before you were taken away, did you know what would happen to you?
BURGER: We never heard anything about concentration camps, no.

13. How many different camps were you in? How many years did you spend in each camp?
BURGER: Before I was sent to the camp in Žilina, I spent three weeks in prison in Bratislava. In Žilina, Jews from all over Slovakia were concentrated. There were a thousand of us. We were put on a train and taken to Auschwitz. I was in Auschwitz from September 19, 1942, until January 1943. Then I was taken to Birkenau. That was the worst camp. In Auschwitz, it was clean, the roads were asphalted, and every prisoner had his own bed. But Birkenau concentration camp, that was hell. We were in stables. We lay in rows of five, and in each of the stables, there were eight hundred men. There was no water; it was hell.

Then they started recruiting typesetters for "Operation Bernhard" in Berlin. They found out that I was a typesetter, and in 1944, I was sent to Sachsenhausen to the "counterfeiters' workshop" where I forged English pound notes. When the Russians were outside Berlin, the 140 or so prisoners from the "counterfeiters' workshop" were loaded onto six freight cars with the machines and tools and taken to Mauthausen concentration camp. That was in the spring of 1945. We were there only a few days before they took us to the subcamp Redl-Zipf in April. This camp had the code name "Schlier" concentration camp. We were supposed to continue our counterfeiting there and forge American dollars. But that never materialized.

At the beginning of May, we were taken on trucks to Ebensee concentration camp. There, we were locked in a small wooden hut above the camp. On May 5, we were taken into Ebensee camp, and on May 6, it was liberated by the Americans.

14. Were you the only member of your family in the concentration camp, or were family members or friends there as well? If so, did you have any contact with them?

BURGER: I was taken to Auschwitz in the same car as my wife. We were split up on the ramp. Before we parted, she whispered to me, "Think of me every evening at eight o'clock! I'll do the same. Then, at least, we'll be together in our thoughts." After that, no more contact with her was possible. Miki [Mikuláš] Šteiner, from Košice, was with me in Birkenau.

15. What were the first things that happened immediately following your arrival at the concentration camp?

BURGER: Mengele asked me, "Age?" I gave my age and state of health. We all stood still. To those who were over forty, he said, "To the left, please." All those over forty and those who said they were sick stood on the left. We stood still. Then trucks came up. They were all loaded onto the trucks and taken to be gassed. We, the ones under forty, went into the camp. We were taken into an office, a card was filled out, and I was given the number 64401. The number was then tattooed. Only then was I given my prisoner's uniform and taken to the block I was to live in.

The encounter with Mengele took place on the ramp immediately after we arrived on the train in Auschwitz. The trucks that took the people away were followed by an "ambulance." This was to make them think they were going to be well looked after, but this "ambulance," which had a red cross on it, contained the poison gas Zyklon B that was used to gas them.

I was also given a yellow badge, which I had to wear on my chest with my number. I didn't like that, so I said to my friend Miki Šteiner, from Košice, "Listen, I'm going to the SS to tell them I don't want this yellow badge, because I'm not Jewish." He said, "You're crazy. They'll kill you." I said, "I don't care. It doesn't matter to me whether they shoot me here or there." So I went and reported to the block senior. "I want to speak to the SS." He had to take me there and wasn't even permitted to ask me what I wanted (*laughs*). Three SS men and some *Hauptscharführers* (master sergeants) were there, and when they saw the yellow badge, they yelled, "What do you want, Jew?" I said, "I don't want anything, I just want this yellow badge removed because I'm not Jewish. I was arrested on the street in Bratislava, stuck on a train with Jews, and now I have to wear the yellow badge." They looked at me and said, "How can you prove it?" I said, "My mother and all my family are at home in Poprad. If you'll let me write a letter, she'll send me documents and the proof of my Aryan lineage." Then one of them said, "All right, write the letter. But if we don't have a reply within three weeks, I'll shoot you." I said, "All right. Agreed."

Then I wrote, "*Dear Mother, I'm very comfortable here, I have enough to eat. Don't send me any food. Just send me my Aryan certificate and the employment record book so I can get a better job.*" When the SS men read what I had written about how comfortable I was and how she shouldn't send me any food, they sent it off. My mother received it and knew immediately what it meant and what I wanted. My stepfather went to the authorities in Poprad with her and said I was his son and consequently of mixed race. The officials in Poprad confirmed this, and I was sent a stack of papers, documents, and all sorts of other things including the confirmation that I was of mixed race. When the SS got all that, they summoned me again. "You told us the truth," they said. "We've already given the order, and you'll have a new number in the block." A couple of days later, I got the number with a red triangle and an S, which meant "political prisoner, Slovak." All the Jews who knew me well found it uproariously funny when I appeared in the morning with that triangle.

16. Why did they shave the heads of the prisoners?
BURGER: How should I know why they did that? They just did. Anyone who was sent to a concentration camp had his head shaved.

17. What prisoner category were you put in?
BURGER: To start with, the Jews. After that, I was a Slovak political prisoner.

18. Can you describe the daily routine in the concentration camp?
BURGER: It was the same everywhere. We had to get up at six o'clock. Then we were given *ersatz* coffee. That was a brown liquid. At seven o'clock, there was roll call; everyone was counted. If everything was in order, we set off for work. Those who went to work took their midday

meal, which was soup, with them. We had to work until five o'clock in the afternoon. At six, there was roll call again. We had to stand there until everyone was accounted for. If everything was in order and no one had escaped, we went to our block. There we were given our evening meal: ten ounces of bread and *ersatz* coffee.

In the "counterfeiters' workshop," it was completely different (*laughs*). We had everything there. I had my own bed with white covers, and there was as much food as we wanted. We were excused from roll call. There was no need for us to take part in it, after all: we were locked in two blocks, 18 and 19, and could never get out. We went to work perfectly normally and printed this money. Then we had one hour's lunch break. Our meals were brought to us, then we worked until five o'clock. But when I went to bed in the evening, I always thought to myself, "You're a dead man on vacation. You'll never get out of here." And yet, here I am.

19. What was the worst thing about the daily routine?
BURGER: In Auschwitz and Birkenau, the worst thing was the hunger. We were hungry all day long because we were only given ten ounces of bread and couldn't organize anything else, I mean any more food. The hunger was unremitting.

20. Did everyday life lead more to solidarity, or did the prisoners try to cope on their own?
BURGER: Every prisoner had a friend, and so did I, Miki Šteiner, from Košice. Everyone got by as best he could. There were thousands of people there, and you had one friend or a group of people who belonged together. When it came to food, it was every man for himself. There was no other way, because everyone only had ten ounces of bread.

21. Was there anything that helped you take your mind off the horror of daily life for a while (such as music)? What gave you strength?
BURGER: Nothing. You went into your block and got your food, ten ounces of bread, and that was it.

In Sachsenhausen, in blocks 18 and 19, things were different. We had evenings when plays were put on and suchlike. But that was only in blocks 18 and 19. There was a ping-pong table there. I played ping-pong with an SS man, *Hauptscharführer* Werner. I always won because he couldn't play. He was an awful player. The others always told me not to be stupid and to let him win. I said, "He shouldn't play if he can't do it." There was absolutely nothing he could do to me. We were under the command of the *Sicherheitsdienst* (Security Service), not the normal SS. But one time I did let him win, and he was more friendly toward me after that.

22. What were living conditions like in the barracks (prisoner allocation, food supplies, hygiene, clothing, etc.)?

BURGER: In Birkenau, the sanitary conditions were appalling. There was no water. You had to go outside and catch a little water. In Auschwitz, we could at least wash, and in Sachsenhausen, they took us to the baths. They saw to it that we kept healthy, but only so we could go on printing money. Blocks 18 and 19 in Sachsenhausen concentration camp were surrounded by barbed wire, and the windows were whitewashed. No one was allowed in except a couple of SS men from the *Sicherheitsdienst*.

The other prisoners didn't know what we were doing there. We only came out once every four weeks to bathe. The camp was closed off, no prisoner was allowed on the street, and no SS man either. We went down the camp road to the baths and back. We didn't have to wear prisoners' uniforms there either.

In Auschwitz, I had my own bed and a blanket. In Birkenau, we lay in rows of five, very close together, and there were eight hundred of us in a stable. In Sachsenhausen, we not only had a bed, but it had white linen, too. It was completely different. In Auschwitz, there were normal toilets; in Sachsenhausen and in Birkenau, there was a wood pole and a ditch.

23. What jobs did you have to do? How many hours a day did you have to work?

BURGER: My job, for example, was in a work detail in which we sorted the suitcases of the new arrivals. But then, all of a sudden, I was ordered to report to *Sturmbannführer* (Major) Höss because they had seen from the card file that I was a typesetter.

Höss summoned me. I went to his room and yelled, "64401 reporting!" He said, "Good, good. You're a printer?" I said, "Yes." He stood up and said, "Herr Burger! We need people like you. You'll be sent to Berlin. You will work as a free man, and I wish you every success." With that, I was free to go, and I almost fell down the stairs.

So they sent me and five other printers to Sachsenhausen. We had printing presses and spent all day, every day, printing English money. The money was then examined, perforated, and made to look old. That was all. I just did the printing. The plates were ready for printing when we got them. They were made not far from Berlin by SS men. We just set them up and ran them off. The team had the code name "Operation Bernhard" and was named after the man in charge of the counterfeiting campaign, SS *Sturmbannführer* Bernhard Krüger. We also forged English postage stamps, and the plan was to start counterfeiting American dollar bills too. We had made samples while still in Sachsenhausen. In Redl-Zipf, we set up the presses and were ready to print the dollar bills, but we never got started: the Americans were already in the vicinity, so the SS came with trucks and loaded the money—the English pound notes that were already in crates—and the presses onto them and threw everything into Lake Toplitz.

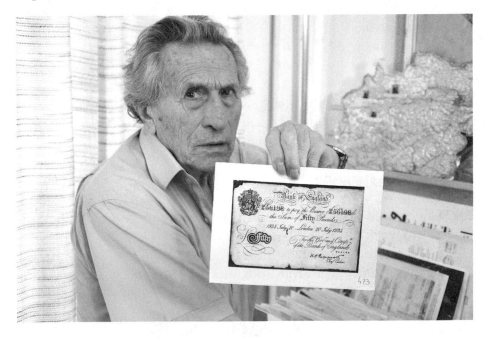

6. *Adolf Burger with a pound sterling note forged in Sachsenhausen concentration camp, 2009*

In Auschwitz, I worked first for the DAW, the *Deutsche Ausrüstungswerke* (German Equipment Works). With ten ounces of bread to eat, you couldn't work very long. I then worked chopping wood because I could no longer stand on the ladder at the DAW, I would have fallen off. In Auschwitz, I also loaded suitcases onto trucks on the ramp. They were the cases belonging to the new arrivals who had already been taken away. I also worked in the sorting detail "Kanada," first in Auschwitz and then in Birkenau. I was given three suitcases. You opened them and spilled their contents on the ground. Their owners had already been gassed. I sorted forks, knives, spoons, forks, knives, spoons, and threw them into a crate. We took the shirts and other things to the women. They then processed them, and everything was sent to Germany.

24. What effect did the slogan "Work liberates" have on you?
BURGER: None whatsoever; we never thought about it (*laughs*). In the camp there was this slogan "Work liberates." We never gave it a second thought.

25. What were the guards like in the camp?
BURGER: In Auschwitz, they were horrible; in Birkenau, even worse. But in Sachsenhausen, they were SS men from the *Sicherheitsdienst* (Security Service) and went about unarmed. What you see in the movie, when they show them yelling, isn't true. That's just the movie [*The Counterfeiters*]. They never yelled at us; they walked among us unarmed. They wanted just one thing: that the machines never stopped. Nothing else. In Sachsenhausen, they behaved like security guards, they weren't typical SS men.

26. Was there any contact between the prisoners and the local population?
BURGER: No, nothing like that existed because the perimeter fencing around Birkenau began about three miles before you reached the camp. Anyone who went near it was shot. And Auschwitz was so heavily protected that no one could get in.

27. Were you aware of how the war was proceeding in the outside world?
BURGER: When we had our "theater evenings," the SS men also watched. The prisoner Oskar Stein would then sneak into the guardroom, because they didn't lock it, and secretly listen to foreign radio stations.

He noted down the key points and then told us about them. That way we got some information. It confirmed our feeling that the war would end soon. But we knew that would mean our end, too, because we would be liquidated on account of what we knew.

28. In the concentration camp, were you allowed to receive letters, food parcels, etc.?

BURGER: Well, we weren't allowed to write at all. I was only ever allowed to write to my mother once, about the Aryan certificate. My brother was in Israel and was trying to get me released. In 1944, I received a letter from Switzerland. It was a certificate saying I was allowed to travel to Israel (*claps his forehead*). The Swiss had no idea what Birkenau and Auschwitz were. They sent it to Birkenau, but I was already in Sachsenhausen, and they were not going to let me go from there.

29. What forms of torture did you suffer?

BURGER: None at all.

30. What was the most frightening moment for you?

BURGER: When they tattooed me in Auschwitz. I didn't know what was going on, and all of a sudden, I had to hold out my hand and they tattooed me.

Also, when I learned in Birkenau concentration camp that my wife, Gisela, had been gassed a week before Christmas 1942. A girl from my hometown told me about it. I was working in the sorting detail and took her the shirts that were then sent to Germany, and that's when she told me.

31. Were there any entertaining or lighthearted incidents that enabled you to forget all the suffering for a moment? Can you describe them?

BURGER: There were no incidents of that kind at all. Except for the theater evenings in Sachsenhausen.

32. What were your day-to-day thoughts while you were in the concentration camp?

BURGER: I don't think we ever had any thoughts there at all. We went to work hungry, came back, were given ten ounces of bread, went to bed, and were constantly hungry. And that was all. In Sachsenhausen, I thought, "You're a dead man on vacation."

33. Was it possible for children to be born in a concentration camp? If so, what happened to these babies?
BURGER: I don't know anything about that.

34. Was it possible to make friends with prisoners?
BURGER: I had my best friend with me, Miki Šteiner, from Košice. He was my friend in Birkenau. Before we were arrested, I had often been to visit him in Košice, and he had visited me in Poprad. He was already in Auschwitz when I arrived there, but he wasn't in the counterfeiters' detail.

35. Who was your best friend during this dreadful time, and how did he or she help you?
BURGER: Miki Šteiner, from Košice. He helped me when I had typhoid fever. When he sorted the suitcases in that detail, he took chocolate and suchlike to the block senior. He then hid me in a bed in block 8 on the fourth floor with the patients who were only slightly sick. I spent three weeks there, without medication. But the SS never even knew I was there. One day he said to me, "You've got to get out of here. The SS are carrying out an inspection." So with a raging fever and no medication, I went back to work, sorting spoons, forks, and knives. That was my job. I was so weak that I fell asleep. Whenever an SS man approached, Miki threw a spoon into my face to wake me up so that the SS man wouldn't see I was asleep.

36. What did you do to relieve the suffering of other inmates?
BURGER: I can't remember anything particular.

37. Were there particular hierarchies among the inmates?
BURGER: Sure. Block seniors and *kapos*. They were in charge in the camps in Auschwitz and Birkenau, and they beat us.

38. Were there any differences in the way the various groups of prisoners (religious, political groups) were treated?
BURGER: No.

39. What diseases and illnesses were prevalent in the concentration camp?

BURGER: In Birkenau, I survived typhoid fever. We had a laboratory for experiments there. Five of us were sent there, and the SS doctor infected us with typhoid fever. He just injected us and let us go. All the others died. But with the aid of Miki Šteiner, I survived without medication.

40. Did you receive a physical injury?

BURGER: I suffered frostbite on one of my toes. A doctor from Poprad—four people held me still—cut off a quarter of the toe. I have a piece missing from it to this day. All they did was bandage it, and next morning, it was in winter, in February, I had to stand for roll call for an hour. That was in Auschwitz.

41. How much did you weigh when you were in the concentration camp?

BURGER: I don't know exactly anymore, but in Auschwitz and Birkenau, about seventy-seven pounds. When I returned home, my weight was already normal again because I had enough to eat in Sachsenhausen.

42. What did death mean to you?

BURGER: It meant the same to me as it had when I was at home. It makes no difference whether ten people die or one. Death is death. We saw bodies every day. In the evening, they were brought on carts from every workplace, laid out, and counted. Everyone was counted—the dead and the living—to see whether everyone was in the camp.

43. What was the closest you came to death?

BURGER: It could happen daily. At any hour, any minute, you could receive a fatal blow to the head from an SS man. You never knew when it might happen.

I once had a narrow escape: they were going to gas me. I was in the wood-chopping detail. That was the last stage for prisoners. You did nothing anymore but chop wood. One day, the SS came and yelled, "Line up! Line up!" We had to stop work and line up. They took us to a block and made us line up in front of it. It was then that I knew things were bad, because wood-chopping was the final stage. And suddenly—all the prisoners knew what was in store for them—they began to shout, "We're not going in!" The SS men began beating people and ordered us to go into the block. In the midst of this confusion, I ran round the corner and got away. It was seven o'clock in the morning. Another group appeared, and I fell in with them. The foreman always wrote down who was working in his group. But he didn't know that I wasn't supposed to be there. He hadn't written the numbers down yet, and I joined the group in order to work with it. So he wrote down my number as well. Half an hour later, SS men were running round looking for me all over the camp because they were one short. But they didn't find me.

The prisoners they forced into that block were gassed in Birkenau concentration camp. I ran away, and I will never forget it.

44. Did you ever build a kind of "wall" to shield yourself from the terrible things that were being done so that the death of a fellow prisoner no longer affected you?
BURGER: No. It didn't affect me, because I watched it every day. You simply accepted it as it was. There was nothing you could do about it.

45. What happened to the dead bodies in the concentration camp?
BURGER: The bodies were taken to the crematorium and incinerated. The ashes were tipped into the river Vistula.

46. Was there ever a possibility for you to be released from the concentration camp?
BURGER: For Jews, it was out of the question.

47. Were there any escape attempts or opportunities to escape? Did you try to escape?
BURGER: Two Slovaks—Alfred Wetzler and Walter Rosenberg, who later went by the name of Rudolf Vrba—broke out of Birkenau in April 1944. They were starting to build new barracks outside the camp in Birkenau and there was already a hole there. They hid under a pile of timber. A Pole helped them. When roll call was taken, two people were missing. We had to stand there until one o'clock in the morning. The SS looked everywhere for the prisoners, but the Pole had coated the outside of the timber with tobacco water. The dogs that searched for them couldn't sniff them out. On the third night, the SS men were called off, and the cordon of guards was withdrawn because they didn't find the prisoners.

So then they were free. They managed to make it to Slovakia and wrote a report to the Allies and the Pope telling them about Auschwitz. They demanded that the railroad from Budapest to Auschwitz be bombed to prevent the deportation of Hungarian Jews to the camp. But the railroad was not bombed.

48. Were there any inmates in the concentration camp who dared to stage a revolt against the camp authorities?

BURGER: I'm not aware of any. How could they have done it? They had nothing, only their bare hands. The SS was armed. What were they supposed to use to stage a revolt? If we would have said in Sachsenhausen, "We won't make the money!" they would have shot us. It was impossible to say, "I won't do that." It couldn't be done.

49. Did you think you would ever make it out alive?

BURGER: I never contemplated whether I would get out alive or not, because I knew I would never get out. Auschwitz was liberated, Birkenau was liberated. But we, the ones who printed the money, were never supposed to get out alive. The counterfeiting of English banknotes was one of Nazi Germany's biggest secrets.

Every time I went to bed, I thought to myself, "You're a dead man on vacation. You'll never get out of here." Because it was like being on vacation for me. I had food. I had my white bed to sleep in.

50. Were there any times when you gave up all hope? If so, why?

BURGER: When I joined the counterfeiting detail, I knew I would be liquidated one day.

51. Did anyone commit suicide?

BURGER: Yes, they threw themselves into the barbed wire and died instantly. But I never saw it myself.

52. During the Holocaust, did you ever consider committing suicide out of sheer despair?

BURGER: No. I was never so desperate that I would have committed suicide.

53. What thoughts, ideas, hopes, wishes, or religious convictions did you cling to?

BURGER: When I saw five thousand Jewish children from Riga being sent to their deaths, I said, "God, have you been sleeping? You didn't see what was going on here. Children being gassed!" Where was God? Where? That's all I thought about. Since then I recognize no god, because none exists. Because if a god had existed, he could never have stood by and watched five thousand children going into the gas chamber. And I had to watch it.

54. Did you lose your faith in God while you were in the camp?

BURGER: There is no God, or God is asleep. God was asleep when the children, the innocent children, five thousand children, went into the gas chamber. Where was God then?

55. What role did your religion play in how you felt about what was going on? Why?

BURGER: When I saw five thousand Jewish children going into the gas chamber, I asked one single question: "Are you on vacation, God, or are you asleep?" That's why I don't recognize any God. There is no God.

56. Did you pray during your internment?

BURGER: Never.

57. Did you ever consider changing your religion (or ideology)? Why?

BURGER: No. I didn't have to change my religion, because I was not a believer. If you don't believe anything, there's no need to change.

58. What was the date of your liberation from the camp?

BURGER: That was May 6, 1945.

59. How were you liberated from the camp, or how did you manage to get out of it?

BURGER: In our detail, it was different, because we had set up the machines in Redl-Zipf and were supposed to start making dollars. But then the Americans arrived. The SS men escaped with the machines and the banknotes, and everything was thrown into Lake Toplitz.

We were taken to Ebensee. But the Americans arrived so fast that the SS ran away. We reached the camp gate—we were a separate group and hadn't been interned in the camp itself—and the prisoners nearly didn't let us in because our heads weren't shaved: we looked good and our prisoners' clothing was clean. They didn't believe that we were prisoners. So we shouted, "We're prisoners! We're prisoners!" and showed them the numbers [tattooed] on our arms. Then they let us in. Then came the Americans, and we were free.

60. How were you treated by the people who liberated you?
BURGER: By the Americans? The first thing was they gave us food. That was the first thing. Then the English arrived by airplane: specialists. They took those of us who had made the money out of the camp to a hotel. There they gave us food and all kinds of things. For three or four days, all we did was make statements. We told them everything. They knew everything, but they submitted none of it at the Nuremberg trials.

They didn't want people to find out that there were over 130 million pounds sterling in circulation.

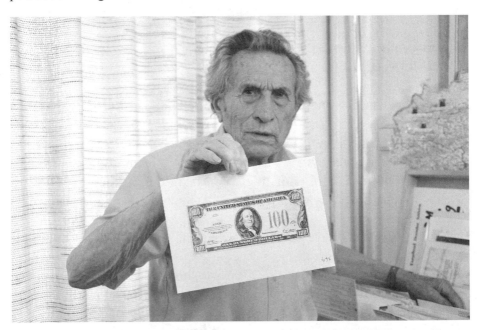

7. Adolf Burger with a sample of a one-hundred-dollar bill made in Sachsenhausen concentration camp, 2009

61. What was the first thing you did after you were liberated?

BURGER: After I was liberated, I went into the village, still in my prisoner's clothing, but armed, and went into the first house I came to.

Inside were a woman with two children and a man who started to scream in fear. I said, "Don't scream." I could speak German, you see, and spoke German to them. "Please, don't scream. I won't harm you. Please lend me a camera and some film." The man said to his daughter, "Go get the camera." Then he gave me the camera and film. I said, "I'll bring it back tomorrow." I went up to the camp and took photos of the people. The photos are in my first book *Číslo 64401 mluví* (*Number 64401 Speaks*).

62. Did you have any problems when you returned home? How did people in your home environment react to you?

BURGER: When I was in Prague, the trains to Slovakia were not yet

8. *Prisoners in Ebensee concentration camp following liberation. Photo by Adolf Burger, 1945*

running. I couldn't go home straightaway. A few weeks later, the trains started running and I was able to go home. I arrived in Poprad in the evening. I ran home, and the apartment was empty, completely empty. There was nothing there. Then our neighbor came, Frau Šeliga she was called; I can still remember that to this day. She was a Catholic. She saved my sister Jaffa by giving her her daughter's identity papers so she could escape. Everything was gone. I asked, "Where are my parents? Where is everything?" She said, "A week before the Russians came to liberate the town, everyone was arrested." My mother was sent to Ravensbrück, my stepfather to Sachsenhausen. No one returned. I couldn't stay there. I would have shot those responsible. I knew the murderers. I knew the members of the Hlinka Guard. I said to myself, "You'll kill five or six people, then spend ten years in prison." That's why I left Poprad, and in the morning, I was in Prague. I couldn't live in Poprad.

63. Were you able to rejoin your family?

BURGER: My wife, Gisela, was taken to Birkenau concentration camp and had to work there in a detail that carried dead bodies out of the barracks. Following a selection, she was gassed in 1942, one week before Christmas. My parents died in concentration camps too. When my mother was arrested, my stepfather didn't have to go with her. But he didn't know where she was being taken, so he went along voluntarily. He was sent to Sachsenhausen, she, to Ravensbrück. My brother, Jitzhak, got away through the regular channels before the war. He had a certificate and went to Israel. The same applies to Malka. Only Jaffa, my youngest sister, fled during the war with Frau Šeliga's papers. My little sister wanted me to come to Israel after the war, but I didn't go.

64. Did you have any acquaintances, friends, or relatives in the camps? Did they survive their internment?

BURGER: The only one who survived the concentration camp was Miki Šteiner, from Košice.

65. What happened to your possessions?

BURGER: The Slovaks took everything.

66. To what extent have you received compensation for your internment?

BURGER: Of course I received compensation. I was also awarded a victims' pension.

67. How did you set about rebuilding your life?

BURGER: Quite simply. When I came back, I went to a printer in Prague 8 and started work. After that, I worked the whole time.

68. How long did it take you to return to a "normal" life after the Holocaust?

BURGER: It took no time at all. I slept soundly the very first day that I came home.

69. What was your life like after the war?

BURGER: I led a normal life. I got married again and had children. I held a lot of talks in schools about my experiences. I have written several books about what I went through. The book *Číslo 64401 mluví*—in English that's *Number 64401 Speaks*—was published in Prague in October 1945. Then I searched for documents, and when I had enough, two hundred documents, I wrote the books *Operation Bernhard: The Counterfeiters' Workshop in Sachsenhausen Concentration Camp* and *The Devil's Workshop*. The first book was made into a film by [Stefan] Ruzowitzky, and I was there during filming.

In 2008, it won an Oscar. I was in Los Angeles. We went over this red carpet, there were journalists everywhere, and we went into the auditorium, no one knowing who the winner would be. Five films had been chosen by the Academy. Suddenly we heard the words "The Counterfeiters," and we were awarded the Oscar.

I was also present in the year 2000 when divers went looking for the sunken money in Lake Toplitz. The Americans invited me to go along, and I was there when they hoisted up the crates containing the English money. During the war, I had to pack the money into these crates. I was on a little boat and gave the Americans interviews for hours on end. I told them all the details, and the guy who was interviewing me said after two hours, "I have to stop. I'm tired." So we went outside onto the balcony. He was so tired that he couldn't go on. I said, "We only just got started."

70. What is your life like today? Do you still often think back to those days?

BURGER: I don't think of those days at all. I live a normal life. I don't read anymore, because it's no longer possible for me. I often watch television. The day is long and the days pass one after the other.

71. What physical and mental scars do you carry from that time?

BURGER: None. A small piece of my toe has been cut off, but that's nothing.

72. Did you have any moral support to help your emotional and social recovery?

BURGER: No. I didn't go into a sanatorium. They wanted to put me in a sanatorium, but I refused. I went back to work in 1945.

73. Has your view of the world changed since that time?

BURGER: No, why? My view of the world only changed when I saw on television, about ten years ago, that every party in the Czech parliament had proposed a law that would help every former concentration camp internee in some way or give them compensation. Since 1945, I had been a member of the Communist party, and the only party that voted against this law was the Communists. When I saw that on television, I went straight to a Communist friend of mine who was in parliament, and I said to him, "How could you vote against prisoners? What's the good of that?" He said, "We want everyone to have that, including those who were at the barricades for a day." Then I said, "You're no Communists," and resigned from the party.

74. Can you think of anything positive that you have gained from your experiences?

BURGER: There was nothing positive about it. What could be positive about the SS? What could be positive about the concentration camps? They were murderers.

75. Have you ever been back to visit the concentration camp you were held in, and if so, what were your feelings?

BURGER: I was in Auschwitz with schoolchildren in a bus they had organized. I was there several times, but I didn't have any feelings at all. I went there, showed them everything, how it was, and that was all. I also went to Ebensee several times. I was often in Sachsenhausen. I was a member of the International Sachsenhausen Committee, and we had a conference once a year in Sachsenhausen. I have stopped going now.

76. Are you still in touch with your fellow internees from the concentration camps?

BURGER: A man who was with me in Sachsenhausen lives in Berlin, but I'm not in touch with him anymore.

77. What did you tell your family about your internment in the concentration camp? How did your relatives react to what you told them?

BURGER: To begin with, I told them about my experiences. We talked about everything in those days. Of course, they were horrified. Then my book was published. If any of the children wanted to read it, they could do so.

78. Do you find it difficult to talk about those days?

BURGER: No. I can talk about them for three hours; it's no problem for me.

79. Which moment from those days has remained most firmly etched in your memory?

BURGER: Mengele! Doctor Mengele! When a transport arrived, and I was standing there, working in a detail that took the suitcases away. When Mengele asked the prisoners, "How old are you?" as they got out of the train on the ramp. If [the answer] was "Forty-two," he said, "To the left, please. To the left, please." [That meant] gas! He did it all with complete composure. I will never forget that as long as I live. A cold-blooded murderer. Like the entire SS. After making this "selection," he went into the women's camp. There was an orchestra there, and he had it play for him.

80. Did you ever see or meet Hitler?

BURGER: No, not Hitler, but Himmler. I did see Himmler. He was in Birkenau with three officers. They went to the crematorium. A special train with three thousand Jews from Poland had been brought for the "occasion." They were forced into the gas chambers, and he and his officers watched them being gassed. He stood there at the window and watched as three thousand Jews who had been brought specially from Poland were gassed. So don't let him tell anyone that he was innocent.

81. What was your opinion of Hitler in those days, and what is your opinion of him now?

BURGER: He was a fascist. He was a murderer. What more can I think of him? Nothing at all.

82. Hypothetically, if Adolf Hitler were still alive and you could have five minutes alone with him, what would you say or do?

BURGER: To start with, I would never sit with him in the same room—except if I were dragged in there. Hitler was one of the thousands of Nazis, SS, SA—murderers. It wasn't only Hitler, it was the others too. They were murderers. I cannot imagine what I would say or do to him.

83. After the war, did you ever meet any of the people who had tormented you?

BURGER: Yes. I went to Germany three times to testify in court as a witness against SS men from Auschwitz and Birkenau. I had to go there. I told those SS men to their faces what I thought.

84. What do you think of the punishments the Nazis received after the war, in the Nuremberg trials, for example?

BURGER: Look, they punished some of them, and that was it. It didn't do any good. In Auschwitz and Birkenau, there were hundreds of SS men who were never punished. The fact that some were convicted at the Nuremberg trials is no use at all. All that counts is telling the truth about what happened there so that it never happens again.

85. Have you forgiven your persecutors?

BURGER: There's nothing to forgive. It was a political situation. It wasn't organized by one man alone. It was a system. If an individual did something to another person, he did it because of this ideology, this system. He didn't think it out for himself, this individual. You can only condemn the system. You can only condemn the ideology; what an individual did was governed by that.

86. What is your opinion of neo-Nazis?

BURGER: That neo-Nazis exist today is the fault of the government. The government is to blame for the existence of neo-Nazis, and they will continue to exist if nothing is done about them. There are neo-Nazis in our country today too. It doesn't matter one bit how they came to be like that. What's important is what the government does. And the government should—on the basis of these experiences, on the basis of these millions of deaths—outlaw every one of these ideologies and do everything to stop their developing any further. If the governments don't do this, we will have neo-Nazis. Every organization that represents this ideology, even a little, should be banned. There should be no democracy for murderers. And this ideology is a murderers' ideology.

87. What do you do to explain to people what exactly happened in the Holocaust?

BURGER: In 1945, my sister, Jaffa, came over from Israel to fetch me, and I asked her, "Why should I go to Israel? What can I explain to the Jews? Most of them were in concentration camps. I'm not going. I have to go to Germany and tell people there what the Nazis did." And I didn't go to Israel. I traveled around to all the cities of Germany. I spoke to groups of three hundred schoolchildren and told them what a Nazi is. They should never become neo-Nazis. I held these talks to warn young people about this ideology. In recognition of that, the German president awarded me the second-highest state honor. That's what I have been doing all these years since the '50s. I have spoken to over one hundred thousand schoolchildren. I have written books, was involved in a movie, and have put together an archive with many photos from all the concentration camps I was in.

88. From today's perspective, how can you explain that "normal people" were capable of such atrocities?

BURGER: That they were capable of it? That was the system. It was the governments, and it remains that way today. If the government doesn't stop these murderous ideologies, doesn't officially outlaw them, they will continue to exist. If that happens, those millions of deaths will have been utterly in vain. It isn't something one man does alone. It's the ideology, and the governments do nothing about it. That's the mistake.

89. What exactly do you feel when you hear that there are still people who claim that the Holocaust never took place?

BURGER: I never had any contact with people like that. As I said, it's the fault of the governments that they don't make it illegal, that they allow such people to say things like that in the name of democracy, even though every child knows it's a lie.

90. What consequences did the proclamation of the "Nuremberg Laws" on September 15, 1935, have for you?

BURGER: They had no consequences for me in 1935, because the Czechoslovakian government didn't allow them. But in September 1941, the "Jewish Code" with its race laws was introduced in Slovakia. Jews had to wear the yellow star and were not even allowed to travel in an automobile. But I was issued an exemption by the government because there were so few printers, and I didn't have to wear the yellow star.

91. What are your personal memories of the "Night of Broken Glass" on November 9/10, 1938?
BURGER: That didn't happen where we were. I heard about it later.

92. What are your personal memories of the beginning of the war in 1939?
BURGER: I don't remember anymore.

93. Did you hear that the National Socialists had decided to implement the "final solution to the Jewish question"—the systematic extermination of Jews in Europe—at the Wannsee Conference on January 20, 1942. If so, when and how?
BURGER: I did go to Wannsee, but ten, maybe fifteen years after the war. I heard nothing about it before then.

94. When you heard that World War II was over, what feelings did you have?
BURGER: I was happy because it meant I was liberated and had survived it. The war had ended, and that meant the terror was over too.

95. Do you think that humankind has learned something from the Holocaust?
BURGER: We should never speak of humankind. We should always say that governments are responsible. They remain responsible today and do nothing, and that's the problem. In the name of democracy, they allow neo-Nazis to march through the streets. They should ban neo-Nazis. If the governments do nothing about it and hide behind democracy, it will have dire consequences.

96. Should the atrocities be forgotten and no longer talked about, as some people wish?
BURGER: Look, whatever people might wish: history is history, it can't be erased. It's just impossible. What happened is history, and that history will always exist. It cannot be erased whether we like it or not.

97. What plans do you still have for the future?

BURGER: I have nothing planned. I live a normal life and make no plans. There's no sense planning anything. You can plan what you like, but it's the governments up there that make the decisions.

98. How would you like to be remembered?

BURGER: It really makes no difference to me what people think about me in the future. For one thing, I don't know who should think anything about me. I stated my views in the book *The Devil's Workshop*, and anyone who has a desire to do so can read it and form his own opinion. Everyone can have his own view about it. It depends on the ideology they have. No one can dictate to another person what he should think. You can write ten, twenty books. There are people who will read them. Someone will think it's important and change his views accordingly, while another person won't. Every person has a brain and must know what he thinks. You can achieve a great deal with books, but not everything.

99. What else would you like to say to us? Which question was not asked?

BURGER: I think you have asked a great many questions. I tried to answer them, but we can never answer everything or ask everything.

100. After all you have been through, what advice can you give us young people?

BURGER: Look, the question should be, "What advice can you give the government?" The type of government you have and the ideology it preaches are absorbed by young people. Through school, through newspapers, in other words, the ideology. And there are countries that still have the fascist ideology. Where that's the case, that's the way the children will be brought up. Nothing happens without a cause. If children are brought up that way, it gets into their heads and determines how they act. You must always be aware—should always be aware—that it's the government that's always responsible for what happens. Because the government has the power, the government has been given the right by the people to decide, etc. And the way the government is, that's the way the people are too.

Leopold Engleitner:
Unbroken Will

Leopold Engleitner, born July 23, 1905
Grounds for persecution: One of Jehovah's Witnesses (Bible Student), conscientious objector
Length of imprisonment: 6 years, 5 months
Country: Austria

9. *Leopold Engleitner, 1939*

10. *Leopold Engleitner, 2009*

Leopold Engleitner was born into a Catholic family on July 23, 1905, in Aigen-Voglhub, Austria-Hungary. As a child, he lived under the imperial and royal Austro-Hungarian monarchy and met Emperor Franz Joseph in Bad Ischl. As a schoolboy, he had to endure the terror of World War I. Following intensive study of the Bible in the early 1930s, he became one of Jehovah's Witnesses in 1932. Religious intolerance during the period of Austrofascism (1934–1938) meant that Engleitner suffered unfair treatment at the hands of the authorities, and he was sentenced to several terms in Bad Ischl, St. Gilgen, Salzburg, and Bad Aussee prisons.

Owing to his faith as one of Jehovah's Witnesses and his refusal to do military service, Engleitner was interned in the prisons in Bad Ischl, Linz, Wels, Salzburg, and Munich, as well as the concentration camps Buchenwald, Niederhagen, and Ravensbrück, and its subcamp Comthurey, from April 4, 1939, to July 15, 1943. He was released on condition that he spend the rest of his life as a forced laborer working in agriculture. On April 17, 1945, he received his call-up papers for the German Wehrmacht. Engleitner fled into the mountains of the Salzkammergut region and hid there until May 5, 1945. After the war, he worked in agriculture and for the road maintenance department in Bad Ischl until his retirement in 1969.

Engleitner's experiences were recorded in his biography *Unbroken Will* and the film documentary of the same name, both of which have been translated into several languages. Toward the end of the 1990s, Engleitner began speaking about his experiences at schools, universities, and memorial sites in Europe and the United States. Even at such a great age, he has traveled over ninety-five thousand miles—almost four times the Earth's circumference—to give talks as an eyewitness who campaigns against forgetting the lessons of history. Leopold Engleitner lives in Austria.

The interviews took place on October 26-27, 2007; December 28-31, 2009; January 3-4, 2010; April 27-28, 2010; and September 12, 2011.

1. When were you born? What was your father like? What was your mother like?

ENGLEITNER: I was born on July 23, 1905, in Aigen-Voglhub [Strobl, Salzburg, Austria-Hungary].

My father, Leopold Engleitner, worked in a sawmill and held quite liberal views. I was closer to my father than to my mother. My mother, Juliana Engleitner, was a strict Catholic. She was the daughter of a large-scale farmer and held very conservative views. I don't remember her ever giving me a hug or a kiss. On the other hand, she was quick to dish out slaps. I grew up with my brother Heinrich who was a year younger. Because of our dire poverty, five other brothers and sisters died shortly after birth or in infancy. My half-brother, Ferdinand [Haas], an illegitimate son of my mother's, didn't live with us, but he often came to visit.

My mother raised my brother Heinrich and me as strict Catholics. We always had to go to church, and every evening, we had to kneel and pray before a picture of the Virgin Mary. I didn't like that at all, because I had been disappointed in the Catholic Church while still a child due to its support of wars. Besides that, during Catholic religious instruction, we would read chapter 20 of the book of Exodus where it says, "You shall not make for yourself an idol . . . You shall not bow down to them or worship them." When I refused to kneel down in front of the picture, my mother was very angry and gave me a hefty slap. I didn't want a second one, so I gave in, but only superficially. Inside I knew that she was telling us to do something that contradicts the Bible. From that point on, I started searching for further confirmation of this discovery.

2. What is your earliest childhood memory?

ENGLEITNER: I spent my early childhood in Aigen-Voglhub. I had a bad experience at the age of four. I was very fond of cats, and I saw a neighboring farmer chop a cat's head off. That gave me a terrible shock. I ran home in tears. My mother then told me that the farmer had killed the cat for food. After that, I was terrified of that farmer. I felt he might chop my head off too. I kept well out of his way. It was as terrible for me as if he had chopped off my own head.

3. What kind of childhood did you have?

ENGLEITNER: Life was very hard. We were always famished because our mother had to save as much as she could. Two pounds of bread had to last us for a whole week. If ever we asked our mother for a small piece of bread, she would say, "I can't! I have to make sure these two pounds of bread last."

We were a very poor family. In around 1910, we moved to my paternal grandmother's house in Pfandl in Bad Ischl. In those days, cows were always herded out into the meadow. The whole village of Haiden still had grazing rights. They were abolished in World War I. Eisl, the youngest son of the biggest farmer there, had to tend cattle in front of our house. We had a few goats. I went with Eisl, taking our goats and tending them alongside the cows. Those were enjoyable moments. We often played children's games, reenacting events we read about in school. We learned a lot about Richard the Lionheart and the Crusades, at the time. According to legend, Richard tore down the Austrian flag during one crusade and dragged it through the dirt. While we tended the cattle, we reenacted that [event] using a branch.

In Pfandl, there was a house next to our grandmother's that was rented out in the summer. A married couple from Vienna always lodged there for a month or so. Everyone wanted to come to Bad Ischl because Emperor Franz Joseph was there. This couple had a son called Fabian who didn't know anyone there. He was only five years old; I was a few years older. The boy's mother liked it when I visited him. She was a hat maker. The boy already had some toys. He had a little train you could pull along on a string. When I visited him, we would play games. It was always a lot of fun. The two of us laughed so much. My mother didn't approve, though, because she didn't like the Viennese and shared the widely held view that the Viennese looked down on people from the country. So I always had to sneak there in secret.

The times were completely different. Technology was still very primitive and older people, very conservative. When the first bicycles appeared, the old folk said, "Who needs a bicycle? We've managed to get everywhere on foot so far." The first automobile I ever saw had the gearshift on the outside, and the driver had to shift gears by hand. It also had a roof that folds back.

In those days, the ruler was Emperor Franz Joseph and he spent the summers in Bad Ischl. During one visit in May 1914, he wanted to see all the schoolchildren in Bad Ischl again. We had to line up along the road from the railroad station to the imperial villa, boys on one side, girls on the other. I saw his chest, all decorated with medals, and his light blue uniform. I found this showiness highly repulsive. We lived in terrible poverty and were constantly hungry. And then the emperor and the nobility came to Bad Ischl in the summer. They lived a life of extravagance and showed off their wealth. I felt this injustice keenly, and that's why I was disappointed in the monarchy. That the Catholic Church showed great support of the emperor and expected us poor people to serve him and pay for his luxurious lifestyle because it claimed that he reigned by divine right was something I could never understand.

I still remember very clearly what caused the outbreak of World War I. First of all, the heir to the throne, Archduke Franz Ferdinand, was murdered in Sarajevo [Serbia] in June 1914. Then, at the end of July 1914, Emperor Franz Joseph signed the declaration of war against Serbia in the imperial villa in Bad Ischl. The villa was only about a mile and a quarter from our house. I was nine years old at the time. The idea of war was greeted with tremendous enthusiasm. The soldiers were so excited when they went to war. The trains were overcrowded; they were even standing on the running boards. They said, "In two weeks, we'll be home again, and Serbia will be beaten." But they were very wrong.

The war lasted over four years. I hated "The Great War," as World War I was known at the time, and suffered enormously because of it. My half-brother, Ferdinand, was also called up and had to fight against Italy. When he returned home, he was furious with the Catholic Church because it supported the war and never went to church again. After the war, I caught the Spanish flu and had a raging fever for weeks on end. I survived; unfortunately, millions of others didn't. So my childhood was not easy, but I survived it.

The awful suffering caused by World War I depressed me greatly, and my desire for world peace and a just government grew stronger and stronger. After the war, I read a saying that became my favorite quotation:

"While empires shattered and fell,
Against tyrants curses swelled.

That war may nevermore plow this earth,
For war, from which all suffering stems—a dearth!
For eternal peace on earth to reign
No more war; aye, war—never again!"

After World War I, I very much hoped that this saying would come true and humankind would never wage war again. But this hope was sadly in vain.

4. How long did you go to school, and what schools did you attend?

ENGLEITNER: I very much enjoyed going to school because I wanted to gain knowledge at all costs and learn many things. But I was only able to go to primary school and couldn't even finish that. When I started school in 1911, at the primary school in Pfandl near Bad Ischl, World War I hadn't even started. The *Titanic* sank in 1912, and I can still remember how we found out about the tragedy from the newspapers. At school, I was especially interested in history. We learned about the Crusades, the emergence and expansion of the Austro-Hungarian monarchy, the American Civil War, and the Napoleonic Wars. In the Salzkammergut region, there were remnants of the Napoleonic Wars. When I was a child, there was still a trench in Pfandl, which was known as the "Frenchman's trench."

My teacher didn't like me. My father had also been in his class. Although I did my best, the teacher said, in front of the whole class, "Your father was my best pupil, but you're an idiot!" After that, the pupils called me "dumb Poidl." During the monarchy, boys were assessed while still schoolboys to see if they would make good soldiers one day. I was born with curvature of the spine and could only stand up straight with great difficulty. So the teacher regarded me as inferior and unsuitable to become a soldier. That's why he excluded me from gym class. I had to stand at the side with the girls and watch the boys. The other pupils scornfully branded me a cripple. That was very depressing. In those days, the teacher taught several grades together in the same classroom. Two pupils who were older and stronger than I was repeatedly beat me up over a period of several weeks for no reason. But I didn't have any school friends who could have helped me. Nobody wanted to be my friend; they would have been embarrassed.

5. What was your adolescence like? What trade did you learn, and what did you do for a living?

ENGLEITNER: My adolescence was hard. It was filled with deprivation and poverty, and moments of happiness were few. Because of our hunger, I was forced to drop out of school after World War I at the age of 13½ and look for work. I worked as a farm laborer for a mountain farmer in St. Wolfgang on Lake Wolfgang for board and lodging only. Conditions on the farm were medieval. There was no running water, and only a kerosene lamp for lighting. You wore the same shirt day and night for a whole week. It was both your working shirt and your nightshirt. I was allowed to wash only once a week, on Saturdays, but only my face, neck, and hands because there was so little water. And the water we had stank of sewage because the well was near the cesspit. Bathing was only possible in summer in the lake itself. The only toilet paper we had was dried leaves. Besides that, I was merely tolerated and had to do hard manual labor. But I always tried to learn things, so I read a lot because I wanted to gain

11. Leopold Engleitner, ca. 1923

knowledge and prevent my mind from stagnating. Opportunities were very limited, though, because in those days, there wasn't much reading material yet. Most of the time, I read newspapers. The farmers didn't like it at all when I read after work in the evenings. They sat round the table and grumbled, "Now he's reading again. We were born to work, not to read." They had very outdated views about life. For them, only work was important, and nothing else mattered. I found it disconcerting. Not only that, but everything was dominated by Catholic tradition, and people didn't question things much; they stuck rigidly to custom.

I wasn't able to learn a trade, because, at that time, fathers had to pay the master craftsman for their child's training. I would have liked to be an electrician, but unfortunately, my father didn't have the money for it. That's why I could only work as a laborer. Mostly I worked for farmers as a farmhand. Sometimes I worked on fortifying and regulating the beds of mountain streams, and once I worked with the woodcutters. So those were my jobs in the 1920s. In the early 1930s, I was out of work due to the economic crisis. Once I had to appear as an extra in a movie filmed in St. Wolfgang starring Hans Moser and Emil Jannings. The movie was called *Favorite of the Gods*.

6. What can you tell us about your family?
ENGLEITNER: Both my grandfathers died before I was born, as did my maternal grandmother. I was very close to my paternal grandmother, Elisabeth Engleitner, and loved her more than I loved my mother. She was more like my father, and not so strict about religion. She also felt drawn to Protestantism. She was a widow for a long time. My paternal grandfather was very sick. He overtaxed himself building their house and, when it was finished, contracted a lung disease and died prematurely. So my grandmother had to go out to work, in a big store in Bad Ischl called Gottwald. When she could no longer work, they gave her a small allowance so she had enough to live on because there were no pensions in those days. I often gave her some of my money too. She died in 1926. My half-brother, Ferdinand, died in December 1918 at the age of twenty-two in a tree-felling accident.

My parents died in 1955 and my brother Heinrich in 1960. I let them live in my house until they died and moved into an apartment with my wife. I got married after the war, in 1949. My wife Theresia had a daughter [Ida] from her first marriage, and later on I adopted her. Although she was thirteen years younger than I, my wife unfortunately died in 1981. We couldn't have any children of our own, because an SS man had crushed one of my testicles with a kick in Niederhagen concentration camp, leaving me sterile. Through my adopted daughter, I now have grandchildren, great-grandchildren, and great-great-grandchildren.

7. Did you use the Nazi greeting "Heil Hitler!" and/or the Nazi salute?
ENGLEITNER: I didn't use the greeting "Heil Hitler" for the reason that "Heil" means "salvation," and salvation cannot come from any person, only from God!

8. Why were you persecuted by the National Socialists?
ENGLEITNER: I was locked up because I was one of Jehovah's Witnesses and refused to do military service.

9. When were you arrested?

ENGLEITNER: On April 4, 1939, in Bad Ischl.

10. Why were you imprisoned?

ENGLEITNER: Because I had gone to the house of my friend Franz Rothauer in Bad Ischl to meet four more of Jehovah's Witnesses and commemorate the death of Jesus Christ and because I refused to give up my faith. Hitler had prohibited gatherings of Jehovah's Witnesses, but I ignored the ban because, for me, the biblical commandment carried more weight.

11. What exactly happened when you were arrested?

ENGLEITNER: All of a sudden, there was a knock at the window. I went to the front door and asked, "What's up?" "Gestapo!" they said. Then I said, "What have we got to do with the Gestapo? We're no criminals." "We'll show you," [they said]. They banged on the door again, so I unlocked it. They burst in, pushed me to one side, and said, "Where are you keeping the *Watchtowers*?" I said, "There aren't any *Watchtowers* anymore, they were prohibited a long time ago. We would be glad if we had one." Then they asked, "What are you doing here anyway?" "We're commemorating the death of Jesus Christ. That's not against the law, is it?" They said, "No, that's not against the law." Then they held a short conference and said, "If you tell us that you have nothing to do with Jehovah's Witnesses, that you're only a small religious group that is entirely devoted to Hitler and does nothing except what he commands, we see no need to arrest you." I said, "You'll have to ask the others. I can't agree with that." The others also declared that they didn't agree to this proposal. Then they arrested us. Only the house owner's wife was allowed to stay at home because she had a baby to look after.

12. Did people know right from the start what was happening in the camps? Before you were taken away, did you know what would happen to you?

ENGLEITNER: In general, not much was known. It was kept very secret. No one was supposed to know exactly what was going on there. All we heard was that it was terrible. The Gestapo threatened us with the words, "You'll get plenty of beatings in Buchenwald!" But I knew more, because at the convention of Jehovah's Witnesses in Prague in 1937, I had met brothers in the faith who had already been interned, and they told us about the dreadful conditions. I had also read accounts of concentration camps in *Watchtower* literature and in the book *Kreuzzug gegen das Christentum* (*Crusade Against Christianity*).[6] That book even had sketches of Esterwegen and Sachsenhausen concentration camps in it.

In the transport to Buchenwald concentration camp, I was put in a two-man cell with Dr. Heinrich Gleissner, the former governor of the province of Upper Austria. He had previously been interned in Dachau concentration camp. He told me he had met Jehovah's Witnesses in Dachau and that they had been treated very badly. He told me that he greatly admired them for their steadfastness, even though they had to suffer so much because of their faith. So it was clear to me that it would be no picnic, and that my faith would be tested to the limit. But I was determined not to let myself be swayed from it.

13. How many different camps were you in? How many years did you spend in each camp?

ENGLEITNER: I was in Buchenwald concentration camp from October 1939 until March 1941, in Niederhagen concentration camp in Wewelsburg from March 1941 until April 1943, and in Ravensbrück concentration camp until July 1943. Prior to that, I had already spent half a year from April through October 1939 in the prisons in Bad Ischl, Linz, and Wels.

It may also be interesting to note that even before the Nazi era, I was sent to prison several times between 1934 and 1937 in Austria during the period of Austrofascism. The reason was that I had left the Catholic Church and had become one of Jehovah's Witnesses. This occurred even though, under Section V, Articles 62 and 63, of the Peace Treaty of St. Germain, there was freedom of religion in Austria. When I lost my job because of the economic downturn, I was even disqualified from receiving unemployment benefits because I didn't belong to a major church.

---

[6]   Published by Franz Zürcher in 1938 from firsthand reports of Jehovah's Witnesses, which included details exposing to the public the atrocities in the concentration camps. See also Simone Liebster, question 12.

14. Were you the only member of your family in the concentration camp, or were family members or friends there as well? If so, did you have any contact with them?

ENGLEITNER: I was alone, with no family and no friends. In the concentration camps, I had Jehovah's Witnesses as friends. The three Jehovah's Witnesses who were arrested with me were deported to other concentration camps.

15. What were the first things that happened immediately following your arrival at the concentration camp?

ENGLEITNER: We arrived in Buchenwald at ten o'clock at night. We were put straight in the bunker because they couldn't register us at night. There were way too few cells in the bunker, so they crammed us in anywhere. We could only stand pressed against each other with our hands at our sides. Each cell was as crowded as the next. Then the bunker supervisor arrived, opened the peephole, and asked each one in turn, "Why are you here? Why are you here? Why are you here?" Then it was my turn. "Why are you here?" I replied, "I'm one of Jehovah's Witnesses." "You're finished, that's the worst," he said. He tore open the door, grabbed me, and dragged me out. Then he put me in another cell that was pitch-black. I couldn't see a thing. Then blows rained down on me from all directions, and I fell down. Next he tried to kick me, but couldn't reach me [because I had rolled under the bed]. He was groaning because he kept banging himself [on the edge of the bed]. Then suddenly the door opened, and in the bright light, I could see that it was a prisoner who had been pounding me.

Now the bunker supervisor dragged me out and took me to his guardroom. In the guardroom, he made me bend over a bench. Then he beat me furiously until he got tired. He said he would have to shoot me but told me to write a farewell note home. When I tried to write, he kept jogging my right elbow so all I produced was a lot of scribbles. Then he said, "Look at this bastard, he can't even write, but he's smart enough to read the Bible." Then he said he was going to shoot me. He took his pistol out of its holster, pressed it against my forehead, and said, "I'm pulling the trigger now! Are you ready?" "Yes, I am," I replied. But there was no report, and no shot was fired. After a pause, he said, "You're too stupid even to shoot."

Then the bunker supervisor—Martin Sommer, his name was—took me back to the cell I had been put in when I arrived. There was a small pot there, full to the brim with urine. He made me carry it to the toilet, warning me not to spill anything. As I walked along with the pot, he kept hitting me from behind, so that by the time I reached the toilet, it was almost empty.

I spent the whole night standing in the single cell from which the SS man had pulled me earlier. Ten prisoners were crammed into it. I was in terrible pain from the beating I had received, my head especially was throbbing, I was slightly dazed, and my hearing was impaired.

Next morning, our particulars were taken down. I was given the prisoner number 6778, prisoner's clothing, and a purple triangle, and my head was shaved. I had ceased to be a man: now I was only a number. As a newcomer, I was detailed to work three months in the feared "Penal Company Quarry."

16. Why did they shave the heads of the prisoners?
ENGLEITNER: To make it harder to escape. If a prisoner escaped, he was immediately recognized outside as a prisoner. The barbers, who were prisoners, came into the barracks at regular intervals and cut our hair. After a while, they shaved a stripe down the middle of our heads from front to back. That made us even more conspicuous.

17. What prisoner category were you put in?
ENGLEITNER: In the Bible Students, as Jehovah's Witnesses were called in the concentration camp. We were a separate category and were given our own triangle by the SS. It was a purple triangle.

18. Can you describe the daily routine in the concentration camp?
ENGLEITNER: At sunrise, an alarm went off and we had to jump out of bed straightaway and make our beds. We weren't allowed to get up before the alarm went off, because that counted as an escape attempt. Then we had to trot quickly to the washroom and the toilet, then back to the barrack. There we had breakfast: a brown brew they called coffee and a morsel of bread saved from the previous day's evening meal.

After that, we had to hurry to morning roll call, after which every work detail had to go to their allotted tasks. At midday, there was another roll call. After that, we were given a very thin stew to eat, which hardly gave us any strength. If you were greedy and ate it very fast, you died sooner. It was important to eat slowly so you digested the small portion properly. A prisoner gave me that advice. That way you could avoid a quick death.

Then it was back to your work detail. At sunset, there was evening roll call when another count was made to see if all the prisoners were present and to make sure no one had escaped. This roll call often went on for two hours because the SS men deliberately prolonged it. Some prisoners were so exhausted by this that they even fainted, especially in very cold or very hot weather.

Then we were allowed back into the barracks and were given an evening meal. There was bread, and sometimes a little margarine or sausage, or an onion. Of course it was nowhere near enough. Then, starving and utterly exhausted, we collapsed into our beds.

19. What was the worst thing about the daily routine?
ENGLEITNER: It was all bad. What I found particularly bad was the persistence in trying to make me give up my faith and the scorn shown by many SS men for the Creator, Jehovah God. When we suffered, they mocked us, saying, "Where's your Jehovah, then? Why doesn't he help you?" Prisoners made fun of us too. That was very hurtful. I was convinced that Jehovah God was giving me the strength to cope with it all, as in fact he was. It was also very depressing to see how men became brutalized. Through my study of the Bible, I learned to love my neighbor and maintain peace, but the SS created a climate of hatred and brutality in the concentration camp, and many prisoners allowed themselves to be contaminated by it.

20. Did everyday life lead more to solidarity, or did the prisoners try to cope on their own?
ENGLEITNER: We Jehovah's Witnesses stuck together and tried to live according to biblical principles despite these adverse conditions. As a result, it was always pleasant in our barrack, and during the day, we looked forward to being together again after work.

21. Was there anything that helped you take your mind off the horror of daily life for a while (such as music)? What gave you strength?
ENGLEITNER: The SS ordered us to sing the camp song when we were on the march, but that didn't give us strength. I always thought of encouraging Bible passages. In Buchenwald, Jehovah's Witnesses had even smuggled in a Bible, which was taken apart. I had the book of Job for several months and hid it in my socks. I could only read it at night. The patience of Job, who was also in adversity, gave me strength. Besides that, I prayed constantly and told God about my troubles.

22. What were living conditions like in the barracks (prisoner allocation, food supplies, hygiene, clothing, etc.)?
ENGLEITNER: There were two rooms in the barracks: a dayroom, where we sat at tables, and a dormitory with bunk beds in which we had to lie on wood wool or straw.

The food was very bad. We were permanently hungry, and sometimes the food we were given was rotten. Sometimes it even happened that the cauldron was already empty when you got there with your bowl. The distribution was not fair, and the *kapos* took the most. In Niederhagen concentration camp, we were so hungry that we even looked for bones in the trash cans. The bones were boiled in the kitchen until we could eat them despite our rotten teeth. We all had scurvy, and in the concentration camp, all my teeth fell out except for a few rotten stumps. In Ravensbrück, one prisoner was so clumsy that he accidentally broke my bowl. I didn't have anything to carry the thin stew in. Then I found a broken cardboard box and carried the stew in that. Most of it dripped out. I couldn't eat it fast enough and ended up with virtually nothing. As a result, I got weaker and weaker.

Hygiene varied enormously from camp to camp. In Buchenwald and Wewelsburg, we Jehovah's Witnesses took great care to keep clean, so we managed to stay free of lice and other parasites. We changed our clothes once a week. In Buchenwald, we were also able to take a shower once a week. We had to undress outside the prisoners' baths in all weathers and dress outside again afterward. That was rough, especially in winter. In Wewelsburg, it depended on whether there was enough hot water. Showers were often canceled there because the order came, "No one is to take a shower because the commandant wants to take a bath!" We could wash every day with cold water. In Ravensbrück, there were no showers at all. It was terrible there. Clothes were only changed once a month, and there were way too few places to wash. I was covered in lice and bites, and had festering ulcers all over my body.

23. What jobs did you have to do? How many hours a day did you have to work?

ENGLEITNER: In the quarry, the worst thing was that there weren't nearly enough tools. In the evening, everything was thrown onto a pile. When the order "Take a tool!" came, the workers fought over them. If you didn't manage to get a tool, you had to dig out the rocks with your bare hands all day. It was so dreadful that young prisoners of fifteen or sixteen went gray in a matter of weeks. The situation was terrible because we were continually beaten by SS men and *kapos* while we worked.

It rained every day. In October 1939, the weather was particularly bad. We got soaking wet every day, but there was no heating in the barracks so we couldn't dry anything. Every morning, we had to put on our wet clothes again. As a result, dysentery broke out after a few weeks. That was in Buchenwald. Following the ten-week dysentery epidemic, a construction firm built a sewage plant at the concentration camp. I was detailed to work on it by *Lagerführer* (Camp Leader) Arthur Rödl. He had a soft spot for me because he had often been to St. Wolfgang.

In Wewelsburg, I worked on fence construction, in agriculture, and sometimes in the castle itself. An electric barbed wire fence was erected round the camp, and the current was switched off while work was in progress. The SS only assigned Jehovah's Witnesses to this task because they wouldn't try to escape. In the basement crypt of Wewelsburg's north tower, Heinrich Himmler had a tomb built for high-ranking Nazis. Only Jehovah's Witnesses were assigned to work on it. It was strictly forbidden to talk to anyone else about what was being done there. Sometimes I had to take gravel and cement to this building site. As a former farm worker, I was also put in harvesting details on nearby farms. I had to harvest potatoes and turnips. The farmers asked the camp commandant to send prisoners. They had to pay for the work we did, but we got nothing. Again, only Jehovah's Witnesses were assigned to these details because we were escorted by only two guards, and they knew we wouldn't try to escape.

The daily working hours varied according to the time of year. They were longer in summer because the sun set later, and shorter in winter.

24. What effect did the slogan "Work liberates" have on you?

ENGLEITNER: It was a huge mockery of us prisoners because no one was liberated by the work. However, the slogan wasn't put up at the entrance of every concentration camp. In Buchenwald, for example, there was the inscription "To each his own" on the front gate. That implied that the prisoners deserved the terrible treatment they received. That was very cynical too.

25. What were the guards like in the camp?

ENGLEITNER: Quite varied. There were very violent SS men like Hans Hüttig in Buchenwald. He struck prisoners full in the face with a dog whip. One time he gave my back a severe whipping. In Niederhagen concentration camp, an SS man crushed one of my testicles with a kick. Another wanted to lure me into a trap so he could shoot me. But there were also some who showed humanity. In Niederhagen concentration camp, I once accidentally crossed the cordon when I was working in the woods, and an SS man saw me. By rights he should have shot me because that was considered an escape attempt. But instead he warned me, and when I asked him, "What good would it have done you if you had shot me?" he replied, "We get two weeks' leave if an escaping prisoners is shot." I was very grateful to him for that. One time an SS man even slipped me his sandwich.

There were also some prisoners who were in charge of work details. These were the *kapos*, and they differed greatly too. Some were extremely violent. In Niederhagen concentration camp, there was Max Schüller, a man with a long criminal record. He wanted to kill me at all costs. One time he wanted to beat me to death with the broken-off handle of a shovel. He rained blows on me, and an SS man stopped him, otherwise he would have killed me.

26. Was there any contact between the prisoners and the local population?

ENGLEITNER: In the concentration camp, there was normally no contact with the population because, as a prisoner, you were completely isolated. In Buchenwald, there was one exception: when I had to work on the sewage plant. The construction company's truck drivers were civilians, and they hid bread and sausage in the loads of sand, and we would eat them in secret.

In Wewelsburg, I came into contact with farmers when I had to work in the harvest detail. However, it was forbidden to speak to them. Once we had an amusing incident. A farmer's wife wanted to bring us something to eat in the field where we were working. That was strictly forbidden. The sentry captain forbade it, and when the farmer's wife turned to go home again, he said, "But you can leave the food here: we sentries will eat it." When she heard that, the farmer's wife started laughing and said, "Out of the question! The prisoners who have to work are not allowed to eat, but those who watch them are? Either the prisoners get something to eat, or no one does!" She was a very determined woman, and it was a very brave thing to do because the SS man could have sent her to the concentration camp for it. But he was evidently very hungry too because he said to her, "Dish it out, then." To us prisoners, he said, "Sit down and eat." We were very grateful to that lady.

27. Were you aware of how the war was proceeding in the outside world?

ENGLEITNER: No, in the concentration camp, I couldn't follow it, because we were cut off from any information about it. It was only from new arrivals in the camp that we heard a few meager accounts.

28. In the concentration camp, were you allowed to receive letters, food parcels, etc.?

ENGLEITNER: Initially I wasn't allowed to write or receive any letters in Buchenwald. Later on, I was permitted to write home once a month. But everything was censored.

Once, permission was granted to write home to say we were allowed to receive clothing, jackets, and so on for warmth. But on no account was food to be sent. When we were summoned to collect our parcels from the SS, they were opened in front of us, and if there was any food inside, the SS guard just threw it out of the window. Then the prisoners threw themselves to the muddy ground and stuffed the grubby food into their mouths. I didn't do that. When the guard asked me why I wasn't joining in, I said, "I can't get down that low, and I'll never be hungry enough to eat muck." So then he told me to hold out my cap, and he filled it with clean cookies, saying, "Eat them out of your cap, then you won't have to eat dirty ones." The prisoner for whom the cookies had been sent saw this. He gave me an angry look, then disappeared. When I had picked up my parcel of linen, I looked for him to give him his cookies. But I couldn't find him, so I ate them myself.

29. What forms of torture did you suffer?

ENGLEITNER: When I arrived at Buchenwald concentration camp, I was brutally beaten by the SS man Martin Sommer. I was also severely beaten while working in the quarry.

In Niederhagen concentration camp, an SS man crushed one of my testicles with his boot. The *kapo* Max Schüller was also extremely vicious toward me and nearly beat me to death with the broken-off handle of a shovel.

30. What was the most frightening moment for you?

ENGLEITNER: My arrival at Buchenwald concentration camp when the bunker supervisor Martin Sommer nearly shot me. So it was the first day in the bunker. It was appalling. But I had to resist this intimidation even though I thought I was done for.

31. Were there any entertaining or lighthearted incidents that enabled you to forget all the suffering for a moment? Can you describe them?

ENGLEITNER: When we didn't have any work to do on Sundays, some of the SS men ordered prisoners to play soccer with them. One time, the SS ordered us prisoners to have a snowball fight amongst ourselves. Because I was so small, a prisoner took me on his shoulders, and I was then the target for everyone else. I was hit by quite a few snowballs, and they sure stung. It was fun for the others, but not for me. Once in a while a *kapo* or SS man would praise us and say, "Well done!" and you were pleased about that. Sometimes we made jokes. When Austria became part of Germany, everyone was saying, "*Heim ins Reich*" (We're going home to the empire). When it became clear that the German empire was coming to an end, we said, "*Heim, uns reicht's*" (We're going home, we've had enough).

32. What were your day-to-day thoughts while you were in the concentration camp?

ENGLEITNER: On the one hand, to keep a strong faith; on the other, I thought about going home again. I firmly believed that, there was never any doubt about it.

One time an SS man said to me, "You have two possibilities of returning home: either you sign, or you go through the chimney." He meant that either I would have to sign the renunciation, which would mean giving up my faith, or I would certainly die and leave the concentration camp as smoke through the chimney of the crematorium. But I was determined to get out of the camp alive and without having made any compromises. So I said, "I will not sign, and I will not go through the chimney. I will go home!" The SS man replied, "You're so fanatical, you think you'll be able to go home one day. You have no other option than to sign." But I was so sure that I would go home again that I bought a suitcase in Niederhagen concentration camp. From time to time, the camp authorities let us prisoners buy the property of inmates who had died and whose home addresses were unknown. On one such occasion, I bought a suitcase so I could pack my things for the journey home. And I really made that journey. I left Ravensbrück concentration camp with that suitcase and went home with it.

33. Was it possible for children to be born in a concentration camp? If so, what happened to these babies?

ENGLEITNER: I don't know anything about that. I had no contact with any women in the concentration camp. In Ravensbrück, the male camp was strictly separated from the female camp. If ever we came across a group of women internees when we were working outside the camp, the women had to either turn their backs on us or kneel down and look at the ground.

34. Was it possible to make friends with prisoners?

ENGLEITNER: There was that possibility, especially with other Jehovah's Witnesses. With them, you were automatically a friend and a brother in the faith. But I also spent a lot of time talking to a prisoner who had a black triangle [asocial element] and we became friends. I often worked with him.

35. Who was your best friend during this dreadful time, and how did he or she help you?

ENGLEITNER: My best friend was Jehovah himself. He helped me in many situations; otherwise, I would never have come home again. He gave me the strength to remain faithful.

36. What did you do to relieve the suffering of other inmates?

ENGLEITNER: I was helpful toward everyone. I had several opportunities to help, and I was happy to do so out of love for my fellowmen.

One time, I was working with two clergymen: one Catholic, one Protestant. I loaded earth into their wheelbarrows. A *kapo* had ordered me to make sure their loads were heavy. They were much too heavy for them, and that met with the *kapo*'s approval. I felt sorry for them, so I helped them. When the *kapo* went away for a while, I wheeled their wheelbarrows for them so they could have a breather. Naturally they were very grateful to me.

In November 1939, an unsuccessful attempt was made on Adolf Hitler's life in Munich by Georg Elser. We prisoners in Buchenwald concentration camp also felt the backlash of Hitler's anger. Our rations were suspended for three days; the Jews' rations, for six days. We never had enough to eat anyway, so this was a terrible torture. When we got some food again after three days, the starving Jews came into our barracks with their bowls to beg for food. Although I myself was famished and could scarcely spare anything, I gave the Jews a few spoonfuls of my stew. Most of the others prisoners did the same. Unfortunately it was not enough for all of them. It cost a tremendous effort, but I felt sorry for them.

In Wewelsburg, a big Russian prisoner collapsed during morning roll call. The other prisoners went away, but an SS man and I noticed him. He was still breathing, though with difficulty. He was a beanpole of a man. I sat him up, pulled him up onto my back, and dragged him to sickbay. I could still feel his breath, so I hoped I would still be able to help him. But unfortunately he died on my back and was already dead when I reached sickbay.

37. Were there particular hierarchies among the inmates?

ENGLEITNER: Yes, there were *kapos*. They were prisoners who acted as foremen in charge of prisoner work details. Some of them were extremely violent. They tried to ingratiate themselves with the SS or to gain an advantage by bullying or mistreating prisoners. They got more to eat too. The block seniors, room orderlies, and table seniors were prisoners who kept things in order in the barracks and supervised the serving of the meals. Some of them abused their position, but there were good ones too. Then there were a camp senior and a camp secretary. They were prisoners who had to work with the camp command and had a higher status. They were able to intervene on behalf of prisoners and sometimes succeeded in persuading the SS to reduce punishments a little.

38. Were there any differences in the way the various groups of prisoners (religious, political groups) were treated?

ENGLEITNER: In general, they were all treated equally. But there were situations in which some were worse off. For example in Buchenwald, when the Jews were not given any food for three days longer than the others. Also, in the camp canteen, you could sometimes buy food or drink. Everyone could buy something, including the Jews. We Jehovah's Witnesses were the only ones who couldn't, because we weren't given the money that was in our accounts. We weren't allowed to do what we liked with the money donated by family or acquaintances. The money they sent was put into an account, and withdrawals were only possible in exceptional cases. When I needed dental treatment, or when I bought the suitcase, I was given the necessary amount from my account.

39. What diseases and illnesses were prevalent in the concentration camp?

ENGLEITNER: There were all kinds of diseases. None of the prisoners was healthy. In Buchenwald, dysentery broke out among the prisoners and even spread to the SS. I was lucky. I didn't get it. We also had scurvy because of the poor quality of the food. My whole body was covered with festering boils. I even had them on my face, with pus always oozing out of them.

40. Did you receive a physical injury?

ENGLEITNER: Several times. When I arrived, I was so badly beaten that my head ached for weeks afterward. My hearing was also damaged, and I had severe pains everywhere.

In Niederhagen concentration camp, an SS man kicked me in the abdomen so hard that I collapsed and could no longer walk. He had crushed one of my testicles. That was very painful. One time, a prisoner beat me so hard across the back with a plank of wood that it broke—and only because I was a couple of seconds late for roll call. I couldn't help it, because I had to tidy up where I had been working beforehand. The others were on time because they didn't help me.

41. How much did you weigh when you were in the concentration camp?

ENGLEITNER: When I was released, I weighed only sixty-two pounds. That was because conditions were very bad, especially in Ravensbrück. I couldn't have survived it for much longer.

42. What did death mean to you?

ENGLEITNER: Death is humankind's greatest enemy and was originally not planned by God. It has brought an unbelievable amount of suffering to humankind. In the concentration camp, I didn't want to let it win, and I fought back. I wanted to live. Sure, I often got lucky. Although in some situations it seemed like death would be a release, things looked completely different again a few moments later.

43. What was the closest you came to death?

ENGLEITNER: I was close to death the whole time. The first time was when I arrived. After that, you had to expect to be shot at any moment. In the quarry in Buchenwald, you could never say in the morning whether you would still be alive in the evening. We were beaten the whole day, and many died.

At the age of ninety-seven, I was very close to death again. I had severe pneumonia followed by weeks of severe diarrhea. I couldn't keep anything down. I vomited everything out again, even water. I was completely dehydrated, and it looked like there was no hope. But in the hospital, they succeeded in stopping the diarrhea after all and I recovered.

I was very ill again in 2011, and twice my condition was critical. But fortunately I survived with the help of my friends.

44. Did you ever build a kind of "wall" to shield yourself from the terrible things that were being done so that the death of a fellow prisoner no longer affected you?
ENGLEITNER: Yes, you had to protect yourself and not let things get to you too much. I'm sure we hardened ourselves to things a little with time. You had no other choice at the time, and you couldn't think about it too much. Death was there every day and everywhere. When I think about it today, I can no longer imagine how I coped with it then. My hope in the Bible helped me get through it, though. The book of Ecclesiastes in the Bible says that death is a state in which we have no feelings, no pain, and no thoughts anymore—like sleep. And I strongly believed that God would resurrect all those innocent people as Jesus Christ promises us in the Gospel According to John.

45. What happened to the dead bodies in the concentration camp?
ENGLEITNER: Normally, they were burned in the crematorium. But to begin with, neither Buchenwald nor Wewelsburg had a crematorium. So the bodies were stored someplace and taken to a crematorium outside the camp. In Wewelsburg, there was a room where the bodies were piled up, and there were so many fat flies in there that the only window was completely black with them. One time, I was detailed to carry the bodies out of there, and the stench was appalling. But just as I was about to start, other prisoners were ordered to take over.

46. Was there ever a possibility for you to be released from the concentration camp?
ENGLEITNER: With regard to us Jehovah's Witnesses, Hitler had decreed, "This brood will be exterminated in Germany." And that's how it stayed. As one of Jehovah's Witnesses, you could only be released if you signed the "renunciation." That was a declaration that you had abandoned the faith and submitted to Hitler entirely. I would have had to go to war. So, of course, there was never any question of my doing that. The offer was often made to me by the SS, but I always refused. As far as the Nazis were concerned, death was the only prospect in store for me if I wanted to stay faithful.

47. Were there any escape attempts or opportunities to escape? Did you try to escape?

ENGLEITNER: Some prisoners tried to escape. In Wewelsburg, I witnessed an escape attempt. In a work detail, we had to march right next to some woods. A Dutchman grabbed the opportunity and suddenly jumped into the woods in order to escape. But a sentry shot at him and hit him in the back of the head. We were immediately made to lie down and stay on the ground until we were allowed to stand up again. Then the prisoner was laid in front of us. We had to gather round him and look at him. The bullet had entered his head from behind and passed through his forehead, taking brains and blood with it. Ludwig Rehn, a vicious SS man, noticed that I couldn't bear to look. He grabbed me and shoved me on top of the prisoner as a deterrent to all the others.

We Jehovah's Witnesses never tried to escape, because if anyone broke out, the whole camp was severely punished. Meals were suspended, or the prisoners in the camp had to do punishment drills. Out of solidarity, we avoided any escape.

I had many opportunities to escape. One time I was assigned to a "harvest detail" to harvest turnips with three other Jehovah's Witnesses. Two young SS men were allocated to us as guards. They looked very tired. One of us asked them, "You look tired today. Didn't you get enough sleep?" "Not nearly enough," they said. "We didn't get home from a night out until four o'clock this morning." Then we asked, "Would you like a nap?" "Yes, if that's possible," they replied. "Yes, it's possible. We'll keep a lookout so you're not caught napping!" we promised. There were two haystacks nearby. They immediately burrowed a hole for themselves and lay down in them. They put their rifles down next to them. When we were done gathering turnips, we woke them up. That's how much trust those SS men had in us.

48. Were there any inmates in the concentration camp who dared to stage a revolt against the camp authorities?

ENGLEITNER: Yes, there were revolts, but I was never in the camps where they happened.

49. Did you think you would ever make it out alive?

ENGLEITNER: Yes, I was absolutely convinced I would. I wanted to survive at all costs to disprove the Nazis' claim that we would never come out alive without giving up our faith, and also so that later on I would be able to tell others what had happened. That's why I always hoped I would get out.

50. Were there any times when you gave up all hope? If so, why?

ENGLEITNER: No, I never gave up hope. It was a close call at the start, but I never gave up hope.

51. Did anyone commit suicide?

ENGLEITNER: Yes, that happened. Now and then, a prisoner would hang himself at night. Anywhere the chance presented itself—in his own barrack, for example. Some prisoners ran into the electric barbed wire fence that enclosed the camp and died that way. Some got themselves shot on purpose. They pretended to stage an escape attempt, knowing they would be shot. In Wewelsburg one time, a prisoner ran off, but the sentry who shot at him missed him twice. So the prisoner ran back to his work detail. Afterward he said he had deliberately provoked the shots. The sentry was punished for his bad shooting. The prisoner got a round hand-sized red patch sewn onto the back of his jacket. That meant he was a potential escapee.

52. During the Holocaust, did you ever consider committing suicide out of sheer despair?

ENGLEITNER: No, I didn't.

53. What thoughts, ideas, hopes, wishes, or religious convictions did you cling to?

ENGLEITNER: To the kingdom of God that billions of people pray for in the Lord's Prayer, and which, one day, will solve all of humankind's problems. That was my dream. Actually, it wasn't really a dream, it was my firm conviction. I wanted to go back to living as one of Jehovah's Witnesses. I always looked ahead. Whenever times were tough, I thought of Psalm 23 where it says, "Jehovah is my shepherd, I shall lack nothing." If God is my shepherd, and I trust in him, he will not abandon me. I've always had those words in my mind, all my life.

54. Did you lose your faith in God while you were in the camp?
ENGLEITNER: No, on the contrary: What I went through strengthened my faith even more because I have personally experienced the fulfillment of Bible prophecies. Jesus foretold our persecution. That was a confirmation for me.

In Buchenwald, we also held secret Bible talks on Sundays. Wilhelm Töllner, a brother in the faith, often used to strengthen our faith with words from the Bible.

55. What role did your religion play in how you felt about what was going on? Why?
ENGLEITNER: My religion played the most important role. Many lost their faith in God. But you cannot blame God for that. People are responsible for the Holocaust. The Bible says that God let man have the earth and gave him free will. Of course God wants us to use our free will for the good of our neighbor. But if he prevented people from doing bad things, it wouldn't be free will anymore.

But God won't allow that forever. He has promised that he has fixed a time when everyone will have to account to him for their actions. Then he will see to it that all the suffering is undone. I firmly believe that.

56. Did you pray during your internment?
ENGLEITNER: Of course I prayed—it was because of my faith that I was in the concentration camp in the first place. So I prayed for God's blessing and the strength to get through it all and remain faithful. I was convinced that he would give those who serve him the protection they need. I prayed at every opportunity and cast all my troubles and fears on God. That's why I didn't worry anymore. In the Bible, he even bids us to throw all our burdens on him. That's in Psalm 55:22.

57. Did you ever consider changing your religion (or ideology)? Why?
ENGLEITNER: No, on the contrary. My convictions were unshakable, and I would never have given them up even though the chance was often presented to me, and doing so would have spared me a lot of suffering. But I wanted to stay true to God.

58. What was the date of your liberation from the camp?

ENGLEITNER: I was unexpectedly released from Ravensbrück concentration camp on July 15, 1943. In 1943, Heinrich Himmler had decided to release certain Jehovah's Witnesses in particular cases without their having to renounce their faith, provided they committed themselves to working as forced laborers in agriculture for the rest of their lives.

59. How were you liberated from the camp, or how did you manage to get out of it?

ENGLEITNER: I was called to the guardroom where they explained that I could be released if I agreed to spend the rest of my life working in agriculture. And I was willing to do that. The camp doctor said to me, "You're still one of those Jehovah's Witnesses, aren't you?" I said, "*Jawohl* (Yes, sir)." Then he said, "We can't really release you, then, can we?" Then he looked me over and remarked, "We'll be glad to be rid of such a wretched creature as you."

To be honest, he was right. I was covered in lice and weighed only sixty-two pounds. I had to get dressed because they gave me my civilian clothes. Two SS men were there, and they were determined to chase me through the cordon of sentries so they could shoot me. They would have thrown my cap beyond the line and shot me as if I had been escaping. But a *kapo* prevented it. He said, "He was a hardworking prisoner, he always worked diligently. He's going home now, that's been decided. He's going home!" So the two SS men were stopped from satisfying their thirst for blood.

60. How were you treated by the people who liberated you?

ENGLEITNER: I wasn't liberated from the concentration camp by the Allies, like many other prisoners were. I was liberated by the Allies in a different way.

61. What was the first thing you did after you were liberated?

ENGLEITNER: Following my release from the concentration camp, I wasn't completely free. I had to work as a forced laborer on the Unterbergers' farm in St. Wolfgang. The owners were very good to me, and I hoped to see out the end of the war without any more problems. But three weeks later, I was summoned to a medical examination for military service. The medical officer examined me and found me unfit for service because of my curvature of the spine. So I was unfit for military service. But a week later, I had to go back for another examination, and this time the same medical officer, without examining me again, read me my medical report, which said, "Fit for active service at the front lines, reserve No. 1."

On April 17, 1945, I received my call-up papers for the German Wehrmacht. I was ordered to go to the front and report to the military base in Krumau in six hours' time. But I was determined not to play a part in this terrible war. The Bible commandment "You shall not murder" carried more weight for me than the government's orders. My only chance of escape was to hide in the mountains of the Salzkammergut region. I fled over the Wirlinger Wand to the southern slope of the Leonsberg mountain. I had to be very careful because I was sure the Nazis would search for me. And if they had found me, they would have shoot me on the spot. I was a deserter and a conscientious objector. Luckily, there was a strong southerly wind, which meant the temperature was pleasantly mild. I was able to spend the night under the trees. I made a makeshift bed with the branches of a pine tree and tried to get some sleep. My great disadvantage was that I had no companion who could take turns keeping watch. I was so jumpy that I awoke at the slightest noise.

After about a week, the warm wind dropped, and there was a dramatic change in the weather. It started raining, and then heavy snow started to fall. The snow was soon half a meter [18 inches] deep in the mountains. I was at an altitude of about 1,000 meters [3,200 feet]. I was wet through and through, half frozen, and utterly exhausted. There was only one thing I could do: I needed an alpine hut in which to warm myself and get dry.

That's why I had no other option but to take refuge in the Meistereben hut. That was very risky because that hut belonged to the farmer I worked for, and it would likely be the first place the Nazis would think of looking for me. I made a fire on the open hearth. I warmed myself and dried my clothes. Then I felt drowsy, so I cleared the fire and pushed the embers into a corner. I put a log down as a barrier to stop myself from turning over into the fire in my sleep. I soon fell asleep on the warm bench by the stove. Unfortunately, the log caught fire, and the flames spread to my clothes. I was literally on fire and was jolted awake by a piercing pain in my back. There was no way to put the fire out other than rolling on the floor of the hut, which was covered with snow. The hut was partly on a stone foundation and raised at one end. That's how the wind blew the snow in up through the cracks in the floor. My whole back was covered in burns. I was in agony.

It was the middle of the night. Somewhere I had to get my wounds treated and find fresh clothes. I had no choice. I had to risk going back to the Unterbergers' farm, although it would put me in great danger of running straight into the arms of the Nazis. I covered myself as best I could with my burned clothes. I was burning with fever, shaking all over, and had a raging thirst. I tried to slake my thirst at every stream I passed. When I arrived at the farm, the farmer's wife immediately sent me away again. She was greatly afraid that I would be discovered under her roof. Because it was already light, all I could do was run to my own house, which was nearby. My parents were living there. They didn't want to let me in either, but I had to stay there. I changed my clothes and looked for a hiding place in the hayloft. I was in tremendous pain, but glad just to be still alive. With a pitchfork, my mother lifted up a damp cloth to cool my burns and some hot soup in a milk can. A neighbor who had already betrayed someone to the Nazis suspected I was in the vicinity and kept asking my parents where I was. They were terrified of being arrested themselves. They complained the whole time.

They told me that Hitler had committed suicide. I knew that the war wouldn't last much longer, but it was still very dangerous. High-ranking Nazis had retreated to the Salzkammergut or were living there. Ernst Kaltenbrunner, Adolf Eichmann, and August Eigruber had houses in Altaussee; Kaltenbrunner even had another one in St. Wolfgang. There were a lot of soldiers in the area, and the Nazis hid there the goods that they had stolen. In the end, I gave in to my parents' pressure and disappeared into the mountains again at dawn two days later.

I looked for a little cave in the rock face. I couldn't even stand up in it. I lined my refuge with pine twigs and moss. The cave was a good hiding place. I had a good view of the surrounding area from it. But then I developed bad diarrhea. Because of the melting snow, water kept dripping through the limestone, making the cave unbearable. I was utterly exhausted and had no strength left at all. I went back to the Meistereben hut, since it was nearby. This time, I took more care when I made a fire.

Then I gathered together the last of the hay to make a bed in the loft. I had a good view of the Attersee [lake] through the back door where I could watch for signs that the war had ended.

But the situation got very dangerous for me one more time. The military authorities had sent out a scout patrol: three Nazis and Franz Kain from my hometown of St. Wolfgang. I used to work with him. The Nazis were forcing him to use his local knowledge to guide them. They had already searched a lot of mountain huts. Then they came to Breitenberg [mountain] near my hiding place. There was a thick fog. Franz Kain suspected I was in the Meistereben hut and had managed to keep the patrol away from it, but now they were dangerously close. The patrol leader stopped on a hill. He looked at his hand-drawn map and said, "There must be another hut down there. Let's search it!" Now Kain saw only one chance of preventing my capture and execution. He protested, "I'm not climbing down there in this weather, in this fog! It's much too dangerous." Then the leader said, "If it's so dangerous, we'll go down some other time." Franz Kain saved my life with this diversion because there was never to be another time.

In the early morning of May 5, 1945, I saw from the hut Allied aircraft flying low over the Attersee. I also heard explosions and saw smoke billowing up when I looked down at the lake. That was a sign that the Allies were blowing up the Germans' ammunition dumps and had finally defeated the Hitler regime. In the evening, I cautiously went back to the Unterbergers' farm. The farmer told me the Germans were going to surrender the next day and that the war was over. So I was liberated by the Allies indirectly and not straight from a concentration camp like most prisoners were.

62. Did you have any problems when you returned home? How did people in your home environment react to you?

ENGLEITNER: I expected people to welcome me with open arms. But the very opposite occurred. No one was interested in my story. Because I was a conscientious objector, they accused me of being a traitor to the fatherland and a coward. The Nazis' propaganda was still in people's minds. It was claimed that only criminals, the lazy, and other bad people who deserved imprisonment had been in the concentration camps. There were many folk who even claimed that concentration camps had never existed. That was very hurtful. My father was afraid of going into a shop because people sneered at him on my account. So then, of course, I went there myself and talked openly about my experiences. In time, those people gradually stopped talking to us like that when they realized that their humiliating remarks were like water off a duck's back to me.

63. Were you able to rejoin your family?
ENGLEITNER: Yes, but my parents and my brother were not persecuted by the Nazis. They were at home during the war.

64. Did you have any acquaintances, friends, or relatives in the camps? Did they survive their internment?
ENGLEITNER: None of my relatives was in a concentration camp, but some of my friends were. I was the only one of Jehovah's Witnesses in the family. My sisters in the faith Pauline Schlägl and Rosalia Hahn, and my brother in the faith Franz Rothauer, who were arrested with me in Bad Ischl, sadly did not survive. They died in concentration camps. I was the only one who came home alive.

65. What happened to your possessions?
ENGLEITNER: While I was in the concentration camp, an attempt was made to take my house from me. But not by the Nazis. No, my own father wanted it, and he wrote a letter to me while I was in the concentration camp saying I should give it to him. But I didn't do it; it remained my property.

The National Socialists took a gramophone away from me that I never got back. Before the war, I used to visit people with the gramophone and play them recordings of talks on Bible subjects. After the war, I once asked the police whether it had been found anywhere. They said, "No, but we'll just take a gramophone from a Nazi and give it to you." But I didn't want that. I just wanted my own gramophone back and didn't want to take anything away from someone else. That would have been unfair.

66. To what extent have you received compensation for your internment?
ENGLEITNER: Immediately after the war, I received nothing at all. The Communists were given support, but not me. Jehovah's Witnesses weren't recognized as victims. My application for a victims' pension was rejected,

even though I had suffered damage to my health in the concentration camp. But then I contacted a former fellow prisoner, Dr. Heinrich Gleissner, who was back as governor of Upper Austria. He made sure that I received a victims' pension. In recent years, I've been awarded larger sums from various institutions as compensation.

67. How did you set about rebuilding your life?
ENGLEITNER: By working hard.

68. How long did it take you to return to a "normal" life after the Holocaust?
ENGLEITNER: I had no other option but to return to a normal life again as soon as possible. I couldn't rest or take time to recover. I had to go to work and cope with everyday life. At first I was plagued by nightmares, but they gradually became less frequent. I had to leave the life in the concentration camp behind me and stop thinking about the atrocities. I got over it quickly. Now, I have no problem with it. I have distanced myself from it all, and it no longer hurts me.

69. What was your life like after the war?
ENGLEITNER: After the war, I worked on the Unterbergers' farm until 1946. Then I wanted a different job. But the labor office in Bad Ischl wouldn't allow it, saying that the commitment from the Nazi days to perform forced labor in agriculture still applied. I told the manager that the end of the Nazi regime must have released me from this obligation, but he didn't agree. He maintained that I was only allowed to work in agriculture. My father wrote to the American military authorities about it, and they made it clear to the labor office in Bad Ischl that this agreement was no longer valid. So then I was free to choose any job, and I worked as a night watchman at a soap factory. From 1951 onward, I worked as a laborer for the Bad Ischl road maintenance department, and in 1969, I retired. After the war, I also added to the house I built in 1931.

The years after the war weren't easy. There was hardly anyone I could talk to about my experiences. No one was interested in them, and when I started talking about them, people either didn't listen or said, "Give it a rest! That was all a long time ago, and we don't want to hear any more about it." I was shunned by society, rejected, and marginalized. That hurt me very much, especially because in the concentration camp, I had always wanted to tell as many people as possible about my experiences so they could learn from them. It looked like my story would be forgotten and no one would be able to gain anything from it, although that would have meant a lot to me.

But then one day in 1994, I happened to meet a young man, Bernhard Rammerstorfer, in the spa gardens in Bad Ischl. He didn't just walk past me like so many others had done before. Instead he took the time to listen to me and asked me a lot of questions. He was really interested in me, and I was able to tell him everything. We talked for hours—for days, in fact. That did me a lot of good. I was able to get everything off my chest. Then we visited the former concentration camps together, and I showed him where everything had happened. He filmed me for a documentary [*Unbroken Will*] and wrote a book [*Unbroken Will*] as well. So now my story has really been preserved, and that makes me very glad. Then with his support, I started talking to young people in schools and universities about my experiences as a witness of history. It's really marvelous to see the genuine interest that the young people show. I hope they learn something from my experiences, live according to just principles, and promote peace.

70. What is your life like today? Do you still often think back to those days?

ENGLEITNER: I feel good and I'm content. These are the happiest days of my life. Until February 2011, I still lived in my own house, and various helpers made sure I had everything I needed. Now I need constant care. I couldn't live alone anymore. That's why my friend Bernhard Rammerstorfer took me in; he and his family care for me round the clock with love and kindness. Life isn't so easy when you're over one hundred years old. Everything is hard work. I have to stick to a strict diet because I have a large gallstone; I can hardly eat any solids because I find it extremely difficult to swallow. So I usually drink through a straw.

My hearing and eyesight are also very bad. But I'm glad still to be alive and able to experience so many nice things, especially my encounters with young people in schools. My daily routine is still governed by my faith and my relationship with God. Every day, I read and study the Bible and Bible literature. I do it either with a closed-circuit television that magnifies the letters, or by friends reading to me, or by listening to the books of the Bible on cassette. My entire life revolves around that. For me, that comes first. I can't remember exactly how many times I've read the Bible, but I can say in all honesty that I've read it one hundred times.

The bad things I went through in the past are not really a burden anymore. I only think back to them when I'm asked about them. I have gotten over that time. I much prefer to look ahead to the future, and I look forward to experiencing what the Bible promises us. That will be a marvelous future. Peace and justice for humankind all over the world. I'm absolutely convinced that it will happen. The only question is whether we'll be worthy to experience it.

71. What physical and mental scars do you carry from that time?
ENGLEITNER: I had a crushed testicle, which has since been removed in an operation. Certain movements cause back pain for me, which is probably due to being beaten with a plank of wood by a prisoner. Since my beating from bunker supervisor Martin Sommer, I have been very hard of hearing in my left ear. The eardrum was damaged. And the concentration camp didn't help my congenital back problems. My time in the concentration camp did cause me psychological problems initially, but I got over all that. One thing I can say about my experiences: physical injuries are not as bad as psychological ones.

72. Did you have any moral support to help your emotional and social recovery?
ENGLEITNER: In general, I was shunned and ostracized by people, so I couldn't expect any support from them. It was more likely to be the opposite.

But I had friends among my fellow believers who sympathized. However my greatest support came from the Bible, prayer, and my close relationship with Jehovah God.

73. Has your view of the world changed since that time?
ENGLEITNER: My view of the world changed when I discovered the Bible. It did not change, because of the Holocaust, and it is still the same today.

74. Can you think of anything positive that you have gained from your experiences?

ENGLEITNER: I feel victorious. I won. I did not give in.

75. Have you ever been back to visit the concentration camp you were held in, and if so, what were your feelings?

ENGLEITNER: Yes, but only to visit them. I went to Buchenwald and Niederhagen in Wewelsburg for memorial events. I was even in Martin Sommer's guardroom where he nearly shot me. Of course the memories came flooding back. In my mind's eye, I saw myself as a prisoner on the roll-call square again, but I didn't have any painful feelings. It's over. Hitler sure made a mess of things. All the trouble he caused there rebounded on him. I now have friends in Wewelsburg and Buchenwald, especially young people.

The faces I see in those places today are different. The wicked faces have all disappeared. Now everyone smiles at me. In the places where maliciousness once reigned, I now feel love and kindness. That's why I'm very pleased to attend the memorial events.

76. Are you still in touch with your fellow internees from the concentration camps?

ENGLEITNER: I used to have close contact with them. I talked to them a lot about what they went through in the concentration camps. I found out a few things I wasn't aware of when I was in the camps. I even met a lot of them for the first time afterward; I hadn't known them in the camps. But unfortunately, most of them have already died.

77. What did you tell your family about your internment in the concentration camp? How did your relatives react to what you told them?

ENGLEITNER: Initially, I wanted to tell them about it, but I sensed that they weren't particularly interested. In their eyes, I was still the internee, the one being punished. Even after the war, my father wanted to take my house away from me. When the judge asked him why, he said, "My son has spent most of his life in prison! He's a concentration camp internee!"

Then even the judge lost patience with him and came to my defense, saying, "Your son has a very good reputation. The sentences he received were not for criminal offenses. He has suffered for a just and good cause and would not abandon his principles even under Hitler. A lot of fathers would be proud of such a courageous son!" That silenced my father, but despite that, he never once offered a word of gratitude to me.

Nowadays I sometimes talk to my grandchildren and great-grandchildren about my experiences, if they ask me. But that's very rare.

78. Do you find it difficult to talk about those days?
ENGLEITNER: No, because what happened in those days in Germany must never be forgotten. What I hold on to is the fact that I can tell the young generation how necessary it is to live according to the principles of justice. That brings life and peace, and it's my duty to talk about these important principles as long as I live.

79. Which moment from those days has remained most firmly etched in your memory?
ENGLEITNER: My arrival in Buchenwald concentration camp, when Martin Sommer put his pistol to my head. That was nearly the end of me.

80. Did you ever see or meet Hitler?
ENGLEITNER: No, I never saw him and had no desire to.

81. What was your opinion of Hitler in those days, and what is your opinion of him now?
ENGLEITNER: When I first heard the name "Hitler" in the 1920s, I thought it was a group like the Boy Scouts that built huts in the woods. The reason was that I misheard it. I thought it was "*Hüttler*," or "hut builder," so I imagined they built huts in the woods during vacation. What the name really stood for, I found out later for myself.

Hitler was a criminal. He only wanted one thing: world domination. He was so self-confident and such a megalomaniac that he firmly believed he would win and put his ideas into practice. At the beginning, he said, "Germany will be transformed beyond recognition!" And it was. Afterward, Germany *was* changed beyond recognition because it was in ruins.

The orders he gave also revealed his megalomania. He even insisted that everyone use the greeting "Heil Hitler!" I didn't do that, because *Heil* means "salvation" and no salvation came from him, quite the opposite. The greeting should really have been "Unheil Hitler!" because *Unheil* means "disaster."

82. Hypothetically, if Adolf Hitler were still alive and you could have five minutes alone with him, what would you say or do?

ENGLEITNER: I would ask him whether he was still so convinced that his ideas were right, or whether he realized what terrible things he had done to people. If he remained unrepentant, I would immediately leave without another word because it would be pointless talking to him. If he were reasonable, I would tell him the "good news" contained in the Bible and recommend that he express remorse for everything and ask God for forgiveness.

83. After the war, did you ever meet any of the people who had tormented you?

ENGLEITNER: Yes, at the trial of Nazi criminals in Paderborn in 1970, I met Max Schüller, the vicious *kapo* from Wewelsburg, and the SS man Ludwig Rehn, who was labor supervisor in Wewelsburg. The positions were now reversed. They were the accused, and I was one of the prisoners who had to testify against them. They were both charged with manslaughter. However, it couldn't be proved, because no one had actually seen them killing anyone. So they were acquitted. I talked to Rehn. I didn't feel any hatred toward him, even though he had caused us so much suffering.

After the trial, most of the former prisoners went for a meal together. We ate in a department store that had a restaurant upstairs. Rehn sat down next to me and said, "It should always be possible to forgive!" I said to him, "Herr Rehn, there are two different things. If you were to punch me now, it would be up to me whether I say, 'Forget it, it's forgiven.' But what happened in the concentration camps was a heinous crime against Jehovah's commandment, 'Love your neighbor as yourself.' So you'll have to sort that out yourself with your creator."

84. What do you think of the punishments the Nazis received after the war, in the Nuremberg trials, for example?

ENGLEITNER: I didn't really follow the trials on television, because they didn't interest me very much. If at all, I only heard about them by chance, but I don't know enough about the punishments. It's always very hard to prove that someone committed a certain crime if the person doesn't admit it, and the Nazis wouldn't have done that. Their defense would surely have been that they felt they were in the right when they killed people.

85. Have you forgiven your persecutors?

ENGLEITNER: Sure, I have forgiven them for what they did to me personally. I feel no hatred. That would only harm me and make life unnecessarily hard. But it's before God that they'll have to answer for all the atrocities they inflicted on millions of other people. He is the judge. But they have to be willing to concede that they did wrong. I did my best to love my enemy, as the Bible tells us to do. It's not easy, but I knew that I should not feel any animosity toward them. The Bible says, "You should love your enemies!" It says you should hate evil, not people. You should hate evil, not the people themselves.

86. What is your opinion of neo-Nazis?

ENGLEITNER: It makes me sad that there are still people around who find something good about this ideology. If such a person were willing to listen, I would tell him about my experiences and recommend that he visit a former concentration camp. Maybe that would help him to see that the Nazi regime was a criminal regime. If he doesn't want to talk, I'll have to leave him with his views and hope that one day he'll find it out for himself.

87. What do you do to explain to people what exactly happened in the Holocaust?

ENGLEITNER: I talk about what I experienced as long as I can and with anyone who asks me. When my eyesight was still good enough, I also wrote letters and answered questions asked by schoolchildren and students. Anyone who reads my biography or watches my film or visits the Internet site about me [www.rammerstorfer.cc] will find more information. People all over the world can learn about my experiences, if they so wish. I personally went through that dreadful time, so I'm really in a position to say what happened. My experiences that I pass on to others are history that I lived through. I talk about it everywhere: when I have visitors at home, or when I have been invited somewhere. Since my biography was published, I have been able to tell my life story to many people in many schools, universities, memorial sites, and other institutions in Europe and America with my friend and biographer Bernhard Rammerstorfer.

12. Leopold Engleitner and Bernhard Rammerstorfer at Harvard University, USA, 2009

Since 1999, we have traveled over eighty thousand miles [over ninety-five thousand miles as of press time] to do this. We traveled all over Austria and were in Germany, Italy, and Switzerland, where I went in the 1930s to attend Bible conventions. We were in the United States three times [four times as of press run], crisscrossing the whole country by airplane, and were even in Moscow, Russia. I was able to speak at the [United States] Holocaust [Memorial] Museum in Washington [D.C.], the Los Angeles Museum [of the Holocaust], the Simon Wiesenthal Center in Los Angeles, and the Illinois [Holocaust] Museum. I was also invited to speak at famous universities like Columbia, Georgetown, Harvard, and Stanford. To be honest, I never imagined I would one day be able to talk about my experiences at a university.

When I think that, as a child, I was described as "dumb" and after World War II was even branded an "idiot" who couldn't even communicate properly, it makes me particularly happy that I was able to speak to so many young people at these universities. They told me that they learned a lot from my story and will do their best to live according to just principles. That makes me very happy and shows me that my activities have meaning and a useful purpose.

13. Leopold Engleitner and Bernhard Rammerstorfer in Moscow, Russian Federation, 2009

Although these journeys are always extremely arduous for me, and are very difficult at my age, I'm always willing to talk to young people. Interestingly, it has always been like a shot in the arm for me. Most times I came home with more vigor than I left with. That was the case when I went to the United States, where the warmth and the pleasant climate in California, and especially in Florida, did me a lot of good. But the friendliness of the people in Switzerland, Italy, Germany, Austria, the United States, and Russia gave me great strength and made me very happy. I'm especially grateful for the many friends I made on these trips, and I hope they will pass my story on so that many more people can learn from it.

14. Leopold Engleitner and Bernhard Rammerstorfer on Clearwater Beach, Florida, USA, 2009

88. From today's perspective, how can you explain that "normal people" were capable of such atrocities?

ENGLEITNER: I have never been able to explain how it is that a human being is capable of such things. The ruler of the world was behind it. He prompted people to suppress what was good for themselves. You can read it in the Bible. But there's one thing that shouldn't be overlooked: many used the excuse that they were only following orders. I myself heard that at the trial in Paderborn. But that a person should train his conscience according to just principles—and that his conscience can stop him from committing such deeds—is hardly ever considered. I too could have said to myself, "I'm just a simple farmhand. Everyone's going to war, even highly intelligent, learned academics. The clergy of the major religions bless the weapons and exhort the faithful to participate in the war. Even the minor religions join in. What can I, a man of no significance, do, and why should I oppose the Nazis and put my neck on the line?" But that kind of attitude was out of the question for me. I knew that, like every other human being, I would have to answer for my actions to God and to my own conscience and that I could not use the excuse that I was just following orders. If an action is bad, then I must not do it, no matter who orders it, or how much pressure is exerted on me. Just because everyone performs a bad deed doesn't make it right. I myself am answerable for what I do. I was always aware that if I had killed someone in the war, my own conscience would have condemned me, and I would have been accountable to God for it. For me that was crystal clear. I wanted a clear conscience before God.

89. What exactly do you feel when you hear that there are still people who claim that the Holocaust never took place?

ENGLEITNER: I'm very disappointed and sad. I experienced it personally, so it distresses me very much when people who were not even alive at the time make that claim.

90. What consequences did the proclamation of the "Nuremberg Laws" on September 15, 1935, have for you?

ENGLEITNER: For me, none. In Austria, the race laws only started to affect the population following the Anschluss in 1938. It was then that many posters appeared in Bad Ischl with the slogan, "*Jude packe schnell dein Bündel, jetzt ist es aus mit dem Gesindel!*" (Pack your bag quickly, Jew, it's over for riffraff like you!). I found this hounding of the Jews utterly repulsive. I was strictly opposed to it because all men are equal in the sight of God. After my arrest, I even told the judge in Wels that I rejected the Nazi race laws.

91. What are your personal memories of the "Night of Broken Glass" on November 9/10, 1938?

ENGLEITNER: Here in the Salzkammergut, I was unaware of it. I didn't find out till later that the Nazis had destroyed Jewish shops.

92. What are your personal memories of the beginning of the war in 1939?

ENGLEITNER: I learned that World War II had broken out while I was locked up in Linz prison. I read it in a newspaper that I was allowed to read there. Of course, it was perfectly clear to me that my opposition to war would be put to the sternest of tests.

93. Did you hear that the National Socialists had decided to implement the "final solution to the Jewish question"—the systematic extermination of Jews in Europe—at the Wannsee Conference on January 20, 1942. If so, when and how?

ENGLEITNER: No, I didn't hear anything about that.

94. When you heard that World War II was over, what feelings did you have?

ENGLEITNER: Good feelings, of course. I was very pleased that I had been able to retain my faith and stay true to my principles and that I had played no part in the atrocities.

95. Do you think that humankind has learned something from the Holocaust?

ENGLEITNER: Individuals have undoubtedly learned something. I know of two former members of the Waffen-SS who were part of the *Leibstandarte SS Adolf Hitler* (Hitler's personal bodyguard) and were on guard duty in the Reich Chancellery in Berlin.

Gottlieb Bernhardt even saw service at Obersalzberg and, in 1945, was appointed adjutant to the captain of Wewelsburg by Heinrich Himmler. There he came into contact with prisoners who were Bible Students and members of the work detail that stayed in Niederhagen concentration camp after its closure. When the Allies were approaching, he even refused the order to liquidate those Jehovah's Witnesses in the camp. A few years after the war, he became one of Jehovah's Witnesses. When I heard about his story in 2010, I wanted to go and visit him, since he was seriously ill. Gottlieb wanted to meet me, but unfortunately died five days before I was due to visit him.

The second one, Eberhard Weimer, also served in the Reich Chancellery. On January 30, 1942, Eberhard was in the guard of honor when Hitler swore in the young officers in the Sportpalast in Berlin. Hitler stopped in front of him and gave him a really hostile, penetrating look that he never forgot. The following night, Eberhard Weimer and Gottlieb Bernhardt were unexpectedly flown to the war front in Russia. When Gottlieb was badly wounded there, Eberhard and some other soldiers administered first aid and took him to the dressing station. Eberhard was wounded several times during the war and, in the 1980s, also became one of Jehovah's

Witnesses. I was delighted to be able to meet him personally in 2010, and he told me a great many things.

Both men bitterly regretted their involvement in the war. They were very young and inexperienced when they joined the Waffen-SS: only seventeen years old. They were taken in by the National Socialists' ideology and thought they were doing the right thing. But during the war, they began to have doubts. They realized they had made mistakes and changed completely. After the war, they devoted their lives to campaigning for peace. So as regards those two, we can say with justification that they learned something from it.

But when I think of the many wars and injustices that have happened since then, and are happening today, I fear I have to say that humankind has learned nothing. Otherwise things would look different.

96. Should the atrocities be forgotten and no longer talked about, as some people wish?
ENGLEITNER: Only when justice and peace reign over the entire earth will it no longer be necessary to talk about them. But today it's important for young people, in particular, that they hear everything.

97. What plans do you still have for the future?
ENGLEITNER: I hope that I still have a long time ahead of me to speak in schools and universities as a witness of history. I would like to learn many new things and keep improving my character.

98. How would you like to be remembered?
ENGLEITNER: I don't want admiration. I just want people to say, "He devoted himself to principles of justice and campaigned vigorously for peace."

99. What else would you like to say to us? Which question was not asked?
ENGLEITNER: I'm often asked how I got to be so old. I usually answer, "I tried to live a healthy life, and I never smoked and never drank too much. I never got angry or worried, because I entrusted everything to God. I always wanted to learn new things and always focused on the future. What I couldn't alter I accepted, and I never regretted missed

opportunities. I was grateful for every day I was allowed to live and always had a positive attitude. And I like a good laugh.

Of course, I know that to reach such a great age many other things are necessary, which you have no control over. But whatever was in my power to do, I did.

I would like to quote a saying that I often use when I'm asked why I'm still alive:

"I am a happy boy. In everything I find joy. But for death and my end, I haven't time to spend."

100. After all you have been through, what advice can you give us young people?
ENGLEITNER: I would like to recommend adopting a healthy lifestyle, always striving for peace, applying just principles, and above all, showing love for your fellowmen.

Renée Firestone:
From Auschwitz to the Kennedy Center

Renée Firestone, née Weinfeld, born April 13, 1924
Grounds for persecution: Jew
Length of imprisonment: 1 year
Country: USA

15: Renée Firestone, 1945   *16: Renée Firestone, 2009*

Renée Firestone, née Weinfeld, was born on April 13, 1924, in Užhorod in Eastern Czechoslovakia [now Ukraine] to a Jewish family. Following annexation of this region by Hungary in 1938, she had her first encounter with repression of the Jewish population at the hands of the Hungarian regime. She was no longer permitted to attend a state school. When the systematic extermination of Hungarian Jews began after Hitler's invasion of Hungary, she, her parents, and her sister were confined in the Užhorod ghetto on April 29, 1944; and on May 26 of that year, she was deported to Auschwitz-Birkenau concentration camp. She was exposed to Dr. Josef Mengele's dreaded selections on a daily basis and encountered him face-to-face on several occasions. In the autumn of 1944, she was sent to Liebau [now Lubawka] female forced labor camp in Silesia, a subcamp of Gross-Rosen concentration camp. She was liberated by the Russian army on May 8, 1945. Her mother was gassed, while her sister Klara was shot after having been the subject of experiments carried out by Dr. Hans Münch. Her father died shortly after he was liberated from the concentration camp. Only her brother Frank survived.

After the war, Renée Firestone lived in Prague, before immigrating to the United States with her family in 1948. She worked as a fashion designer and ran a successful boutique. In 1998, she told her story in Steven Spielberg's Oscar-winning documentary *The Last Days*. She regularly speaks about the Holocaust to young people in schools, at the Simon Wiesenthal Center in Los Angeles, and at the Los Angeles Museum of the Holocaust. Renée Firestone lives in California.

The interviews took place on May 28, 2009; August 4, 2011; August 12, 2011; September 14, 2011; October 23, 2011; November 2, 2011; and November 13, 2011.

1. When were you born? What was your father like? What was your mother like?

FIRESTONE: My name is Renée Firestone. I was born Renée Weinfeld on April 13, 1924, in the very eastern part of Czechoslovakia in a city called Užhorod. My father Morice [Moritz] had a textile and tailoring business, which was quite lucrative. We were upper-middle-class Jews. He built a beautiful home for us: we had a lovely villa. My mother Johanna [née Rosenfeld] did not work, as I remember. I understand that she did work with my father when they first got married: my mother was a career woman before her marriage, which was very unusual at the time. She had a millinery shop in Vienna with her two sisters, and they told me that the royal family was among their customers.

I had a brother who was four years older than I—his name was Frank, in Czech František—and a sister who was four and a half years younger than I. Her name was Klara.

2. What is your earliest childhood memory?

FIRESTONE: I remember that I started to dance at a very early age. I also used to skate, and then later I learned ballet, and my recollection is that my mother used to make our costumes for us, and I used to entertain at events for organizations. I still have some pictures of that. I also remember going to kindergarten at the age of four. I had a Czech teacher who had a daughter my age, and we were very close friends. So I have a lot of good memories of my childhood.

17: Renée Firestone, ca. 1938

3. What kind of childhood did you have?

FIRESTONE: Basically, I had a very beautiful childhood. We lived partway up a hill, and above us, on top of the hill, was another villa that was owned by a Czech congressman whose daughter and son were friends of mine. His name was Zajíc. Zajíc in Czech means "rabbit." Above us was a beautiful Greek Orthodox Church and nunnery; it was like a fort. I remember also that there was a tree in front of the fort, and we used to climb the tree and sit on top of the fort. Our parents were always scared that we would fall off.

My parents were well-off and we had all the things that, by European standards, were luxuries. Both my brother and I—my sister was much younger—did all kinds of sports: we skied, we skated, and we played tennis. I was a gymnast and my brother was an athlete, and so we really had a very wonderful childhood until the Hungarians occupied Užhorod in 1938.

18. *Renée's sister Klara, and brother Frank Weinfeld, ca. 1940*

4. How long did you go to school, and what schools did you attend?
FIRESTONE: I went to Czech elementary school and then to the *Realgymnasium* (secondary school) for three years. When the Hungarians came, I could no longer go to school. After the war, I settled in Prague and went to the Academy of Fine Arts. Later I decided that I should perhaps do something more practical, so I changed to commercial arts and completed my courses at the Academy in Prague.

5. What was your adolescence like? What trade did you learn, and what did you do for a living?
FIRESTONE: Most of my adolescence was spent under Hungarian rule because I went into the camp at the age of twenty. But up till then, I was living at home. I went to a private home to a woman who taught me to make artificial flowers and to embroider. She was an art teacher, and she had a few students who came to her house for lessons, and that's what I did until I went into the camp.

6. What can you tell us about your family?

FIRESTONE: After the war, I found my brother Frank, and we settled in Prague. Since he was thought of as a war hero, the Czechoslovakian government gave him a beautiful apartment in Prague. One day, we met a friend of his with whom he had been interned in the forced labor camp. This friend kept coming to visit. That was Bernard Feuerstein. He was in a Hungarian forced labor camp, and then, sometime during 1944, he was taken to Mauthausen concentration camp. He was liberated on May 8, 1945. We got married in 1946. So did my brother; he married his girlfriend who had been hiding in Budapest during the war. My daughter Klara was born in 1947, also in Prague. In 1948, we came to the United States and changed our name to "Firestone." Bernard was a schoolteacher in Europe for a while, and then went to law school in Prague, but he never graduated because we left for the United States. He never went back to school. I became a fashion designer; he learned pattern-making, and we became business partners. We were in business for a long time. He died in 2001. I have one granddaughter, called Johanna, and three great-grandchildren.

7. Did you use the Nazi greeting "Heil Hitler!" and/or the Nazi salute?

FIRESTONE: No, we didn't. First of all, the Nazis did not come to Hungary until 1944, and then we were immediately taken away. So no, we didn't even have a chance.

8. Why were you persecuted by the National Socialists?

FIRESTONE: Well, because I was Jewish. And of course we know what [Hitler's] basic aim was: to wipe out the Jewish people.

9. When were you arrested?

FIRESTONE: I wasn't arrested. We—the whole city—were immediately notified when the Germans marched in. In 1944, by the way, when Hitler was pushed out of the Soviet Union, the German army was pressed against the Hungarian border. At that time, we already knew that England and America were fighting on the Western Front, so we believed that we were going to be saved, that we would be the only Jews to escape deportation. Well, what happened was that Hitler found out that our president, Horthy, was double-crossing him and was negotiating with the Allies. Then he [Hitler] invited Horthy to Schloss Klessheim near Salzburg; in the meantime, his troops marched into Hungary. As soon as they marched in, we were notified that we were going to be relocated. That happened on April 29, 1944.

10. Why were you imprisoned?
FIRESTONE: Well, you know it was very interesting because we were lied to. We were told that we were going to be taken to Germany. We were told that Germany was in trouble, and they needed people harvesting, producing food for the army, and working in the factories, and that's what we thought: that was where we were going. I remember we got to the railroad station, and we were very surprised that we were not traveling in passenger trains. But among themselves people were trying to excuse the Germans, and they were saying that Germany was in such trouble that they needed all their trains to evacuate their own soldiers, and that was why we had to go on cattle cars. We didn't know where we were going until we got there. We thought we were going to Germany.

11. What happened exactly when you were arrested?
FIRESTONE: Well, as I say, we were not arrested. We were told that we were going to be shipped out, and I remember questioning my father because, somehow, I didn't trust the Germans. We knew about mass graves; we knew that Jews were being shot and buried in mass graves in Poland; so I was sort of worried. My father explained to me that even though Hitler could not be trusted, he probably needed us as workers, so I was satisfied. I thought we were going to Germany.

We were taken from the house to the Užhorod ghetto. It was in a brick factory, and we stayed there for about three weeks until they transported us out. We were packed into cattle cars, of course. In the cattle car I was in, there were about 120 of us, so there was no room to sit down. We hardly had room to put our suitcases down. I remember that, being twenty years old, healthy, strong, and having a few friends there—boys and girls my age—we tried to help the older people. We let them sit at the edges of the cattle car so they didn't have to stand. I remember we took infants and children from mothers who were holding them in their arms to make it a little more comfortable for them. We placed the infants in the laps of those who were sitting. The cattle cars were locked from the outside. They did not give us any food or any water. In one of the corners of the cattle car was an empty bucket, surrounded with a little bit of straw, and we realized that it was to be our bathroom. The journey lasted three and a half days. Every night the train would stop, and the Nazi soldiers who were escorting our train banged on the walls of the cattle cars and told us that if we were hiding any money or any valuables, such as jewelry, gold or silver, we should give them up, or we would suffer the consequences. And while they were talking to us, we could hear screaming and shooting outside, and we thought that maybe they were searching people and killing them. In fact, when we left our homes, there was a place where all the valuables had to be turned over, so really nobody dared to hide anything. But who knows why they were shooting? The transport ended at Auschwitz-Birkenau.

12. Did people know right from the start what was happening in the camps? Before you were taken away, did you know what would happen to you?

FIRESTONE: Well, first of all, we had no idea that camps existed. We knew nothing about the Wannsee Conference. We had never heard of it. We didn't know that six extermination camps had been built in Poland, so we really believed that we were going to Germany to work, and so nobody was worried. When we arrived in Auschwitz, we still had no idea: we still thought that we were in Germany. We had no idea what was going on.

13. How many different camps were you in? How many years did you spend in each camp?

FIRESTONE: We went to Auschwitz on May 26, 1944. I was in Auschwitz-Birkenau till fall. Then I was sent on a "death march" to Krakow, and from there, I was taken to Silesia to a camp called Liebau. There, I became a slave laborer for Nordland, which belonged to the Krupp Company, till the end of the war. On May 8, 1945, I was liberated by the Russians.

14. Were you the only member of your family in the concentration camp, or were family members or friends there as well? If so, did you have any contact with them?

FIRESTONE: First of all, my brother was already in a Hungarian forced labor camp when they took us away. And my mother was taken to the gas chambers on arrival, as soon as we arrived from the railroad station. My father, on the other hand, was taken to Auschwitz I, and my sister and I went to Birkenau. About a week after we arrived, a group of men came into our camp to fix something . . . we didn't know [them] . . . a working group of men; and while we went looking to see who they were, I saw my father. And of course we were not allowed to speak to them or to make contact with them. But I remember when I realized that my father was there, I wanted to hide; I did not want him to see me this way—with a shaved head in this rag, so I was trying to move behind somebody, and at that point, we connected—we looked at each other, and I saw my father's tears coming. He was crying, and of course I was crying, and that was the last time I saw him in the camp. My sister, on the other hand, stayed with me for six months; and after six months, Dr. Mengele separated me from her. And we used to see each other at the [barbed] wires every morning just to say to each other that we were alive; and I remember that in 1944, on the High Holy Day, on Yom Kippur, she didn't show up; and I thought that maybe she was upset because of the holiday. So I figured, "Tomorrow I'll see her." But she never came, and I knew then that she was probably gone.

15. What were the first things that happened immediately following your arrival at the concentration camp?

FIRESTONE: Well, first we were processed into the camp, which meant that we were stripped of our own clothes. When we were coming into the camp—as we were coming out of the bathhouse to be shaved—I still had my hair and was totally naked, and Mengele walked in with another doctor. I think his name was Dr. Klein, and they were standing under a light, and we were going into the place where they were shaving the heads.

And a friend of mine was behind me, and she tapped me on the shoulder and she said, "You know that Nazi is asking [for] you . . ." And I looked over and I saw Mengele going like this (*makes a beckoning gesture*), and I turned away, pretended that it was not for me, and ignored it. She tapped me on the shoulder again and said, "You better go over there. This Nazi wants you." And I had never even got undressed in front of my father—here I was totally naked—and I looked over again, and he again (*makes beckoning gesture*) invited me. So I tried to cover myself, went over there, and he took his [whip]—he used to carry a little baton, like a whip—and he put it under my chin and lifted my head to the light and he said to me, "*Warum bist du da?* Why are you here?" And I said, "*Ich bin eine Jüdin.* I am Jewish." And he says to me, "Well, who in the family—which parent—wasn't Jewish?" I said, "Both parents, *beide* [were Jewish]." So then he said, "What about your grandparents?" And he starts asking me: my mother's father, my mother's *Mutter* . . . , and I kept saying, "*Alle, alle Juden* (All, all Jews)," and he turned to this Dr. Klein and he said, "*Aber das ist unmöglich* (But that's impossible)." Well, I had long blond hair, I had blue eyes, and I was in very good physical condition. Yes, I did look like any German girl, any *Hitlerjugend* (Hitler Youth); and while they were still discussing me, I saw that my sister was already at the shaver, so I turned around, ran away, and I ran back to my sister. I was afraid that if they shaved her head, maybe I would lose her; I would not recognize her. A *kapo* came after me and started beating me and yelling at me in Polish, "*Psiakrew, cholera jasna,*" cursing at me, telling me how stupid I am, that I'm lucky that I wasn't shot by Mengele, that nobody runs away from Dr. Mengele. That was my first experience with Mengele.

Then when he separated me from my sister, I hoped that she would run to me. I kept telling her to run to me. She did not, so I tried to run back to her. Mengele caught me and turned me over to the *kapo*. The *kapo* beat me, but again I was lucky because they said that usually Mengele would have shot me. The third time I met him was just before we were liberated. He told me that if I survived, I should have my tonsils removed.

Our heads and bodies were shaved; then they sprayed us with DDT, a pesticide, and they handed us a recycled piece of rag to put on our bodies; and as we were leaving the bathhouse, they painted a yellow streak on our backs, from the top of our shaved heads down our backs. And that was the way they took us into the camp. It was total darkness; it was in the middle of the night. We didn't know whether there were any people around us or any buildings around us, and we were standing there; people were crying and screaming and talking. Nobody knew what was going to happen; everybody thought that maybe they would bring a machine gun now and they were going to finish us off. Well, while we were waiting there for many hours in the middle of the night, all of a sudden, out of four brick chimneys fire and smoke started to blow into the sky. And the sky became red, and the whole place looked like hell. We didn't know what all those fires were, why the sky was red; ashes were falling all over the ground; the ground became white with ashes; and everybody was screaming, and we had no idea what was happening.

And I remember one of the prisoners started to tell us, "Don't worry, those chimneys must be the factories we're going to be working at." And of course, we wanted to believe that she was right, and everybody was hoping that maybe, maybe those *were* factories, maybe we *would* work. And then many hours later again, another prisoner had another idea. She thought that those were bakeries. She smelled something burning. She says, "Don't you smell something burning? They are baking bread for us." This was the fourth day without food for us, so everybody wanted to believe her that it was baking, [that] they were baking bread. But of course, next morning at daybreak, the *kapos*, the overseers, arrived and began to beat us into these lines.

This went on all day long. They didn't tell us what they wanted from us, so we didn't know. We would have lined up if they had told us what they wanted. They were just beating and pushing and shoving. Late that same afternoon, we realized that we had been formed into lines, and they were yelling something in German, which sounded like "*Zählappell*"; but nobody knew what *Zählappell* was. So I figured, when we were standing in line, that those who lay in front of us were those who had been beaten to death; and I remember some of them were still moving. I thought maybe *Zählappell* meant that was the way they were going to kill everybody, and I thought that after the next *Zählappell*, it would be I or my sister lying there, so I was frightened.

And it was then that my sister started to cry and asked me to find out when we were going to be reunited with our parents. We did not know where our parents were. So in my ignorance, I walked over to one of the overseers, one of the *kapos*, and asked her very politely, did she know when we were going to be reunited with our parents? Well, it was then that she pointed to one of the chimneys, and she said, "You don't see the chimney and the fire and the smoke? There go your parents! And when you go through the chimneys," she said, "you will be reunited." And I had no idea what she was talking about. So I kept asking the prisoners, "Why would I go through the chimneys? What does that mean?" Well, we found out later.

I was tattooed [with the number A-12307] maybe two weeks after we arrived. Tattooing was random; you know, there was no rhyme or reason for it. Whenever they decided that they wanted to play around with a group, they decided to tattoo. Many were not tattooed at all.

16. Why did they shave the heads of the prisoners?
FIRESTONE: They said that they were afraid of lice, of course, but I think that it was just to humiliate us whichever way they could. I think all of the mistreatment was just plain humiliation.

17. What prisoner category were you put in?
FIRESTONE: What category? Well, where I was we were all Hungarian Jews. In that particular *Lager* (camp), we were all Hungarian Jews. But each *Lager* had different groups. I was in C *Lager*.

18. Can you describe the daily routine in the concentration camp?
FIRESTONE: We had to wake up between three and four o'clock. The *kapo* whistled, and we had to jump off the bunk. We had to go outside and line up for *Zählappell*, for roll call. We stood there sometimes till ten, eleven o'clock until Dr. Mengele came and counted us. After the morning count, they brought some barrels of liquid. The liquid was called "*Ersatz*." It resembled coffee or tea. I don't know what it was made of; it was always full of dirt. We found safety pins in it and pieces of combs, pieces of glass, it was full of garbage. We stood in columns of five, and they gave the first prisoners a little bowl, which, by the way, I don't think was ever washed. The first prisoner had to go to the server, and the *kapo* gave her some of the *Ersatz*. She had to come back and share this bowl of liquid with the five of us. I don't have to tell you we were all starving. By the time the bowl reached the fourth or the fifth prisoner, there was nothing in it, so then you had to wait until the afternoon lineup because in the afternoon, around three o'clock, we had another roll call, which lasted till about nine at night. Then we were fed again. They brought the same liquid; this time they called it "soup" and served it the same way; and with the soup, we each received a slice of brown bread: a kind of rye bread, cut into eight slices; and one of those slices was our daily intake.

On Sundays, if we were not being punished, they brought us something "special": we had to put our hands out like this (*holds out cupped hand*), and they put a spoonful of marmalade in it, made of sugar beet, which we always craved because we were starving for sweets. Or they gave us a slice of horse salami. Those were the delicacies on Sundays. But if we were being punished, we didn't get them.

19. What was the worst thing about the daily routine?
FIRESTONE: The worst thing was that we stayed out all day. We were not allowed to go into the barracks, and the bunks were scrubbed all day long. We had no blankets; we slept on wooden bunks, and they were always wet. Because of that, there were many cases of tuberculosis and other diseases and illnesses. That was probably the worst part. Also, being outdoors—whatever the weather—was bad: in summertime, when the heat went up to over one hundred degrees; and in the wintertime, in the snow, though actually the winter was not as bad as the fall was; in the fall, it was pouring rain, and the mud was knee-high. So it was unbearable to stay outdoors. Nevertheless, we were not allowed to go inside. So those were the worst things.

20. Did everyday life lead more to solidarity, or did the prisoners try to cope on their own?
FIRESTONE: Some did, some didn't. There were prisoners who never socialized at all, who were always separate—on their own—and there were some who tried to be together. But it was difficult because we were watched from the towers by guards with machine guns, and if they saw any gathering, they would shoot, so we tried to conceal any gathering. Even when we talked to each other, we were sort of sitting apart so they couldn't see us as a group. We didn't really make very close friendships, because we knew that any day the other person could be taken away and it would be just more heartbreak.

21. Was there anything that helped you take your mind off the horror of daily life for a while (such as music)? What gave you strength?
FIRESTONE: Well, I don't know if it gave us strength, but because we were starving, we "cooked" (*laughs*). We exchanged recipes when we had a chance, and we tried to "cook" by talking about food. It sort of satisfied our needs somehow.

22. What were living conditions like in the barracks (prisoner allocation, food supplies, hygiene, clothing, etc.)?
FIRESTONE: Okay, hygiene: there was none. We were always full of lice even though they tried to wash the bunks all the time. The bunks were three rows high, and about six [feet] by six [feet]. We were twelve in a bunk, six facing one way, six the other. We had no blankets. We slept on the wooden bunks, and what kept us warm was being so close to each other. That actually kept us warm during the night. So the conditions were totally inhuman and totally indescribable.

The Germans even took care of menstruation, because in our food, there was a drug called bromide. Bromide was a sedative, but it also stopped menstruation immediately. So they had figured out everything scientifically. That's why I say the difference between genocide and the Holocaust is that the Holocaust was carried out by scientists and educated people who planned it totally scientifically.

23. What jobs did you have to do? How many hours a day did you have to work?

FIRESTONE: What jobs? In Birkenau, nothing. That was probably the worst part: that we knew we were useless and that any minute we could be picked for the gas chambers. Later, after I was taken to Liebau forced labor camp, I worked for Krupp in a factory producing snow chains for German tanks. We worked twelve-hour shifts, a day shift and a night shift. I did a few different jobs, like soldering, and I was also one of the few that knew how to put the pattern together on the table, because the chain was arranged in a pattern. Because of that, the engineer who was running the factory took a liking to me: he saw that I knew some of the things that he needed, and occasionally he would bring me a little food. He would hide it somewhere and then whisper to me where it was and that I should go and get it. This same man, after the war was over, came into the camp and took me to his home to introduce me to his wife and his children. I am really sorry that I somehow never kept in touch with him, because he really was good to me.

24. What effect did the slogan "Work liberates" have on you?

FIRESTONE: First of all, I didn't see it. The sign *"Arbeit macht frei (Work liberates)"* is on the gate of Auschwitz I, and we never went to Auschwitz I. We heard that there was such a sign on the gate, and of course, we thought that it was just another trick they were playing on us. Of course, after the war, I did see it.

25. What were the guards like in the camp?

FIRESTONE: Brutal. Plain brutal. There is no other word for it. They were inhuman. In our camp, the *Lagerführerin* (female camp leader) was a woman, Irma Grese. Dan Brown wrote a book about her. She was one of three women who were tried and hung after the war. So you can imagine how brutal she was.

Her *Lagerälteste* (camp senior) was a prisoner, and she had a rank and traveled around with Irma and Dr. Mengele. She now lives in Australia. When we started to interview for Steven Spielberg's film, we wanted to interview her, but she declined. Then later she contacted us and agreed to it. I haven't seen the interview yet.

26. Was there any contact between the prisoners and the local population?
FIRESTONE: Absolutely not.

27. Were you aware of how the war was proceeding in the outside world?
FIRESTONE: We didn't know anything until September. In September, some American planes flew over Birkenau. They were flying to Auschwitz III, which was Buna where the I. G. Farben Auschwitz factory was. In this factory, they processed all the goods that the Jews brought in their suitcases and then shipped them to Germany.

These American planes flew over to bomb Buna and then they flew back. Some people knew that they were American, so we knew that the United States was in the war. That's about all we knew. Then when we were already in Liebau, just before the war ended, the Russians carried out bombings, and we knew that it was the Russians because they had these "Stalin candles," flares on parachutes to light the place they were going to bomb. So we knew that the Russians were close by.

But the problem was that the Germans told us that if the war ended and even if they lost, we shouldn't be happy about it, because they would finish us off beforehand. So we were worried about the end of the war, knowing that they might kill us.

28. In the concentration camp, were you allowed to receive letters, food parcels, etc.?
FIRESTONE: We had no connection with the outside world. The only contact was when we arrived; they made us write a note home saying that we were in this beautiful forest, that we were being taken care of, and that everything was fine. I sent one to my brother at the forced labor camp; he received the note, but had no idea where we were.

29. What forms of torture did you suffer?
FIRESTONE: Well, just being there was torture. I mean, you slept on a wooden bunk, you froze, or burned from the heat outside, you sat on the ground all day long, you were starving. Isn't that enough torture?

30. What was the most frightening moment for you?
FIRESTONE: It was all fear, the whole process. Everything was fear. It was frightening when I got off the train and realized that my parents had disappeared, then not knowing what was going to happen to us, where we were going, what they were going to do to us, where we were, not knowing what this place was, and being in charge of a fourteen-year-old sister. Our whole existence was terrifying.

31. Were there any entertaining or lighthearted incidents that enabled you to forget all the suffering for a moment? Can you describe them?
FIRESTONE: Well, occasionally. There were some very talented people there, and I remember there was a young woman who was a mime; occasionally she would perform around the barracks. I remember she had a scene where she pretended to be skating, and every time she did that, I cried because, of course, I remembered my own skating days. So they were very few, but there were some occasions.

32. What were your day-to-day thoughts while you were in the concentration camp?
FIRESTONE: No thoughts. There were absolutely no thoughts. That's what bromide did. You were like a zombie. You didn't think. You knew that you were doomed; I never thought that I would get out alive.

So there were no thoughts. As I say, sometimes we "cooked" because we were hungry, and that sort of satisfied our palates.

33. Was it possible for children to be born in a concentration camp? If so, what happened to these babies?
FIRESTONE: Yes, there were some babies. There were women who came in pregnant. If the pregnant woman was caught, she was killed. But there were a few that were in hiding. If the prisoners realized that there was a pregnant woman amongst them, they would be kind and help her hide from Dr. Mengele.

143

There was a woman, from my hometown by the way, who now lives in Los Angeles, who did give birth in the barrack. The midwife showed the child to the mother, then wrapped the little boy in a blanket, took him to the latrines, and drowned him in the human waste. If there is any more inhuman way of dying . . . I think there is no worse way than that. But this woman survived, got married, and has three beautiful children.

34. Was it possible to make friends with prisoners?
FIRESTONE: Yes, it was possible, but we didn't. We didn't make close friends for fear that the other person could be taken away at any time, and that would just cause more pain.

35. Who was your best friend during this dreadful time, and how did he or she help you?
FIRESTONE: My sister was my best friend as long as I was with her. Later, I didn't have any close friends, but just before we were taken away from Auschwitz, I had strep throat, and the night before, I had a very high temperature.

There were a mother and daughter who slept in the same bunk with me, and when we were called for roll call, in order to be selected, she told me to come, and I told her that I couldn't get up, I was so weak. I was burning up. So the mother, her name was Mrs. Farkas, went away and from somewhere, I don't know where or how, she got a blanket. She came back with this blanket and wrapped me up in it, and we went out for roll call.

When we were selected—who was selected to go, and who to stay—I was assigned to those who were going. We had to get undressed so that our clothes could be disinfected. I was standing in the pouring rain—and it was freezing rain—naked, without shoes, all day long, and after that we marched to Krakow. In Krakow, they put us into cattle cars, and by the time we arrived in Liebau, the freezing rain had taken my temperature down and I was well again. My throat was clear, and my friend who was with me arrived with pneumonia. I had thought I was going to die. So life is totally unpredictable and it's all a matter of luck.

36. What did you do to relieve the suffering of other inmates?
FIRESTONE: There was nothing you could do. You could help spontaneously like this woman helped me, but there was nothing that you could preplan.

37. Were there particular hierarchies among the inmates?

FIRESTONE: In the *C Lager*, there were female *kapos*, there were the runners, and there was the *Lagerälteste*. Sure, there were ranks. The *kapos* watched to make sure that we were in our bunks at nine o'clock, that we didn't talk to each other, that we didn't communicate; and it was they who served us our food. The *kapo* was responsible for the barrack. Each barrack had a *kapo*.

38. Were there any differences in the way the various groups of prisoners (religious, political groups) were treated?

FIRESTONE: I wouldn't know that. We do know that the *Sonderkommando* (special unit) was treated differently. Those were the people who worked in the gas chambers and the crematorium. They were always men, by the way. They had everything they needed, but they also knew they were going to live only three months. Every three months, they were rotated. They were killed.

39. What diseases and illnesses were prevalent in the concentration camp?

FIRESTONE: There was a lot of tuberculosis and, of course, typhoid. Typhus was the main problem. In some camps, there were typhus epidemics. Thousands and thousands died of typhus.

40. Did you receive a physical injury?

FIRESTONE: Physical injury? Oh, well, I was beaten a few times, but suffered nothing that would have made me a cripple.

41. How much did you weigh when you were in the concentration camp?

FIRESTONE: When I was liberated, I weighed seventy pounds. I weighed myself at home, and I was 5'2" tall at that time.

42. What did death mean to you?

FIRESTONE: What did it mean to me? I didn't think about it too much; death was around me all the time, so I knew I was not going to survive. We saw bodies by the hundreds every day. I was not preoccupied with it. I just knew that eventually it would come.

43. What was the closest you came to death?

FIRESTONE: Well, being in Auschwitz was close enough because there were selections [for the gas chambers] every day. So I could have been picked anytime, any minute by Mengele. The possibility of death was there all the time. Mengele was our biggest fear. He was a very handsome man—he looked more like a gypsy than a German. But his reputation was horrible, so whenever he came around, all we wanted to do was hide from him because after every roll call, which was taken twice a day, he selected people out of the lineup. That's how my sister was taken away.

44. Did you ever build a kind of "wall" to shield you from the terrible things that were being done so that the death of a fellow prisoner no longer affected you?

FIRESTONE: No, the bromide took care of that. We were zombies; we really did not think much.

45. What happened to the dead bodies in the concentration camp?

FIRESTONE: They were burned. They were taken to the crematorium and burned.

46. Was there ever a possibility for you to be released from the concentration camp?

FIRESTONE: No way! No way! I don't know of anyone who had the possibility of release. Once you got there, there was no way out—only through the chimneys.

47. Were there any escape attempts or opportunities to escape? Did you try to escape?

FIRESTONE: Oh, there was no way. Nobody tried. But in the underground, there were two Czechs who did escape. What happened was that the underground buried these two men. I understand that they covered the place where they were buried with tobacco so that the dogs could not sniff them out. They waited till the Nazis finished searching and then dug them up. And they escaped. They went to London and told Churchill what was going on in Auschwitz. So they [the Allies] knew. They knew.

48. Were there any inmates in the concentration camp who dared to stage a revolt against the camp authorities?

FIRESTONE: There was a *Sonderkommando* revolt in Auschwitz while I was still there. We didn't see it or know about it intimately, but we knew that the *Sonderkommando* blew up the crematorium. We also knew that three girls who worked in an ammunition factory brought the [explosives] for the underground. And among the *Sonderkommando*, there was also a member of the underground. So we knew about it, but we did not see it. We had no contact with them. The girls were hung.

49. Did you think you would ever make it out alive?

FIRESTONE: No, I did not. I really did not think I would make it out alive.

50. Were there any times when you gave up all hope? If so, why?

FIRESTONE: Well, from the minute we got in and found out what was going on, we realized where we were, and we gave up.

51. Did anyone commit suicide?

FIRESTONE: Oh yeah, many. It was very easy to commit suicide because the wires were charged with high-voltage electricity, and all you had to do was go near the wires and you were killed. Many, many people threw themselves onto the wires.

52. During the Holocaust, did you ever consider committing suicide out of sheer despair?

FIRESTONE: There were times when I thought about it, but never really attempted [it]. Then, when my sister was taken away, I thought maybe I should end it, but my will to live was very strong. I was young. I really wanted to live.

53. What thoughts, ideas, hopes, wishes, or religious convictions did you cling to?

FIRESTONE: None, absolutely none. I was not religious at home, so my religion was not strong enough for that, and otherwise there was nothing.

54. Did you lose your faith in God while you were in the camp?

FIRESTONE: Never in God. Never in God because I always thought that if I started blaming God, then I was going to excuse men, and this was really done by men, by humanity. And I will never blame God for something that he equipped us to deal with.

God gave us a mind and a heart, and free will, and he did not say, "I am going to take each of you by the hand and take you through life." So it was only man who was responsible for the Holocaust and is responsible for all the genocides that are going on now.

55. What role did your religion play in how you felt about what was going on? Why?
FIRESTONE: Well, as I said, I was not religious. So my religion played no role in anything.

56. Did you pray during your internment?
FIRESTONE: No, I didn't.

57. Did you ever consider changing your religion (or ideology)? Why?
FIRESTONE: No, I never did. Actually, I think I became a Jew in the camp! I did not know much about Judaism, my religion, but in Auschwitz, I gave some thought to why we were there, and I thought there must be a reason why we were persecuted, and that's when I really became a Jew.

58. What was the date of your liberation from the camp?
FIRESTONE: I was liberated on the very last day of the war, May 8, 1945.

59. How were you liberated from the camp, or how did you manage to get out of it?
FIRESTONE: We already knew that the Russians were close by, and one day we were not called for roll call. So we were afraid to go out because they told us we were going to be machine-gunned at the end, so we stayed indoors. I remember that in the late afternoon, one of the prisoners went crazy; she opened the door and ran out. The *Umschlagplatz* [the yard where prisoners were split into groups] was right in front of our barrack, and she ran out into it and turned around, raised her hand like this (*gestures*), then started to run back. We thought she was facing a gun. She was yelling, "German kaput, German kaput." There were no Germans.

The Germans had escaped during the night, and a few hours later, a Russian officer rode into our camp on horseback, and of course, he didn't know who we were. But he saw these women with shaved heads and in rags. So he asked us in Russian, "*Evrei*, Jews?" We were afraid to tell him that we were Jews. We didn't know why a Russian would ask us; the Germans asked, but why would a Russian ask us? But he kept asking, "Jews?" So one of the girls said, "*Da, da*, yes, we are Jews." This Russian officer, whose uniform was covered with ribbons and medals, jumped off his horse and came around and started to hug the women and started to cry. We wondered why he was crying. We should be the ones crying! Suddenly he straightened up and started to beat his chest and yell at us again in Russian, "I am also a Jew!"

Then he explained to us that this was the first time that he was able to tell somebody that he was a Jew, because in the Russian army it was not safe to be a Jew. And we looked at this man, this decorated hero who had four big stars on his shoulders but was afraid to say in his own army that he was a Jew! How was I going to go back into that same world where I would have to lie or be afraid to say who I was? So those were terrible awakenings. It was also then that we realized that most likely our parents had not made it. Some of the prisoners knew their brothers or sisters had not made it. You know, people always think that liberation was a joyful day. Liberation, for me, was probably the worst day of my life! There were a lot of things that came to mind that day, and I wondered how I was going to live in the same world that had put me in there.

60. How were you treated by the people who liberated you?
FIRESTONE: We were not lucky enough to be liberated by the Americans or the English like other prisoners. The Russians just opened the gate and said, "You're free! Go!" And then we had to roam around in the Russian zone where the Russian soldiers were looting and raping. So it was very dangerous. Those were difficult times.

61. What was the first thing you did after you were liberated?
FIRESTONE: Absolutely nothing. We stayed in the camp, and the engineer who ran the factory came for me about a day later. He took me to his house. I had dinner with him and his family, then he brought me back to the camp. The Russian officer had told us not to leave right away, but to wait until the Russian army had marched through the city; he said that he would come back and tell us when it was safe to leave.

So we stayed a week and a half in the camp, and then we just left. We found out that we were six kilometers [about three and three-quarter miles] from the Czech border, so my aim was to go to Czechoslovakia right away. There were about nine of us girls who stayed together. We were afraid to be alone because of the Russians, and we crossed into the city of Trutnov, where I saw a restaurant. I walked into this restaurant, and the owner immediately recognized where I came from, with my shaved head and my wooden clogs. He came over to me and asked if I came from a concentration camp, and I told him, "Yes." He said I should go to the kitchen and ask the cook to feed me. I said, "Well, I can't, because I have eight other people waiting outside." So he came out with us and showed us how to go into the kitchen through the back. He fed us and told us that if we came back later, he would let us stay overnight in the restaurant. That was my first night of liberation. After that, we just left and roamed around Czechoslovakia for a while. We partly hitchhiked, partly walked, and partly rode on the train. We were homeless and took whatever transport we could to get to Hungary. It was in Budapest that I ran into my brother.

62. Did you have any problems when you returned home? How did people in your home environment react to you?

FIRESTONE: I did not have much contact with anybody. I went to my house. The Russian commander was living there. I told them that we were the owners of the house, and the Russians were very polite and told me I could take a room if I wanted to stay. I said, "No, thank you," and that same day, I left and went back to Prague. That was about three months after liberation.

63. Were you able to rejoin your family?

FIRESTONE: I found my brother Frank, and then we found out from a stranger that my father was in Theresienstadt, in the hospital. We found him there dying of tuberculosis. He died four months later. He had been on a death march from Buchenwald to Theresienstadt.

19. *Renée's father, Moritz Weinfeld, Buchenwald Concentration Camp photo, 1944*

My mother died in Auschwitz the day we arrived, and my sister six months later. My brother was in a Hungarian forced labor camp. The Hungarians didn't

150

take Jewish men into the military; all Jewish men of military age were taken to forced labor camps, and he was of military age. He was there from 1940 till 1944, till we were taken away in April. He escaped from the forced labor camp and became a partisan in Slovakia.

After the war, when Frank was already married and had a one-year-old boy, he and his family went to France. In France, they were contacted by the *Haganah*. The *Haganah* was recruiting people to fight for the State of Israel. So Frank joined the *Haganah* and went fighting for the State of Israel. He remained in Israel for fifteen years and fought in all the early wars. One day, fifteen years later, he wrote me that he was now too old to fight, and that was when we brought him and his family to the United States.

64. Did you have any acquaintances, friends, or relatives in the camps? Did they survive their internment?

FIRESTONE: Yes, one of my girlfriends from home was with me till the end. She was liberated with me. When she came home, she found her father in Užhorod, so she remained in Užhorod. Later, she moved to Budapest, and I was in touch with her. And I had a cousin who married a girl from Marmaroschsiget, which was in Romania before it was occupied by the Hungarians. She lived in Los Angeles. Both have since passed away.

65. What happened to your possessions?

FIRESTONE: Who knows! Whoever could steal something stole it! I don't know what happened to them. They were gone. When we got home, everything was gone. The only thing left in the house was the furniture, which was so heavy they couldn't take it! Someone lived in the house during my time in the camps, but I don't know who. When we got there, the Russian commander was living there. I have no idea who lived there before. I know who lived there afterward: when we did the film *The Last Days*, I went back, and there were three Russian families living there.

66. To what extent have you received compensation for your internment?

FIRESTONE: For many years, I didn't claim any, because I thought, "Are they going to pay me for my dead parents or what?" I didn't want anything. Then sometime in the 1980s, I realized that it was stupid of me.

Even if I were planning to give it away, I should take it. So I applied, and now I'm getting around $300 a month from Germany.

But what gratifies me more than material compensation is that I have received several unexpected honors. I received an honorary doctorate in educational justice from Redlands University. I met two American presidents, Bill Clinton and George W. Bush. And in 2006, I was a presenter to Steven Spielberg at the Kennedy Center Honors in Washington, D.C. That was a great honor for me.

20. *Left to right: Bill Clinton, 42nd US president; Renée Firestone, Steven Spielberg, film director and producer; and Douglas Greenberg, director of the Shoah Foundation, in the Shoah Foundation conference room, which Steven Spielberg dedicated to Bernard Firestone (top right in the photo), 2001*

67. How did you set about rebuilding your life?
FIRESTONE: It just automatically happened. I came to America, and I realized that I had to carry on. When I came to America, I became successful as a fashion designer.

68. How long did it take you to return to a "normal" life after the Holocaust?

FIRESTONE: Actually, till I came to America. I came in 1948, so I lived in Prague for three years. It was hard to get back to a normal life; first of all, my father was buried there [in Prague], and we were still refugees. In America, I started to live somewhat of a normal life, and I did not talk about the Holocaust, so it was tolerable. And I was very lucky. I didn't have nightmares. Most survivors had nightmares. I already had a family, and for a long time, I tried to forget, actually until 1977 when people from the Simon Wiesenthal Center came to interview me. Until then, I never really spoke about the Holocaust.

69. What was your life like after the war?

FIRESTONE: In Prague, we had to earn a living somehow. I went back to school, and my brother was an artist. I remember we bought some English parachutes and made skirts out of them, since at that time it was fashionable to wear big skirts; we painted designs on these skirts, and that was how we made our living in Prague.

Also, I want to tell you a story: When I found my father, he asked me whether I had been back home, and I said, "Yes." He asked me whether I had found a little aluminum can in the backyard at home. I said, "I wasn't looking for it. What do you mean?" He said, "You go back home and see whether you can find a little aluminum milk can in the backyard." He didn't want to tell me why, but I went back home, went into the backyard, and found it dug up. I think the Hungarians dug it up first, looking for something we might have buried. Then the Germans came, and they dug it up again; then the Russians came, and they too dug it up, so the backyard was a shambles. There was a big mound of dirt. On top of it was this little milk can. I ran over to it, of course, because

21. *Renée Firestone with her husband, Bernard, 1947*

153

I wanted to know why my father wanted me to find a milk can. I opened it up, and rolled up in it were three hundred American dollars. Needless to say, that was a fortune at the time. When I came back, my father told me he had these dollars on him as we were leaving, and he knew if the Nazis found them, they would kill him; so in desperation, he found this little milk can, rolled the money up in it, and tossed it into the backyard. They had dug up the backyard so many times looking for treasures—found nothing—and there it was, sitting in plain view. So we had that money and made those skirts, and that's how we made our living in Prague.

In 1948, we immigrated to the United States. We were refugees. We were often called refugees. We were actually called the "Greeners" [people looking for "greener pastures" or a better life], and nobody wanted to hear our stories. It was just as well. Every time you started to say something about the Holocaust, people said, "Oh forget it. Look forward. You're in a free country now." So we didn't tell our stories for many, many years.

We came to Pennsylvania. My husband had a sister in Pennsylvania, and we stayed there for a few months. In April 1949, we came to Los Angeles because I had an aunt—my father had a sister here. So we came here just to visit, and we stayed. I loved it. I was very lucky. I immediately got a job as a designer. Then, only a few months later, my boss was killed in an accident, so I was on my own again. That's when I decided to go into business for myself. I started a business and was very successful. I had the business in Los Angeles till 1992.

70. What is your life like today? Do you still often think back to those days?

FIRESTONE: I am now in my mid-eighties, and I take every day as a gift and try to make the best of it. I'm not rich, but I'm not poor, so I'm satisfied. I have a very nice life. I manage the building I'm living in, by

22. *Renée Firestone with her daughter Klara upon their arrival in New York, USA, 1948*

the way, and I give presentations almost every day as a public speaker for the Simon Wiesenthal Center. I used to travel a lot: all over the United States, even overseas.

I also worked for Steven Spielberg at the Shoah Foundation, so I was kept busy. Well, now I talk about it all the time, so of course I often think back to those days.

71. What physical and mental scars do you carry from that time?
FIRESTONE: I don't think I have any physical or mental scars. I talk about the fact that we're much stronger than we think we are. I didn't think that I could survive such a life. And even thinking back, I can't imagine how I survived. So apparently we are physically much stronger than we know [we are].

72. Did you have any moral support to help your emotional and social recovery?
FIRESTONE: My husband was my moral help. He was a very good man and he loved me, and that's all I needed.

73. Has your view of the world changed since that time?
FIRESTONE: Yes. Before the Holocaust, I thought people would treat each other kindly. But I learned that people can be crueler than animals. I don't even want to compare us with animals, because animals don't do such things to each other. It was a shock to me to realize how cruel human beings can be.

74. Can you think of anything positive that you have gained from your experiences?
FIRESTONE: Nothing positive from my experiences themselves, but I do hope that through my work and talking to young people, they will perhaps realize that the world has to change, and maybe they will change it. That's my hope. Otherwise, I wouldn't be doing it at my age. I would be sitting at home, knitting.

75. Have you ever been back to visit the concentration camp you were held in, and if so, what were your feelings?
FIRESTONE: Oh, I've been back many times. I take high school kids to Auschwitz. And each time, it's very difficult. That's the burying ground

of my mother and my sister, so for me, going there is like going to a cemetery.

76. Are you still in touch with your fellow internees from the concentration camps?

FIRESTONE: I was in touch with the two I told you about, Elisabeth Gottlieb in Budapest and Rose Jackson, the one who lived here in Los Angeles. Her name had been Jakubowicz. She changed it to Jackson. But both of these ladies passed away in 2011. And I am in touch with many Holocaust survivors, not necessarily those who were interned with me, for I belong to quite a few Holocaust organizations.

77. What did you tell your family about your internment in the concentration camp? How did your relatives react to what you told them?

FIRESTONE: The only relative I spoke with was my husband's sister who was very understanding and tried to be very kind to me. I didn't have a very good relationship with my aunt who lived here. So I really didn't talk much about my internment. But with my brother Frank, I exchanged stories all the time. He told me his partisan stories, and I told him my concentration camp stories.

78. Do you find it difficult to talk about those days?

FIRESTONE: Not anymore. In the beginning, I had a hard time, but now I almost remove myself [from the scene]. When I speak to a group, I just remove myself, and I tell the story of the Holocaust.

79. Which moment from those days has remained most firmly etched in your memory?

FIRESTONE: In 1998, I went back to Auschwitz, and I found out what happened to my sister. And ever since I have known that she was shot after she was experimented on, I constantly have one thought in my head: How did that fourteen-year-old feel when she was taken to be shot? She knew that she was being taken to be shot. What did she feel? Was she crying? Was she scared? Was she numb? That's constantly in my head!

80. Did you ever see or meet Hitler?

FIRESTONE: Not personally. In the movies, of course, many times, but never in person. In the movies, they used to show newsreels. He was always in the newsreels. We knew what he was doing in Germany. We never thought it was going to happen to us.

81. What was your opinion of Hitler in those days, and what is your opinion of him now?

FIRESTONE: Well, at that time we were just afraid of him—we hoped that he would never reach us. Today, what do I think of him? I think that he got what he deserved. Although, maybe not, maybe he deserved more suffering than the way he died; and I hope that there will never be another human being who will imitate him, even though we know that there is one [Mrs. Firestone refers to president Mahmoud Ahmadinejad] whom we fear now in Iran. So I don't know; I'm just skeptical about the human race in general.

82. Hypothetically, if Adolf Hitler were still alive and you could have five minutes alone with him, what would you say or do?

FIRESTONE: I cannot even imagine what I would say or do. I have no idea, absolutely no idea. What would I say to a man who is responsible for [taking] fifty-five million human lives? What do you say to him? I cannot think of anything that I could say to this man. What would I say? You're an animal? You don't deserve to live? You should be tortured the way you tortured millions of people? I don't know. I have no idea what I would say. I am not sure that I really would want to meet him.

83. After the war, did you ever meet any of the people who had tormented you?

FIRESTONE: In 1998, I was taken back to Auschwitz because we were making a movie with Steven Spielberg called *The Last Days*, and in the archives of Auschwitz, I found a document which was telling me that my sister was experimented on in a place called the Hygienic Institute. I asked the archivist, "What does that mean?" He showed me that there was a name on that same paper, which said, "Dr. Münch." He explained to me that this Dr. Münch was the head doctor of this institute and that was where they were experimenting mostly on women and children. He also told me at the time that he had the address of this Dr. Münch, and he said, if I wanted to write to him, then he would give me the address. While I was talking to the archivist, the director of our film came over to me and he told me that what was happening here was a miracle because he had an appointment with Dr. Münch to interview him for our film! Coincidence? So we flew to Munich the next day, and I had a chance to confront Dr. Münch with this paper, asking him what kind of experiments he performed on my sister. And he said, "We did only harmless experiments," and I said, "If they were harmless experiments, Dr. Münch, why did she die?" And he had the audacity to turn to me and to say, "Well, she didn't die in the experiments, but we couldn't send her back to the camp to tell everybody what we were doing there, so we had to get rid of her." And that's how I found out that she was shot afterwards.

Dr. Münch said that he was working under Mengele, and what a great man Mengele was, and [praised] what he did for humanity. He asked me, "How long was your sister in the camp?" So I said, "Six months." He said, "You were there, you should know. Six months was the average time to survive in Auschwitz." I said, "Well, I was there much more than six months." He didn't answer that. Well, I just got up. I was afraid that I was just going to attack this man, so I just got up and walked out.

I was told that Dr. Münch was tried by a tribunal that was held in Auschwitz by the Russians, and he convinced them that he was taking care of the non-Jewish prisoners in Auschwitz; so they decided that he was a good doctor but should be punished for being a Nazi. They sent him to Russia to a denazification camp for four years, and then he came back to Munich and practiced medicine. The interesting part was that right after we interviewed him, *Spiegel* magazine also interviewed him, and the editor of *Spiegel* was so upset about some of the things he said that he went to the government and said, "Why is this man free? Why isn't he incarcerated?" So they arrested him, but released him a few weeks later, saying that he was no longer competent to stand trial. He was then nearly ninety.

84. What do you think of the punishments the Nazis received after the war, in the Nuremberg trials, for example?
FIRESTONE: Some of them were tried and received punishment, but thousands of them did not. There are thousands of them who escaped to South America, or even lived in Germany under different names. There were many, many Nazis who committed crimes and were never tried. Some even came to the United States.

85. Have you forgiven your persecutors?
FIRESTONE: Have I forgiven? I have no right to forgive. Who am I to forgive them for eleven million lives? God should forgive them. I came

out of the camps hating and wanting punishment and wanting retribution. So my daughter was born, and one day I was standing over her crib, and I looked at this innocent little baby, and I thought to myself, "How am I going to raise this child? Is she going to be like me, hating and angry all the time?" And it was then that I realized that those whom you hate do not know you hate them; they do not care. So who are you punishing? You are punishing yourself only. You have this energy all the time, pushing you in the wrong direction. So it was then that I felt that I had to start working on myself and using this energy somewhere else, and that is what I did. And I was successful, and I am very grateful that I had the strength to do that.

86. What is your opinion of neo-Nazis?

FIRESTONE: I think that the neo-Nazis are worse than the Nazis because they already know the truth. We may say that some of the Nazis, when they became Nazis and followers of Hitler, didn't yet know what they would have to do or what they would have to become; but the neo-Nazis already do know. And I think becoming a neo-Nazi in peacetime is much worse than being a Nazi in wartime. So I hope that they are eliminated somehow.

87. What do you do to explain to people what exactly happened in the Holocaust?

FIRESTONE: I'm telling the story. That's all I can do. I can tell the story and hope that people understand and realize how horrific it was; I hope they realize that humanity must change, or else we're going to destroy ourselves. Eventually this kind of hatred, this kind of murderous attitude, will destroy the whole of humanity. So I hope that the children I speak to, who write me wonderful letters, will change the world.

We have quite a few Holocaust organizations here. I'm a board member of the Los Angeles Museum of the Holocaust and a public speaker at the Simon Wiesenthal Center. I have been involved with the people who help survivors of the new genocides. I met children of Cambodian survivors; in London I met with Rwandan survivors; and here in Los Angeles, a group of us organized a rally to make our government acknowledge that what happened in Darfur was genocide and not an isolated incident. We try to make the world aware of what's going on, and try to see if there's any way we can help engage people in the issues.

88. From today's perspective, how can you explain that "normal people" were capable of such atrocities?

FIRESTONE: I can't. I still wonder how one man could convince not just one nation, but many nations, to become murderers. I cannot explain that, and I cannot understand it; and there are much smarter people than I, trying to figure it out. There is just no way that it can be explained.

89. What exactly do you feel when you hear that there are still people who claim that the Holocaust never took place?

FIRESTONE: Well, I think anybody who claims that the Holocaust never existed or never took place is a total ignoramus: just an ignorant human being! Germany acknowledges it! Germans themselves acknowledge it. I mean, how can anybody say that it didn't happen? You can go to Poland and see all the camps there. Thousands and thousands of people are flocking to these camps every single day—to *see* them. Only a totally ignorant human being could say it never happened.

90. What consequences did the proclamation of the "Nuremberg Laws" on September 15, 1935, have for you?

FIRESTONE: Of course, none in 1935, because I lived in Czechoslovakia. In Hungary, similar laws came about in 1939. When we were occupied by Hungary, the first effect was that I could not go to a public school anymore. Then we were stripped of our rights in the same way as the Nuremburg Laws stripped the German Jews of theirs. Later on we were stripped of our possessions. We had to turn in everything of value to the government; so naturally, it had a great, great effect on us. And we had to wear the yellow star, of course, the Star of David.

91. What are your personal memories of the "Night of Broken Glass" on November 9/10, 1938?

FIRESTONE: We found out about *Kristallnacht* through newsreels in the movie theaters. We saw how they burned the synagogues. That was what we knew about it. We did not know about the men being taken to Dachau, but we knew that the Jews were being persecuted and that the synagogues were being burned. And at one point we saw a synagogue on fire, with the people being burned inside it. It was in a news film.

92. What are your personal memories of the beginning of the war in 1939?

FIRESTONE: In the beginning, we still had radios, and we also saw it in the newsreels. Newsreels were like today's television news, but were shown in movie theaters before the movie started. We just knew that Germany had invaded Poland. We didn't know that they had made a deal with Russia. We were very surprised when we found out that Stalin was involved in that. But we heard that Poland had been invaded by Germany, and then, of course, soon after, when they started to shoot the Jews into mass graves, rumors of that came from Poland, and of what else the Germans were doing there.

93. Did you hear that the National Socialists had decided to implement the "final solution to the Jewish question"—the systematic extermination of Jews in Europe—at the Wannsee Conference on January 20, 1942. If so, when and how?

FIRESTONE: We knew nothing about the Wannsee Conference. We knew nothing about concentration camps. But I'll tell you what we did know. And we did not believe it. Some of the workers in the forced labor camps from Hungary were taken to the front when the war started, and a few months later, a group of young men was brought back from the front. They were in the hospital, and the Jewish community told us girls to take cookies to these young Jewish forced laborers. I met a young man who was with a group of twelve. They were in the hospital, but they were not wounded, so I wondered what they were doing there. They told me that they had contracted typhus at the front, but had now recovered; some of them had died, but these twelve had recovered. So the Germans brought them back to Hungary and were using them as so-called "lice feeders." They put little boxes of lice all over their arms and legs so that the lice would suck their blood, and from their blood, the Germans would make a serum, an antidote for typhus.

This young man used to come to my house for dinner, and at the dinner table, he would tell us stories. He told us that where he had been at the Ukrainian front between Germany and Ukraine, the Germans had gathered Jews by the truckload every Friday night and had taken them to a place, which they could see from a distance was surrounded with barbed wire. And he said, "We never saw those Jews again." A few days later, the trucks came back carrying soap. My parents said to me, "You know, the typhus must have affected this young man's head, and now he's telling these terrible stories." Well, we found out later that they were making soap out of Jews' fat, so he was telling the truth, after all. These were the only things he knew. Nothing else. He didn't know that it was a concentration camp, or an extermination camp, so we knew nothing about that.

94. When you heard that World War II was over, what feelings did you have?

FIRESTONE: Well, I was glad that I might be free, but of course I knew that my parents most probably would not return. I also knew that my little sister was probably not coming back. So there I was, twenty-one years old, an orphan; I had never been alone before, and I wondered what my future was going to be, how I was going to exist, where I was going to go. I knew I didn't want to go back home, and fortunately, I found my brother. Otherwise I have no idea what I would have done.

95. Do you think that humankind has learned something from the Holocaust?

FIRESTONE: Of course not. Humankind learned nothing from the Holocaust. If they had, there wouldn't have been genocide in Cambodia, or in Kosovo, or in Rwanda, or in Darfur. So it looks like they learned absolutely nothing.

96. Should the atrocities be forgotten and no longer talked about, as some people wish?

FIRESTONE: Never! They should never be forgotten. We should talk about it all the time, and that's why I'm talking about it. I hope that maybe young generations', future generations', learning about it and understanding it will change the world. That is what we are hoping for. That is the only reason why we have Holocaust museums.

97. What plans do you still have for the future?

FIRESTONE: What plans do you make at my age? Who knows, if I live as long as Leopold [Engleitner], I can have some plans. In the meantime, I just do what I can every day. As long as I can, I'll be speaking about my experiences to groups of people, and I am trying to stay healthy so that I can do it.

98. How would you like to be remembered?
FIRESTONE: I am not a special person, but I think I will be remembered because I appear in a few movies. I also wrote a memoir. So I hope that my memoir, not me, will be a reminder of my story. And an exhibition of my designs [took] place in the Los Angeles Museum of Design in 2012, so that also will be a reminder.

99. What else would you like to say to us? Which question was not asked?
FIRESTONE: When I was packing my suitcase to leave, I wanted to take something to remember my childhood by, and I came across this bathing suit. My father had brought it for me from one of his business trips. He always used to bring us some gifts. And I remember asking him, "What did you bring?" He opened a box, and out of the box came the most beautiful bathing suit. It was the first latex, stretch-fabric bathing suit I had ever seen. It had a print of multicolored flowers on it. So I was holding this bathing suit, thinking I should pack it. As I was holding it, I remembered when I first wore it and how I paraded around the swimming pool and how the boys whistled at me, and I thought to myself, I should take this with me. Whenever I'm sad or upset, all I have to do is look at this bathing suit, and I will remember my father's love and the good times. But then I decided not to, because I thought it was sort of trivial to think about a bathing suit in such serious times. So I left it and packed my suitcase. When the Hungarian gendarmes (policemen) came to pick us up, I thought maybe I should take it after all, so I ran back and put it on under my clothes. I put it on, then I put my dress on; that's how I left for Auschwitz.

When we got to Auschwitz, we were in the bathhouse, and they told us to get undressed. I undressed, and there I was standing, wearing the bathing suit, and I could not take it off. I had a premonition that if I left the bathing suit, I would leave everything that was ever good to me in life: my parents' love and the good times I had experienced as a child. A Nazi soldier came over and hit me, saying, "Take it off!" I took the bathing suit off; my sister started to cry because she was afraid I was going to be beaten again. I folded the bathing suit very neatly and left it on top of my clothing. Of course, when I tell the story to children, I tell them that with that bathing suit I did not just leave my good memories in Auschwitz, I left my whole family there.

I have another story to tell about a young man who, when we were still at home, was a nuisance. He used to follow me around when I was a little girl and threaten me with all kinds of things because I didn't want to talk to him. Then when I was growing up and starting to date, he used to follow me around and threaten my boyfriends. I came from an upper-middle-class family, and he came from a very poor family, so I ignored him most of the time; but he became so annoying that I used to come home to my mother crying, upset that he was following me around and was being so annoying. My mother used to say, "Just ignore him. He'll go away." Then one day, he did go away, and I didn't know, of course, that he went to a forced labor camp; I was just glad that he was not after me anymore, and I forgot about him.

One day I was sitting in Auschwitz—it was after my sister was taken away from me—and I remember I was very depressed. I was sitting against the barracks, and a group of workmen came through. Usually, we would all run over to them, calling out names, hoping that somebody would remember a brother or a father. Well, I was not in the mood even to get up. All of a sudden, one man left this group and came towards me. I was sitting there, and he looked at me and said, "Oh my god! What did they do to you?" And I ignored him; I didn't know who he was, or what he was questioning me for. Then he turned to me and said, "Are you hungry?" Of course, I answered, "Oh yes, I'm very hungry!" He reached into his uniform and took out three raw potatoes and dropped them into my lap. I looked at these potatoes, and my first thought was, "How am I going to eat these? If my fellow prisoners find out that I have three potatoes, they will kill me for them." So I tried to wrap them in my skirt so that nobody could see them, and he ran away, back to his group. As he ran away, the voice reminded me of somebody. I kept thinking, and I said to myself, "My gosh, that's the boy who used to follow me around!" And I found myself crying—my tears were running—and I don't know what, but something happened to me at that moment. I kept thinking, "My gosh, he is saving my life here, and I was so cruel, so ugly to him!" I couldn't get him out of my mind for a long time after that.

Then I came to America. Many years later, I went to a New Year's Eve party. A woman from my hometown was there, and she knew that I was working for the Simon Wiesenthal Center, so she asked me, "What do you do there?" I said I told my story and stories about the Holocaust. "What kind of stories?" I started telling her about this boy, and she said, "Who was this boy?" I told her the name and she said, "You know that he is alive?" "No, where is he?" She said, "He lives in Hollywood," and she gave me a telephone number. The next day, of course, I called the number and asked him if he was "so-and-so" and he said, "Yes." I said, "Were you in Auschwitz?" and he said, "No." I said, "Oh, I'm so sorry. I'm looking for someone with this name, someone who was in Auschwitz. Forgive me." I went to hang up and he said, "Don't hang up! You're looking for my cousin. He's in New York." He gave me his cousin's telephone number, and I called him in New York, and sure enough, it was the boy. He remembered me, of course, and remembered giving me the potatoes in Auschwitz. Then, a few months later, he called me to say that he was going to Las Vegas and had decided to come to Los Angeles to meet me. He came with his wife, and we met. Of course, I apologized to him and asked him for his forgiveness. He went back to New York, and a few years later, he died.

100. After all you have been through, what advice can you give us young people?

FIRESTONE: I want young people, first of all, to get to know each other. I usually ask them, "Do you know the person whom you sit next to in school? Do you know anything about them? Do you know, when they go home, are their parents there? Do they have any brothers or sisters? You know, we find that people hate each other not even knowing each other, not knowing anything about each other. I found some students in Poland, for example, who never saw a Jew. Yet, I heard them say derogatory things about Jews, and I keep telling our students that there is only one race—and that is the human race—and we are all created by the same God, and we should respect one another. We do not have to love each other, but [we must] respect one another and get to know each other. So we can understand, if we are angry at somebody, why we are angry at [that person], or why we don't like somebody; but most of the [reasons for] hatred are totally unknown. What did some of these people know about us [that incited them] to murder us? What crimes did we commit? Did they think that we committed some kind of a crime [for which we were] to be killed or executed? So basically I think that just to respect the fact that we all belong to the human race would be enough [reason] not to kill each other.

I usually also tell young people what I do and encourage them to find a cause—a cause for humanity. There are so many students who need tutoring, for example, so I tell them, "Find a younger student who needs your help. You will find out how rewarding it is to help somebody, to do something kind for another person. There are also older people who need help. Go and help them." We now have some students doing that, and I hope that it will catch on and that young people will start performing some kindnesses for other people. It is very important for me, for example, if I do something kind for another person: it makes me feel good and it helps humanity.

Frieda Horvath:
Stolen Youth

Frieda Horvath, née Schröder, born July 18, 1926
Grounds for persecution: Sintiza (gypsy)
Length of imprisonment: 2 years, 2 months
Country: Austria

23. *Frieda Horvath, 1949*

24. *Frieda Horvath, 2009*

Frieda Horvath, née Schröder, was born on July 18, 1926, in Słupsk in Pomerania, Prussia, Germany, to a family of Sinti. In March 1943, she, her parents, and eight brothers and sisters were arrested. On March 14, 1943, they were deported to Auschwitz-Birkenau concentration camp and interned in the so-called Gypsy Camp in Birkenau. After about a week in Ravensbrück concentration camp, Frieda Horvath was transferred to Graslitz, a subcamp of Flossenbürg concentration camp, at the beginning of August 1944. There, she had to perform heavy labor in a munitions factory. When the factory premises were bombed by the Allies, Graslitz subcamp was evacuated in mid-April 1945, and she had to join the death march. At the end of April 1945, Frieda Horvath was liberated by the Americans. Her parents and three brothers died in concentration camps. After the war, she married Johann Horvath, a Roma who had also been in a concentration camp, and they had five children. Earning a livelihood was an enormous struggle; she worked very hard and begged for alms. For decades, she was forced to move from one refugee camp to another before finally obtaining an apartment in Linz an der Donau, Austria, in 1971. Cooking is her great passion, and she likes nothing better than treating her large family to a sumptuous meal. Frieda Horvath lives in Austria.

The interviews took place on February 2, 2009 and September 15, 2011.

1. When were you born? What was your father like? What was your mother like?

HORVATH: I was born on July 18, 1926, in Słupsk in Pomerania [Prussia]. At that time, it was part of Germany. After the war, it was taken over by the Poles. My father's name was Albert Schröder, my mother's, Johanna. Her maiden name was Laubinger. My parents had nine children. They were good parents. We were five boys and four girls. The girls' names were Erna, Herta, Lola, and Frieda. The boys were called Waldemar, Max, Siegfried, Heini, and Willi. Willi was the oldest.

We were a Sinti family. Our grandparents lived with us as well. They were my father's parents. My grandmother died at home and so did my grandfather. I only rarely saw my grandparents on my mother's side.

2. What is your earliest childhood memory?

HORVATH: Somehow I can't really put my finger on anything specific. In summer, there was always a kind of fair, with merry-go-rounds and so on. As children, we often went there after school. We didn't have much freedom. Our parents were much too strict for that.

3. What kind of childhood did you have?

HORVATH: Well, what can I say? Growing up, I had to look after the two children who were younger than me. The older boys were all working. The youngest brother, Heini, was born in 1931. When I came home from school, I did my homework, and in summer, I had to go and work in the field. In the winter, it wasn't so bad, we tended our farm at home. We had a little farm. My father built a house and leased a small piece of land.

We grew lots of potatoes and vegetables on it so that we and the animals had something to eat. We had three sheep, a pig, a horse, chickens, and Angora rabbits. They were very nice, and we used to shear them. Our mother then knitted socks and pullovers. When my brothers and sisters came home from work in the evening, we had to cook pots and pots of food. I helped my mother. We cooked and then served food for eleven. We needed three to four loaves of bread per day. In the evening, we baked bread to be taken to work or school. We needed a lot. Sausage, meat, and so on. If a person works hard, he has to eat. That's obvious. This went on until I was fifteen or sixteen years old.

At school, no one ever called me a gypsy. No one dared, because I would have beaten them up if they had. Maybe they said it secretly to each other. I had one cousin who was very dark-skinned and whose left arm was crippled. They always bullied him, but I always stepped in to put a stop to it. I fought a lot. I always stood up for him in school.

4. How long did you go to school, and what schools did you attend?
HORVATH: I was only able to do eight years of primary school. I wanted to learn something, but I never had the chance.

5. What was your adolescence like? What trade did you learn, and what did you do for a living?
HORVATH: I couldn't learn any trade. When I left school, I was supposed to do labor service in the BDM [*Bund Deutscher Mädel*] (League of German Maidens). My father managed to have me exempted because he was sick, and I had to help him cultivate the field. I stayed at home and looked for a job: delivering newspapers, which I did on my bicycle. When I was done, I went back to the field to work or helped my mother at home, doing the laundry and so on. I was only there to work; I didn't have an adolescence. And after? We were arrested.

6. What can you tell us about your family?
HORVATH: In 1949 I married Johann Horvath. He was a Roma from Burgenland and had also been in a concentration camp. With my husband, I had five children: Johann, Franz, Hermine, Martin, and Renaldo. I also have twenty grandchildren, twenty-four great-grandchildren, and two great-great-grandchildren. My husband died in 1991, my son Franz, in 2007.

7. Did you use the Nazi greeting "Heil Hitler!" and/or the Nazi salute?
HORVATH: Yes, in school after the war had started. But not at home in the family.

8. Why were you persecuted by the National Socialists?
HORVATH: Because we were Sinti. We were Sinti, and that's why we were all taken away—the whole family.

9. When were you arrested?
HORVATH: In March 1943.

10. Why were you imprisoned?
HORVATH: Because we were Sinti. All the Sinti were taken away, from the entire area, from everywhere.

11. What exactly happened when you were arrested?
HORVATH: We were told we all had to report to the local council office, the whole family. We had to take our identity papers with us and wear our warmest and best clothes. We didn't suspect anything, but my father already knew what was going on because he must have sold the house before then, since we never got it back. He must have sold the house before because he had the money. We asked him, "Papa, where did you get that money from? Where's our house?" And then, in prison, he explained it for the first time: "I sold the house because they're taking us all away." Then we all cried. We didn't know it before. Then he said, "It's good that the house has been sold. At least it has someone who will look after it." He had sold it, and everything in it, to some Germans.

We didn't know where they were taking us. We were locked in a cell in the prison—the entire family. We spent the night there, and in the morning, a train came to transport us away. We were taken as far as Danzig [now Gdańsk, Poland]. In Danzig, we all had to get in a freight car that was normally used for cattle. There was straw on the floor and a bucket of water. There were already a great many families in there. We had to use the bucket as a toilet. It was unbelievable. You can't describe such a thing anymore. We stopped at a lot of stations, and many cars were uncoupled. Where they went, we didn't know. Some of our relatives were in them. Our car went on to Auschwitz.

12. Did people know right from the start what was happening in the camps? Before you were taken away, did you know what would happen to you?
HORVATH: We had absolutely no idea about anything. At the council office, they told us we would be given a small plot of land that we could farm there [in Auschwitz]. And in reality, it was an extermination camp. They led us all by the nose.

13. How many different camps were you in? How many years did you spend in each camp?

HORVATH: After the prison, we arrived in Auschwitz-Birkenau on March 14, 1943. In July 1944, all the girls and young women who were still strong were sent to Ravensbrück. I was in Ravensbrück for about a week. Then we were examined. Those who were still fit were sent away again. In August 1944, I was sent to Graslitz to work in a munitions factory. That was a subcamp of Flossenbürg concentration camp. I was there until mid-April 1945, when we had to march out of the camp. At the end of April, we were liberated by the Americans.

14. Were you the only member of your family in the concentration camp, or were family members or friends there as well? If so, did you have any contact with them?

HORVATH: I didn't have any friends; I was with my family. Then my grandmother and grandfather, my mother's parents, also arrived at the concentration camp. My father's brothers and sisters were in Birkenau. The families were put in different barracks. All of my family was in one barrack. We had two "boxes," wide bunk beds for six people on top and six underneath. The men slept on top, the women underneath as was customary with the Sinti. After all, you don't sleep with your own brothers or parents. Then the kitchen was set up. For months on end, we were given only beetroot and potatoes to eat. But we were so hungry that we were glad to get that. Then "barrack no. 1" was built for the people who worked in the kitchen. On the right was the cooking space, on the left the peeling space, where the potatoes were peeled. My brothers were assigned to the kitchen because they could cook. That meant they could no longer be together with the rest of the family, because they had to be clean when they cooked. So then we had more room to sleep. Later on, I was assigned to the kitchen too.

In the summer of 1944, we older children were moved from Birkenau. When we arrived in Ravensbrück, my sisters and I had to walk through an iodine bath. That was to disinfect us so that we didn't carry any germs in. My youngest sister, Lola, cut her foot open going through the bath, and a large mark developed. As a result, she had to stay in Ravensbrück concentration camp. The other two, Erna and Herta, came with me to Graslitz. My mother and Heini stayed in Birkenau. The other brothers were sent to Sachsenhausen and Buchenwald concentration camps.

15. What were the first things that happened immediately following your arrival at the concentration camp?

HORVATH: On arrival, we were lined up in families. Then the doctor came and tattooed us. There, on the arm. I was given the number 3359. The little children were tattooed on their backsides. That really hurt. My arm swelled up to a huge size. But we weren't given any ointment. It took a few weeks for everything to heal. No one helped us.

We were also taken into a barrack for a shower. Then our new clothes were taken away from us. We had to undress completely. To be completely naked in front of our brothers and our father was humiliating for us. That is not customary for us Sinti. The boys cried their eyes out. If you covered yourself with a piece of cloth, you received a beating. Then the water came. At first we wondered if it was gas. We were frightened because the water came out in such streams that we all thought it was gas.

Later we heard that the gas chamber was behind the showers. That was where people were gassed. After we were there for a few months, they opened the gas chamber once. Very many Jews were gassed there, but we didn't know what that was. The older generation knew it, maybe, but we youngsters were just afraid the whole time that they would kill us.

After our shower, they gave us someone else's clothes. The clothes belonged to the people who had gone before us, while our clothes were given to those who came after us. We weren't given a prisoner's uniform, we were given civilian clothing with a black triangle. That was the gypsy's triangle. Our numbers were tattooed on our arms. We had a strip with our number on it fixed to our clothes only when we were in a work detail outside the camp.

When we arrived in Auschwitz, there was a barrack with women and doctors inside. They looked at us all and divided us up. The sick ones were laid to one side. I was put in barrack 8 in the gypsy camp in Birkenau. We, the whole family, had to walk from the main entrance of Auschwitz to Birkenau. It was March, and there must have been a deluge because there was so much mud and dirt. Our shoes got stuck in it. We marched for almost a whole hour. Then we reached the barrack where there were rats and mice. There were blankets there that were so filthy that lice were living in them. It was inhuman.

16. Why did they shave the heads of the prisoners?
HORVATH: Because of the lice, and because I worked in the kitchen. My head was shaved after a few months. I had very long tresses. It was so humiliating for a Sintiza. I cried my eyes out on account of my hair. It looks so stupid, running around with a bald head. It's unbelievable. My mother had a headscarf and said, "Here, take this!" I tied the headscarf round my head and poked a few of my hairs under it at the front. When I went into the kitchen like that, they asked me, "How can you have hair when it's all been shaved off?" Then the female guard who was there took away the headscarf. I received a beating and a punishment. I was confined to the barrack and had to clean and do barrack room duty.

17. What prisoner category were you put in?
HORVATH: In the gypsy camp in Birkenau, there were only people who were persecuted on racial grounds. These included Sinti and Roma. Czech, Hungarian, and Polish gypsies were also there.

18. Can you describe the daily routine in the concentration camp?
HORVATH: We young people all went to work in Birkenau. The older ones, Father and Mother, didn't have to work. They stayed in the barrack. So did my sister, who had just given birth. And they didn't take the two youngest children, Lola and Heini, with them when they went to work. Early in the morning, there was roll call, winter and summer. You stood outside and they counted everyone. In summer, it was all right, but in winter, it was the worst.

In the morning, we only got a morsel of bread and blue tea. The family was given a loaf of bread and a little bit of butter, but that was all. I don't know what kind of tea it was, but it was blue and tasted horrible. We had no sugar, nothing. We had to work until midday, when they gave us a concoction to eat. They boiled beetroots, potatoes in their skins, and carrots all mixed up in one pot. Then we had to go back to work until the evening.

19. What was the worst thing about the daily routine?
HORVATH: The worst thing was working outside the camp in a detail and worrying about our parents. They were in the barracks. We were outside and didn't know what was happening there all day. When we came home again in the evening, we were dead tired but glad to see our parents again and [glad to] lie down. It got easier for me when I started working in the kitchen.

20. Did everyday life lead more to solidarity, or did the prisoners try to cope on their own?

HORVATH: We only had to take care of our own family. I often went over to see my grandmother. Then my grandmother and my grandfather both died.

21. Was there anything that helped you take your mind off the horror of daily life for a while (such as music)? What gave you strength?

HORVATH: There was nothing at all. All you did was go take a look to see who was still alive. There was a prisoners' band, but it only played when we went out in our work detail. We had to march out and back in again to music. Now and then a man would go round the barracks playing gypsy music on a violin, but that was forbidden. I always wanted to get up and dance. One time I said to my brother Max, "Come on, let's go for a little dance, he's playing so beautifully." But when the block senior appeared, we stopped immediately.

22. What were living conditions like in the barracks (prisoner allocation, food supplies, hygiene, clothing, etc.)?

HORVATH: I can't remember how many people were in one barrack in Birkenau. I should think there were thirty families at least. There was a sliding door, and behind it the makeshift toilet made of wood. In winter, everything was frozen, and the rats came. They were enormous and came right into the barrack. We weren't sure whether they had bitten us or not. There were so many rats and lice too. It stank dreadfully in the barack. The people were from many different nations. Each one had a different smell, and the stench from the toilet also wafted in. We weren't allowed to use the shower. But I wanted to have a wash because otherwise I couldn't have borne it. In winter, I even rubbed snow on my skin and then crept into bed beside my mother. We always had the same clothes. We had to wash them ourselves. In Graslitz, we lived in the factory. The living space was upstairs. There was a big dayroom and a dormitory. Between thirty and forty people were served their meals in the dayroom.

23. What jobs did you have to do? How many hours a day did you have to work?

HORVATH: In an outside work detail in Birkenau, we had to cut out pieces of turf and lay them out in the camp near the entrance. To the right was the place where the musicians were, and to the left, we laid this turf because everything was so dirty. In summer, that's what we did from morning to evening. In the end, it all looked nice. I was treated well because I did my job well. No one said anything mean to me. For months, I also did barrack room duty. In Birkenau, I was assigned to the kitchen where the potatoes were peeled. I peeled potatoes there until we were taken away. In Ravensbrück, I was kept in quarantine until I was taken away from there.

In Graslitz, I was in a munitions factory. Only women worked there, and I had to work at a machine that was as big as a table. Our job was to drill holes in pieces of iron. I don't know exactly what for. The pieces of iron were round, and we had to place them on a rod. Then we had to drill a hole. Next, two stabilizers were attached. We put twenty-five of these items in a crate, and by evening, we had to have finished twenty crates. It was all done at top speed. I had a German foreman who always helped me and showed me what to do. He was a good man and often brought me bread. He asked, "Are you a German?" I said, "Yes." He always brought me a slice of bread and butter and said, "I brought you some bread."

24. What effect did the slogan "Work liberates" have on you?
HORVATH: That was over the entrance in Auschwitz. We didn't take any notice of it when we went in.

25. What were the guards like in the camp?
HORVATH: In Birkenau, there was a camp *kapo*, and the SS sometimes held inspections.

None of them hurt me, except one SS man who hit me on the head, and on one occasion the camp *kapo*. Smoking was not allowed outside the barrack. One time, I went to my grandmother and took her some cigarettes. I had a cigarette in my hand too and didn't notice the camp *kapo* and an SS man coming toward me. They were carrying out an inspection. The SS man himself had occasionally given me a cigarette to smoke while I was working, but now he shouted, "Stand still!" I extinguished the smoke behind my back, and the ash lay on the ground. I had to stand at attention and give my number and my name. He looked at me and asked, "Did you just smoke?" I said, "No, I didn't." He knew my name and said, "Frieda, don't lie to me! You just smoked." I said, "No, I didn't smoke!" Then he raised his hand and struck me in the face in front of the camp *kapo*, breaking off a piece of my tooth.

176

Next day, I met the SS man at work again and he said to me, "Why did you lie to me?" I said, "And you had to hit me so hard that a piece of my tooth broke off?" He then suggested I go to the laboratory because they had all the teeth from the dead bodies stored there. He said, "Have a tooth put in, and make it a gold one while you're at it. I'll go with you." To which I replied, "You better shoot me. I'm not having a tooth from a dead person put in." He said, "You can't leave it like that. I'll do it for you." "No," I said, "take your pistol and shoot me at once. I will not have a tooth from a dead person put in." Then he said, "Then get lost! And next time, tell the truth. I had to do that because the camp *kapo* was there." And I said, "I'm not saying another word to you." He wanted to make it up to me, and later I relented and forgave him.

26. Was there any contact between the prisoners and the local population?
HORVATH: No! We never got out because we weren't allowed to. In Birkenau, there was a fence, and if you went up to it, you were caught in the electric current. We didn't have much room to move.

27. Were you aware of how the war was proceeding in the outside world?
HORVATH: No, we never got to hear anything about that. The only thing we heard were bombardments. Graslitz was bombed once. I had just come into the dormitory from night shift and should have been in bed. We weren't allowed to work during a raid; that's why we were all in the room. The shrapnel shattered the windows. One piece of shrapnel embedded itself in my pillow. It could have hit me. A train carrying prisoners was also bombed. They took a great many of the wounded straight to a hospital in Czechoslovakia. I didn't really realize what was happening, but my sister shouted, "Get up, get up! There's a raid on, and they're taking prisoners away down there. Maybe our brother's there." So we looked out of the window and could see everything. But our brother wasn't there.

28. In the concentration camp, were you allowed to receive letters, food parcels, etc.?
HORVATH: Who could we have written to? We had no one. We didn't have any acquaintances on the outside either. Regrettably, our relatives were all gone and no one was at home. It might have been possible if we had had someone [on the outside].

29. What forms of torture did you suffer?

HORVATH: Torture? I can't complain too much on that score. Except for one time in Graslitz when I was made to stand in water up to my stomach from early morning until noon. When Göring and Himmler came to the camp, we got very good food for once: roast pork with dumplings and potatoes. I said, "I'm surprised we're getting good food today." I didn't mean to say it loudly, only quietly, but an SS man heard it and said, "Since when do they get bad food, then?" An older tall female SS guard was standing next to me. "Well," I said, "we always get water to eat, and the good solid stuff is distributed to her friends here. What's that all about? We're the ones who have to work hard, not them; they're inside doing housework." The SS guard said, "That's not true." I retorted, "It *is* true! The others don't dare say so, but I do. Because I have to work on a big machine. If I ever fall over, it will rip my head off. It's already happened to one person!" When the SS men who were accompanying Himmler and Göring had gone, the SS man said that in the future the food must be shared properly so that everyone got her portion. If not, a complaint would be lodged. Then they left, and the SS guard summoned me and said, "You will not go to work tomorrow. You will stand in water until noon!" We were on the early shift. So from the early morning until about two o'clock, I had to stand in a barrel of cold water. I kept leaning on the rim, but it was still cold. Afterward I massaged my legs to stimulate the circulation again. I ran up and down until they "thawed out" a little and wrapped them in blankets.

30. What was the most frightening moment for you?

HORVATH: The worst thing was when I lost my family. When my mother and my little brother Heini were gassed and when my father died. My mother and Heini were gassed after we older children had been taken away from Birkenau.

My father died in mid-1944 when I was still in Birkenau. He was already dying, and he was put in the barrack where seriously ill prisoners were brought. If you survived that, you were all right. If not, you died, or they gave you an injection that sent you straight to sleep. That's what happened to my father. He caught abdominal typhus and was taken into this barrack. I said to the block senior of the barrack for the sick, "I want to visit my father often, and when I come, I'll clean your office in return." He said,

"Okay, you can come." He always let me in to see Father. Then they gave him an injection. The block senior told me they had given him an injection and that he had died. There was a room at the back of the barrack where all the dead were laid. I went in again and saw my father. Then a car came, and they loaded him and the other deceased into it and drove them off to be cremated. The rats were running around. It was simply indescribable.

31. Were there any entertaining or lighthearted incidents that enabled you to forget all the suffering for a moment? Can you describe them?

HORVATH: It was when it was time to fetch the midday meal. In Birkenau, I was on barrack room duty one time. The block senior said, "Who will fetch the food now?" Heavy fifty-liter cauldrons of food had to be carried from the kitchen from barrack number 1 to barrack number 8. Two poles were put through an iron ring so the cauldron could be carried. I said to the block senior, "I can do that too. I'll show you!" He said, "You'll never manage that in a month of Sundays." I said, "If I get something that I can give to my mother, father, and the children, then I'll manage it." My mother said, "My child, you can't carry that, it's impossible." "Oh yes, I can, Mama," I replied. And then I really did carry that cauldron together with a young man who was eighteen years old. Then the block senior said, "You'll collapse now, though, won't you?" "No," I said. As a result, my mother got a bowl of food. I was given a loaf of bread and a packet of butter. We were really happy to have gotten that. The boy I carried the cauldron with got something too. The block senior set it aside for us.

I couldn't complain; I wasn't in such bad shape. Thankfully, I wasn't often sick. I didn't catch anything, because I always worked as hard as I could. If you had let yourself go in the concentration camp, you were finished. You had to go on working to build up your strength again.

32. What were your day-to-day thoughts while you were in the concentration camp?

HORVATH: My only thoughts were that it was possible to go on living. Mostly I only looked after my brothers and sisters and my parents. I was the only one who did that; my brothers and sisters would never have been able to do it.

33. Was it possible for children to be born in a concentration camp? If so, what happened to these babies?

HORVATH: Yes. My sister Erna gave birth after we had been in the concentration camp for a month. Prior to that, she had been suffering from a touch of typhus. Then she was given a Caesarean section. In one of the barracks, there was a "laboratory." The women who had just given birth were put in there. My sister never got to see her child. She just kept shouting, "Where's my child?" It was gone, but it had been alive. After the birth, it had been taken away immediately and killed. She suffered a great deal, and her nerves were never the same again. At the time of her arrest, she was eight months pregnant. She had wanted to get married, but the child's father had gone home to visit his parents in Berlin and couldn't leave the city again. He just wrote a quick letter saying he and his parents were being taken away, but they didn't know to where, yet. He was also brought to Birkenau, and I saw him once.

34. Was it possible to make friends with prisoners?

HORVATH: I was young, and even if I had wanted to be friends with a boy, it was simply not an option. It was not something that interested you at all. You always had to focus on your own life and on your brothers, sisters, and parents—and on nothing else.

35. Who was your best friend during this dreadful time, and how did he or she help you?

HORVATH: Who could have been our friends there? That kind of thing simply didn't exist. There were no friends there. All I had was a slight acquaintance, but she wasn't a close friend. She was a Hungarian gypsy called Sophie. When we were all split up and sent to different camps, I didn't see her anymore. It was only after the war that I met her once in Linz.

36. What did you do to relieve the suffering of other inmates?

HORVATH: I looked after my parents, brothers, and sisters. When we were being allocated to Graslitz in Ravensbrück, I went to an SS doctor and said, "I would like my two sisters to come with me." He said, "If you're all healthy, we can do that." So I said to my sister Erna, "Get your nerves under control. Don't do anything stupid, then I'll be able to take you with me." He let me take both of them. They couldn't do any heavy work, only light duties.

37. Were there particular hierarchies among the inmates?
HORVATH: The camp *kapo* and block seniors had a higher status than all the other prisoners. Otherwise there were no differences.

38. Were there any differences in the way the various groups of prisoners (religious, political groups) were treated?
HORVATH: No, none.

39. What diseases and illnesses were prevalent in the concentration camp?
HORVATH: Typhus and typhoid fever. Those who had abdominal typhus generally died. Abdominal typhus empties the stomach. The intestines are drained and you dehydrate. Then it goes to your head. My sister Erna had it but recovered. I had a very slight case of abdominal typhus. I was careful and didn't eat everything. That's why I didn't immediately catch the same illnesses that the others did. Of my family, I remained the healthiest.

40. Did you receive a physical injury?
HORVATH: In Birkenau, I received a blow on the head when the food was being served, and one time a piece of my tooth was knocked out. The meals for the detail that worked outside were brought in cauldrons. Two SS men stood guard. But the girls were so hungry that they didn't want to work anymore. When the cauldron with the food arrived, they rushed at it with their bowls. I and a lot of other women stood to one side because we didn't dare join in. Then the SS men started beating back the girls, and I received a few blows as well. I was hit on the back of the head (*points to it*) with a baton. The blood poured down. I said to him, "Why did you hit me? I wasn't doing anything." He wasn't at all disagreeable. He was a young man, this SS man, and he said, "Because you were standing there. I thought you were one of them." I said, "You should look more carefully." Then he parted my hair, took a Band-Aid. and stuck it on my wound. He himself did that.

A terrible thing happened to my cousin in Graslitz. I must tell you that. We were working and she wanted to switch the machine off. She had long hair, and some of it got caught at the front in the machine. The machine kept turning. From the hairline to the back of her head, her whole scalp was torn off. I was working next to her, there was only a passage between us that the guards walked through. She screamed at me to help her. I went to switch the machine off, and when I bent down, my hair nearly got caught in it as well. My foreman came in and switched it off. There was nothing I could do to help her. She lay on the ground, the blood pouring out. She screamed and screamed. She was immediately taken to the hospital. A skin graft was taken from her thigh and grafted onto her head. We were not allowed to visit her, and they didn't release her either. She lay in bed, and when she came out of the hospital, she had to march with us on the death march, even though she was seriously injured. But I had my two sisters to look after and couldn't help her. But another woman helped her.

41. How much did you weigh when you were in the concentration camp?
HORVATH: I can't say. I wasn't in such bad shape.

42. What did death mean to you?
HORVATH: Yes, you do get frightened. You think, "All those people had to die; now you'll have to die too." When you still have your youth ahead of you, you get frightened, that's perfectly natural. Many young people died in the concentration camp. They would have liked to carry on living, but they couldn't go on. I always thought, "I hope God helps us to get out of here."

43. What was the closest you came to death?
HORVATH: There was only one dangerous situation, when shrapnel embedded itself in my pillow during an air raid in Graslitz. But I saw death all the time. In Birkenau, there was a crematorium with a gas chamber right next to our barrack. It was separated from us only by a fence. I could see how the sick, the lame, and the frail went in and how the prisoners assigned to the task carried out the bodies. The SS men would never have touched them. Truckloads of Jews kept arriving who were then taken in there.

When there were too many bodies to burn in the crematorium, they built a large bonfire pile outside, threw all the bodies on it, and lit it. The bodies first rose up, then sank down again. No one was allowed to leave the barrack as long as the fire was burning. We had to shut all the doors and windows, but I always peeped out through the gap near the barrack. If you have seen something like that, it stays with you day and night. Even after my release, these images were still etched in my mind for years afterward.

44. Did you ever build a kind of "wall" to shield yourself from the terrible things that were being done so that the death of a fellow prisoner no longer affected you?

HORVATH: I blanked that straight out. I always thought, "I'll just do my work, and hopefully I'll be able to go on." We always thought that either we would die or we would survive.

45. What happened to the dead bodies in the concentration camp?

HORVATH: The bodies were burned in the crematorium or on the fire. There's a peculiar smell when people burn. I had never smoked a cigarette in my life, but my father said to me, "If you manage to get cigarettes from anywhere, girl, smoke them." I said, "Why should I smoke?" He said, "Just smell the 'gas' that comes out when people burn. You inhale it." Then I said, "Everyone has to. That's no reason for me to smoke, and where am I supposed to get cigarettes from?" There was a canteen there, and those who had money could buy odds and ends.

My father still had plenty of money, even though they had taken a lot away from us at the council office. I had plenty of money too. I had smuggled a few hundred marks into the concentration camp. I always hid it under my long hair at the back of my head. The prisoner in charge of the canteen was a Hungarian Sinto. I got on well with his sister, Sophie. She always went with me and said, "Come on, let's go see him and get some cigarettes." I always bought two or three packs. I also took some without paying (*laughs*), and he always said, "You've taken some cigarettes again, haven't you?" I replied, "No, honestly, I didn't! I paid you for them!" His sister stood up for me and said, "No way. She doesn't take anything."

46. Was there ever a possibility for you to be released from the concentration camp?

HORVATH: No, not for me. But the young men were offered the chance to join the army and fight for Hitler. They were told that if they did, their parents would be released. There were lots of families whose sons put their names forward. They didn't return home from imprisonment until after the war, in 1947 or 1948. And the parents really were released. They lived down in Burgenland in Unterschützen.

47. Were there any escape attempts or opportunities to escape? Did you try to escape?

HORVATH: In Graslitz and Auschwitz-Birkenau, there was no chance for me to escape. The fence in Birkenau was electrified. In Ravensbrück, I couldn't go anywhere, because I was in the barrack, and we weren't even allowed to go outside. I had relatives there in the camp, but I wasn't allowed to visit them.

In Birkenau, there were two men who had either given up hope long ago or wanted to stage an escape attempt. They got stuck on the electric fence. One of them was a Sinto, and they laid him on a stretcher and carried him through the barrack. They didn't cover him up and went through, showing him to everyone. Everyone saw him, even the children. He had open wounds and severe burns. Two SS men were there and they said, "The same thing will happen to anyone who tries what he did." Everyone stood there in shock, crying.

48. Were there any inmates in the concentration camp who dared to stage a revolt against the camp authorities?

HORVATH: I didn't see any. The only thing I remember was that I complained about the food in the munitions factory (*laughs*).

49. Did you think you would ever make it out alive?

HORVATH: I always said, "I must get out!"

50. Were there any times when you gave up all hope? If so, why?

HORVATH: I never gave up hope, although there were days when I was in despair. The work I had to do on the big machine was really very strenuous. Many times at night I couldn't feel my hands anymore. I thought to myself, "My god, if only it were over at last!" We always had the hope that the war would end one day, we would really be liberated, and the hard labor would stop. If the food had been sufficient, we wouldn't have been so desperate. But when you go to work with just a small piece of bread, when you get tea to drink in the morning and have to work hard until noon, and then you go into the dayroom and are given "vegetable soup" with two or three potatoes in it . . .

51. Did anyone commit suicide?

HORVATH: I can't say. The Sinto they carried around the barrack might have committed suicide. We all knew that anyone who wanted to get out of there just had to run into the electric fence. You just never got out of there.

52. During the Holocaust, did you ever consider committing suicide out of sheer despair?

HORVATH: No, that could never have occurred to me.

53. What thoughts, ideas, hopes, wishes, or religious convictions did you cling to?

HORVATH: I simply believed in God; just as I believe in God today, I believed in him in the camp. "Lord, help us to get out of here!" That was the only thing you thought about. You thought only of God and that he can help you.

54. Did you lose your faith in God while you were in the camp?

HORVATH: No, never. I still haven't.

55. What role did your religion play in how you felt about what was going on? Why?

HORVATH: It helped me. I don't know whether the Lord did anything for me. Today I can't say. But I survived it and came out happy.

56. Did you pray during your internment?

HORVATH: I prayed for myself and that my brothers and sisters and parents would all come out again, but unfortunately, that didn't happen.

57. Did you ever consider changing your religion (or ideology)? Why?

HORVATH: No.

58. What was the date of your liberation from the camp?

HORVATH: In mid-April 1945, we were sent on a death march starting from Graslitz. At the end of April 1945, we were liberated by the Americans.

59. How were you liberated from the camp, or how did you manage to get out of it?

HORVATH: The munitions factory was bombed. When that happened, the SS got scared. We couldn't work anymore, and they left with us. The prisoners had to pull a cart. They loaded bread and other food on it, but they only gave us bread. The SS ate the sausage and the other stuff themselves. There were six or seven SS women. They gathered there in a group and then marched off with us. We marched to Czechoslovakia, to the vicinity of Pilsen and Krakow. I can't remember the names of all the places exactly. We marched from early morning till the evening, when they would take us into a barn on a farm. They would boil potatoes, and we were all given potatoes in their skins and a piece of bread. We had to sleep in one stable after another. Then, at the end of April, they left us standing on the square in the middle of a village because the Americans were coming. The SS women had all disappeared. They took prisoners' clothing and disappeared with it. Among them was the one who had made me stand in the water. I would have hunted her, and if I had caught her, I would have turned her over straightaway. But there were also two or three good-natured SS girls among them; they must have been twenty-five or twenty-eight years old. They were really nice. There was another incident on this death march. One time I went to fetch potatoes from a farmer, and my older sister, Erna, and my cousin whose scalp had been torn off ran away. I looked for them but couldn't find them.

60. How were you treated by the people who liberated you?

HORVATH: Not badly. The Americans gave us packets of food.

61. What was the first thing you did after you were liberated?

HORVATH: We were taken to a collection camp in Pilsen, and that was where I met my future husband. The Americans were in charge. Then we had to get on a transport and were taken to a big square where the Russians were. I was so frightened that I thought I was going to die now, because the Russians were dangerous. But my future husband took charge of me and the other girls who had stayed together. That's how I got together with him. We went away on foot and made sure that we made it to Burgenland. The Russians were there too.

62. Did you have any problems when you returned home? How did people in your home environment react to you?

HORVATH: There were no major problems, because everyone had had a hard time. Except that to the people in Burgenland I was a foreigner. I was the Imperial German there, and they didn't like me.

There were few men and a lot of women, and they were jealous of me. They bitched about me: "Why is he bringing that Imperial German here, of all people?" They weren't all like that, only the people in Schreibersdorf, my husband's home village. All the others were friendly

63. Were you able to rejoin your family?

HORVATH: My parents and three brothers—Heini, Siegfried, and Willi—died in the concentration camp. The other brothers and all my sisters survived. Herta went with me to Burgenland. Later, I found out that my sister Erna, who ran away on the death march, was still alive. She and my other brothers and sisters looked for me with the Red Cross at the beginning of the 1950s, and she came to visit me. I also met my youngest sister, Lola, again. After the war, it was a long time before I found out what had become of everyone.

64. Did you have any acquaintances, friends, or relatives in the camps? Did they survive their internment?

HORVATH: Yes.

65. What happened to your possessions?

HORVATH: My father sold my parents' house in Pomerania before we were arrested, but the region is now part of Poland. We couldn't go back again afterward. The Germans who were in the house fled with their families.

66. To what extent have you received compensation for your internment?

HORVATH: I received compensation for my internment from Germany in the 1960s. In Austria, I only receive something from the victims' fund as the surviving dependent of my husband.

67. How did you set about rebuilding your life?

HORVATH: My goodness, I rebuilt it on a pittance. I had no spoons, no plates, nothing. I had to beg to get those things so that I had at least something. Later it was easier. I came to Linz, but down in Burgenland, I had nothing at all apart from my clothes. I went to the farmers, begging for food. They laughed at me because I spoke high German. That's just how it is when an outsider arrives. But they had their fun. They always said I was too good to work. Then they said, "Well, let's give her something then." They gave me food. That's how I coped. In Ebelsberg, I worked for the farmers, helping to bring in the potato and sugar beet harvests.

My husband worked for the ESG [electricity and tramway company]. Then he contracted a serious lung disease and spent a lot of time in the hospital. I was alone with my children most of the time, but I brought them up very well. They did what they were told because they knew I was on my own with them. They came home from school and immediately did their homework. They ate at the table and kept themselves clean. I came under welfare protection because I received welfare payments. My children were well-behaved and respectable.

68. How long did it take you to return to a "normal" life after the Holocaust?

HORVATH: It kept coming back to me when I was lying in bed. Especially in the immediate aftermath. It was years before I could shake it off some. Even today I can't shake it all off, because sometimes something comes back to me. Then I reflect and think back to it. As long as my children are by me, it's all right, but when I'm sitting there alone, everything comes back to me. But I want to forget. I don't want to think about it anymore, because it's over and life goes on. I have my good children, and that's all I need.

69. What was your life like after the war?

HORVATH: Following liberation, we went from Czechoslovakia to Burgenland. My husband thought he would find his parents or his brothers and sisters there, but there was nobody there. They had all died in the concentration camp. The only family member he met was a cousin.

I didn't like it in Burgenland, and we moved to Linz into a former barracks on Garnisonstrasse. The Americans were in charge of that area. We were given a large room where there were already a lot of concentration camp internees. They were Sinti. The Americans supported us and gave us packets of food. In 1947, Johann was born. But we didn't get an apartment, and we wanted to cross over the river to the other side of Linz, Urfahr. My husband was already over there with Johann, and I was standing by the Nibelungen Bridge on the far side, waiting to cross. I had a German passport. The Russians wouldn't let me over. I cried and sobbed and said, "That's my husband and my child!" Then an interpreter came and told the Russians that we intended to get married and that I didn't want to lose my husband and my child. Then they allowed me to cross, and we went to the shelter for the homeless on the Danube. Later on, they closed it down and we got an apartment in the Bachl camp in Urfahr. It was there that I had Franz in 1948.

In 1949, we got married. Then my husband started working at the ESG, and the Bachl camp was closed down.

25. Frieda and Johann Horvath, 1949

From there we went to another camp, in Traun. In 1950, my daughter Hermine was born in Traun. Then they closed down that camp as well. Next, I went to the Marinewald camp in Ebelsberg and from there to a camp in the Kleinmünchen district of Linz until I obtained my first proper apartment in 1971 in the Neue Heimat part of Linz. That all happened in rapid sequence. My husband, the children, and I went from one camp to another. In 1952, Martin was born, and in 1963, Renaldo. I had virtually no youth at all. Children, a sick husband, work, and that was all.

Until 2003, I didn't even have my own shower or toilet in the apartment; all of that was outside in the hallway. My children put in a shower for me.

70. What is your life like today? Do you still often think back to those days?

HORVATH: Now I feel content. I have my bathroom and my fine apartment. I have my children around me, and that's all I need. I have my life, I have enough to eat, and I don't need any more than that. But cooking is my life! I think when I die, I will take my stove with me. A saucepan, a spoon for stirring, they will have to bury that with me. Cooking is my life.

71. What physical and mental scars do you carry from that time?

HORVATH: I have a lot of problems with my feet from the time I stood in the water. I often have cramps and my joints hurt. My nerves have also been affected, but I don't go to the doctor. Some concentration camp internees find it hard to live with the tattoo on their arm. It doesn't bother me at all. When I traveled by bus in the summertime, I didn't even put a Band-Aid on it. Some Sinti always covered their tattoos with a Band-Aid, but I never did. People I know often asked me, "Say, Frieda, what's that number you have there?" I replied, "Oh, I always forget my telephone number. So I got it tattooed." Some said, "Aha," and others, "Wow, you're clever!" I'm not about to tell just anyone that I was in a concentration camp. Now, if anyone asks, I tell them that I was in a concentration camp. I was in the hospital one time, and the doctor saw my number. He said, "Frau Horvath, what's that number you have there?" I told him, "Doctor, I was in a concentration camp many years ago." "I would never have thought it," he said. "Yes," I said, "if I told you everything I went through, you would treat me differently!" He said, "But I'm not treating you badly." "No, no," I replied, "I was just kidding."

72. Did you have any moral support to help your emotional and social recovery?

HORVATH: No, I didn't.

73. Has your view of the world changed since that time?

HORVATH: No.

74. Can you think of anything positive that you have gained from your experiences?

HORVATH: Maybe that I learned not to let myself go in order to survive. That's still the same today. Whenever I'm in pain, I say, "I won't let myself go. I want to go on living."

75. Have you ever been back to visit the concentration camp you were held in, and if so, what were your feelings?

HORVATH: No, I couldn't bear to. The children went to Auschwitz, and I had the chance to go with them, but I didn't. I would have collapsed, I would have died. Because everything comes flooding back when I see those things again. I would have seen all my brothers and sisters and my parents again. I would have broken down, I couldn't have done it. I have often received invitations to Ravensbrück, but I won't go.

76. Are you still in touch with your fellow internees from the concentration camps?

HORVATH: My youngest sister, Lola, is still alive and lives in Germany. But we can't make such a long journey anymore and can't visit each other. Sometimes we talk on the phone.

77. What did you tell your family about your internment in the concentration camp? How did your relatives react to what you told them?

HORVATH: I told my children a lot. They know what I lived through. I always said they should remember what I went through. When they were children, they didn't really understand what that meant, but now that they're older, they do.

78. Do you find it difficult to talk about those days?

HORVATH: For me, it's difficult to recall everything to mind. When I'm lying in bed, it all comes back to me, and then I can't sleep.

79. Which moment from those days has remained most firmly etched in your memory?

HORVATH: The worst thing was losing my parents and brothers. That was the most terrible thing. Those were the hardest days for me.

80. Did you ever see or meet Hitler?
HORVATH: No.

81. What was your opinion of Hitler in those days, and what is your opinion of him now?
HORVATH: We never even realized what Adolf Hitler was planning to do. All the boys and girls had to join the Hitler Youth or the SS. But none of us knew that a war was being planned.

The boys just loved playing soccer. When they won a game, they got a picture of Hitler. I said, "What are we supposed to do with this picture?" The children answered, "We have to put it in the window." So we had to put Hitler in the window. When we were arrested I said, "See, Hitler's in the window, and now they're locking us up." If I caught him today, I would wring his neck. I would kill him.

82. Hypothetically, if Adolf Hitler were still alive and you could have five minutes alone with him, what would you say or do?
HORVATH: I would say, "Put him on the gallows and torture him. Cut him up, piece by piece, like he did to those other poor people."

83. After the war, did you ever meet any of the people who had tormented you?
HORVATH: No, not one.

84. What do you think of the punishments the Nazis received after the war, in the Nuremberg trials, for example?
HORVATH: Well, what am I supposed to think of them? My brother Waldemar had to give evidence at a trial. I didn't really follow the trials and didn't watch them on television. If I had been a judge and had an SS man in front of me, I would have had him hung straightaway. We were the ones who suffered, not them.

85. Have you forgiven your persecutors?
HORVATH: No. I would go out of my way to avoid them and spit at them for good measure. That would be revenge. They had better not cross my path.

86. What is your opinion of neo-Nazis?

HORVATH: I hope the Hitler era will never return. Neo-Nazis are too lazy to go to work. They ought to learn something! They ought to go to work, then they wouldn't need to make such a fuss. They're real Nazis, and they hate the gypsies too.

87. What do you do to explain to people what exactly happened in the Holocaust?

HORVATH: What is there to explain? They quite simply must never do that again! I was at a school for refugees in Vienna. I told them how old I was and all the things I went through. I also told them they should take it to heart and never call anyone at school a gypsy or foreigner. I said, "You must stick together!" My grandson Christoph did his *Zivildienst* [compulsory community service instead of military service] at the Mauthausen Memorial. He acted as a tour guide for visitors to the concentration camp and told them about its history. My son Renaldo is head of the Ketani Association that looks after Sinti and Roma.

88. From today's perspective, how can you explain that "normal people" were capable of such atrocities?

HORVATH: How can people do that? I don't know either. No one knows. And there are many people who don't believe what folk like us went through.

89. What exactly do you feel when you hear that there are still people who claim that the Holocaust never took place?

HORVATH: I think to myself that they're not normal, because they must have seen something on television. They must have seen how concentration camp prisoners were shot during the Hitler regime. To me, people like that aren't normal, because under normal circumstances, they should follow the example set by others and accept the truth. It can't be a lie if it's told by someone who experienced it firsthand.

90. What consequences did the proclamation of the "Nuremberg Laws" on September 15, 1935, have for you?

HORVATH: A gypsy wasn't allowed to associate with a German woman. It was another matter if they went out together in secret. My brothers mixed with German women instead of gypsy women, but they had to make sure they never got caught. They always went dancing in secret, or met somewhere, for example, secretly in an apartment. But much earlier, it was the custom among the Sinti that the men have no relations with German women. Nowadays no one cares about this custom anymore.

91. What are your personal memories of the "Night of Broken Glass" on November 9/10, 1938?

HORVATH: It happened where we lived in Pomerania too. They destroyed everything the Jews had, robbed them, and beat them. Then they were all taken away. We saw that because their shops were all around the neighborhood. I always went shopping at the Jews' shops. The shops were destroyed and everything in them was seized. They were wealthy Jews. At the time, we didn't think that it would happen to us as well. Maybe my father knew something, but we didn't.

92. What are your personal memories of the beginning of the war in 1939?

HORVATH: I didn't know anything about it. We had a little radio receiver, but our father was the only one who listened to it because we were in school, of course. No one said anything about it in school, either.

93. Did you hear that the National Socialists had decided to implement the "final solution to the Jewish question"—the systematic extermination of Jews in Europe—at the Wannsee Conference on January 20, 1942. If so, when and how?

HORVATH: No, we didn't hear anything about that. Maybe the grown-ups knew something, but they didn't tell us young ones things like that.

94. When you heard that World War II was over, what feelings did you have?

HORVATH: I thought, "Thank God it's over and we have our liberty." That was the only thing I wished for.

95. Do you think that humankind has learned something from the Holocaust?

HORVATH: I certainly hope they have learned a lesson from the war years and take it as an example. They must remember how they suffered in the past. But nowadays, when people have a few more possessions, they no longer think back to the bad times.

96. Should the atrocities be forgotten and no longer talked about, as some people wish?

HORVATH: Children in particular should be told about them. Children should learn about them so they don't turn into bandits. On the other hand, we shouldn't keep stirring up things we have long since forgotten. You can never completely forget anyway. Something always remains in your heart.

97. What plans do you still have for the future?

HORVATH: I would like to live a little longer because I still want to go dancing.

98. How would you like to be remembered?

HORVATH: As a good person, certainly not as a bad one, because I'm good to everyone. If a poor man comes to me, I'll give him something. I have suffered myself, and when I see that a person is hungry, I give him something to eat, whether he's a relative or a stranger.

99. What else would you like to say to us? Which question was not asked?

HORVATH: What else could I say? My grandchildren and my own children have all been brought up well and visit me every day. I'm very pleased with them.

100. After all you have been through, what advice can you give us young people?

HORVATH: When you leave school, you should do an apprenticeship, take the exams and do them well, and learn. Later, when you have finished your apprenticeship, you should look for work, be sensible, and obey your parents.

Josef Jakubowicz:
Back from the Dead

Josef Jakubowicz, born October 10, 1925
Grounds for persecution: Jew
Length of imprisonment: 5 years, 2 months
Country: Germany

26: Josef Jakubowicz, 1946   *27: Josef Jakubowicz, 2008*

Josef Jakubowicz was born on October 10, 1925, in Oświęcim [Auschwitz], Poland, to a Jewish family. As a fourteen-year-old, he had to work on construction of the *Stammlager* (base camp) Auschwitz I without knowing what this concentration camp was to be used for. So that he could do this work in place of his father, he had his birth certificate manipulated to say he was four years older.

Because of his Jewish parentage, he was interned in a total of eleven concentration, forced labor, and transit camps from 1940 until his liberation from Bergen-Belsen concentration camp on April 15, 1945. These were the forced labor or transit camps Sakrau, Annaberg, Rava-Ruska, Gross-Masselwitz, Breslau-Neukirch, and Markstädt, and the concentration camps Fünfteichen, Gross-Rosen, Flossenbürg, Mittelbau-Dora, and Bergen-Belsen. In 1944, he escaped to a farm near Prague during transportation. His escape attempt failed, and he was recaptured a day later. His parents and most of his family members were murdered during the Holocaust. Josef Jakubowicz survived and started a family. He rebuilt his life in Nuremberg, managing a jewelry store. Although he finds it very hard and it causes him great distress, he speaks about his experiences in schools and documented them in his autobiography *Auschwitz ist auch eine Stadt* (*Auschwitz Is Also a City*). Josef Jakubowicz lives in Germany.

The interviews took place on December 21, 2008; August 12, 2011; and October 4, 2011.

1. When were you born? What was your father like? What was your mother like?

JAKUBOWICZ: I was born on October 10, 1925, in Oświęcim in Poland, to a Jewish family. Oświęcim is in Upper Silesia and is called Auschwitz in German. Our house was about five hundred yards from the future *Stammlager* (base camp) Auschwitz I.

My father, Jehuda, was a very musical, jolly, and kind-hearted man. He was well-known in the town and was a member of various cultural institutions and synagogue associations.

My mother, Ernestine, was a very astute businesswoman and made sure her children received an education in religion, languages, and at commercial schools. She devoted a lot of time to looking after the children and also managed the family business with our father in Katowice. The shop sold animal intestines that were bought by butchers to make sausages. I had three sisters, Helene, Felizia, and Mathilde, and one brother whose name was Samuel.

2. What is your earliest childhood memory?

JAKUBOWICZ: At age four, I was taken to a Jewish primary school. I can still remember that day with absolute clarity. I remember the way there and that I was wearing a sailor suit and cap. In the school, I was received by "Klein-Rebbele," which means "little teacher." He really was very small, only about five feet. I can also remember another event when I was eight years old. A great celebration was held in our town. A prominent learned rabbi from Galicia was given a reception. It was Rabbi Shlomo Halberstam from Bobov. He was very well-known. Today he has followers living in London, Antwerp, and the United States. There are still a few thousand of them in New York. He arrived by train and was brought into the town in a white coach drawn by white horses. The people greeted him with Chinese lanterns and lined the road all the way from the railway station to the temple where he got out, a distance of one and a half miles. Christians were there too. His journey from the station to the town was accompanied by music and singing. The whole street was jammed with people. For me as a child, it was a hugely impressive spectacle. He held a talk that was broadcast everywhere. He quoted many passages from books, from the Talmud, and from scholars who studied religion. He also appealed to the people regarding social aspects, saying they should help the poor and so on. That is right and proper. It's a law, a very important law for Jews. It was a very colorful celebration, and it stayed in my memory for many, many years.

3.   What kind of childhood did you have?
JAKUBOWICZ: My childhood was full of fun. Carefree. I played with a lot of other children, played sports, and went swimming in the river. There was a fine river near us. I often met a lot of friends there and played with them. The Germans were not yet in power in Poland. The country was occupied in 1939. Up to 1939, the days were still full of fun for us children.

4.   How long did you go to school, and what schools did you attend?
JAKUBOWICZ: I started at the Jewish primary school when I was only four. I was a very industrious pupil and liked going to school. The first things we learned were morning prayer, evening prayer, and bedtime prayer. I learned Hebrew in school. When I was six, I moved to the Christian primary school, and in 1933, to the Jewish morning school. From 1935, I attended a Hebrew high school in Oświęcim. My parents wanted me to go to a Hebrew school. The teachers there were very good. I attended this school until the war broke out in 1939. The war and the abolition of all Jewish institutions by the National Socialists meant that was the last school I ever attended.

5.   What was your adolescence like? What trade did you learn, and what did you do for a living?
JAKUBOWICZ: All I did as an adolescent was go to school until I was thirteen. Then, in September 1939, the war broke out. The persecution of Jews and anti-Jewish decrees had already started. It was clear immediately after the German troops invaded which way the wind was blowing, that the predictions people had made were true. And we were worried. Mild panic broke out in the town. The German government installed a mayor in our town. That was unusual, since in other parts of Poland, military commands were set up. But the town of Oświęcim was annexed to the old Reich immediately after the German troops invaded, and they installed a mayor. He put up posters and issued a number of decrees ordering the Jews to bring their jewelry, gold, foreign currency, radios, and fur coats and hand them in. That's how it began after the German troops invaded.

Then they ordered our Jewish community to provide people between the ages of eighteen and forty-five who were fit for work. The SS came and took them to do forced labor in the barracks. The work was construction of Auschwitz [I] concentration camp: barbed wire fences, lookout towers, roads inside the camp, and barracks. That was outside the town, about a mile and a half from the town center. The workers had to line up at about six o'clock in the morning. They were then picked up, taken to work, and brought back to town again in the evening. They were tortured while they worked and beaten. Some were beaten to death. Sometimes they brought back a few dead bodies with them. The SS had just beaten them to death.

My father was chosen for this work a few times. My mother then said it would be better if I went instead of him. She was thinking ahead and suspected that I would be deported if I didn't work. But it wasn't possible because I was fourteen, and you had to be eighteen to be chosen.

My mother found out that the mayor was a certain Dr. Juliusz Grünweller and that he had his office in the castle. She went to see him. The mayor was from the same town as my mother, and they went to the same school. That was a coincidence. She recognized him and he recognized her. So he did her a favor and issued a birth certificate for me that said I was born in 1921 and not in 1925.

So from February 1940, I was able to join the workers and went to the barracks with the others, taking the place of my father. We did construction work there, but we didn't know what we were building. We only did jobs like road construction, building barracks, putting up barbed wire fences, and fixing electric wiring round the perimeter of the camp. We did various jobs, forced labor. The SS put us under constant pressure; they were real sadists. Any false move, any slip, and they beat the workers and bullied them. In the evening, we went home again. That lasted until around mid-1940. In mid-1940, they brought the first prisoners. When we got to work, we saw men running around in striped uniforms. We didn't know why, because we weren't allowed to have any contact with them. We were kept apart from them and only found out about it after a few days. We thought maybe they were from the sanatorium, the hospital, or the madhouse. They had on these peculiar striped uniforms. Then we realized that they were the first prisoners brought from the protectorate, from occupied Poland. Warsaw, Lodz, Tschenstochau (Częstochowa), Lublin, from all over the occupied territories. And these people were intellectuals, doctors, priests, rabbis, writers, journalists, and Polish nationalists. They [the Nazis] had lists [of these people] someplace, herded them all together and put them in the camp.

One evening, instead of being taken home, we were taken to the railway station. We were forced into cattle trucks and taken to Silesia to a small town called Annaberg [now Chałupki]. That was the first labor camp I was interned in. Straight from the building site in Auschwitz to Annaberg, by way of Sakrau collection camp. We never went home again and couldn't take anything with us.

6. What can you tell us about your family?
JAKUBOWICZ: After the war, I married Jente Schwarzberg in 1947. I have two children, a son and a daughter, Jehuda and Ernestine. My wife and her family were confined in Sosnowitz [now Sosnowiec] ghetto in 1940. She was separated from her family and had to work in a flax factory in Gräben forced labor camp. She became totally emaciated and was put in sickbay in Bergen-Belsen. That's where I met her, and she told me her parents had died too. After liberation, Jente and I moved from the English zone to the American one because we were told that Jews were treated better there. That's how I came to Bavaria, and here I stayed. I also married here. My wife died in 1991. I have three grandchildren and one great-grandchild. These days I live with my partner Rose Wanninger in Nuremberg.

7. Did you use the Nazi greeting "Heil Hitler!" and/or the Nazi salute?
JAKUBOWICZ: Whom should I have used it for? We had no contact with Germans, and they were the ones it was meant for. We were separated immediately after the invasion. We had to live in particular streets, and certain roads were closed to us. There was no one to greet.

8. Why were you persecuted by the National Socialists?
JAKUBOWICZ: Because I'm of Jewish descent; and after the race laws were passed, we knew what was planned for the Jews. Hitler, Goebbels, and Göring held speeches. Every speech indicated that the Jews in Europe were to be exterminated. It was already clear what was going to happen. But it happened systematically because first they gathered them all

together in one place, concentrated them to have them under control in ghettos in certain parts of the town, and from there, they were all deported to the camps. They needed people who could work. They sent us to labor camps, to forced labor camps. We worked on the Reichsautobahn, the Reich railroad, on building sites for Krupp Arms Works—anywhere they needed people. Those who were unfit for work were sent to the extermination camps.

Concentration camps included labor camps and extermination camps. The extermination camps were Majdanek, Treblinka, Belzec, Sobibor, and of course, Auschwitz, and Auschwitz-Birkenau. In these camps, women, children, and the elderly were immediately sent to the gas chambers. Those who were able to work were made to work for as long as they could. When they could no longer work, they were killed too. And the slogan they mounted on the gates, "Work liberates," was bogus.

9. When were you arrested?
JAKUBOWICZ: It wasn't an arrest in the true sense. I was sent to do forced labor in the barracks in Auschwitz, instead of my father. That was in February 1940. From the site of my forced labor in Auschwitz, I was taken to the forced labor camp in Annaberg by way of Sakrau. I was there from February 1941.

10. Why were you imprisoned?
JAKUBOWICZ: Because of my Jewish descent.

11. What exactly happened when you were arrested?
JAKUBOWICZ: I wasn't arrested. The reasons they gave us were like this: there's a war on, and we have to work in the arms industry because a lot of men have been drafted into the Wehrmacht. After a while, we'll be released again! That's how they explained it to us.

12. Did people know right from the start what was happening in the camps? Before you were taken away, did you know what would happen to you?
JAKUBOWICZ: Before they came to take us away, we knew absolutely nothing about the camp. We didn't find out that such a thing existed until they took us there. We didn't know before. They were only just starting to build them. But in the beginning, we had no idea. It wasn't until a year or

two later that we learned there were more camps and what was happening there. We discovered it from a number of different sources.

13. How many different camps were you in? How many years did you spend in each camp?

JAKUBOWICZ: After I had to work on the construction of Auschwitz [I] concentration camp from February 1940, I was in eleven different forced labor camps and concentration camps. The first one was the Upper Silesian forced labor camp Annaberg. Prior to that, I was briefly in Sakrau transit camp. Then I was sent to Rava-Ruska for forced labor in the eastern occupied territories. In 1941, the Reich railroad needed people when the war with Russia broke out. We had to lay the tracks. The site was a couple of miles beyond Lviv, where there was no camp anymore. We lived in open freight cars all winter long—with no heating, no sanitation, no proper food—and worked on the Reich railroad. Then we had to drop everything because a typhoid fever epidemic broke out. The guards were worried and took us back to Germany. I was sent first to Gross-Masselwitz [now Maślice Wielkie] and a few weeks later to Annaberg again. After that, I was taken to Breslau-Neukirch, where I worked on the railroad again.

Next, I worked on a large construction site. There were forty-five thousand people working there. That was in Markstädt [now Mieścisko] near Breslau [now Wrocław]. A Krupp factory for the manufacture of anti-aircraft guns was being built there. Some worked on construction, some, on production for Krupp.

From January through October 1944, I was interned in Fünfteichen concentration camp. I was there until the Russians drove the Germans back and advanced further and further into German territory. After that, they began evacuating the camps because most of the forced laborers in the concentration camps were in Lower Silesia. They didn't want them to fall into the hands of the Russians when the Russians invaded and so drove them further west on death marches.

So I was held in Gross-Rosen concentration camp for a few weeks. Then we had to march toward the Sudetenland. In the towns of Parschnitz [now Poříčí] and Tratenau [now Trutnov], civilians spat at us and yelled, "War criminals!" at us. We covered a lot of ground on foot; sometimes we were shut in railroad cars. At that time the trains could no longer run properly because the bridges had been blown up, or there were other obstacles. I came to Flossenbürg concentration camp in Bavaria on a couple of trains and on foot. I was there from December 1944 through February 1945.

The next camp I was in was Mittelbau-Dora. In Dora, we were taken to the quarry. That was a dangerous business. V2 and V1 rockets were made there too, though we didn't work on those. We worked in the tunnels. Explosives were laid in the mountain to make the tunnels wider. We had to carry all the rubble out. That was real heavy labor. Our rations diminished from day to day, and many prisoners died. We always had to carry the dead back into the camp. Then my friend Jasny Leizer and I said, "We have to do something. If we stay here working in the quarry every day, we won't survive for long." One evening, we came back into the camp from work and there was a line of prisoners waiting to march out. We quickly ran across the road to join this group. No one saw us, so we were able to march out with this group. At a small railway station, we were loaded onto freight cars. We didn't know where they were going, we were just glad to be out of Dora.

We were taken to Bergen-Belsen concentration camp. That was mid-February 1945. I was liberated from Bergen-Belsen on April 15, 1945.

14. Were you the only member of your family in the concentration camp, or were family members or friends there as well? If so, did you have any contact with them?
JAKUBOWICZ: I only had a few friends, but I wasn't in the concentration camp with my family. I had no contact with my family.

15. What were the first things that happened immediately following your arrival at the concentration camp?
JAKUBOWICZ: When I arrived at the first concentration camp, Fünfteichen, we were given a number. We weren't tattooed. I was given the number 24327. We had to sew it on our chest and trousers, and our names were gone. Prior to that, in the forced labor camps, we had still been called by our names, but in the concentration camp, we were given a number. We were no more than a number. You didn't know your fellow prisoners' names, only the numbers (*his eyes fill with tears*). You wore your number right to the end.

We didn't have a triangle. The Jews all had a yellow minus sign in front of the number. The political prisoners, Jehovah's Witnesses, saboteurs, and homosexuals, on the other hand, had a triangle. Prisoners interned for serious crimes had a green triangle pointing down; "normal" criminals had one pointing up. Political prisoners had a red triangle. I think Jehovah's Witnesses had a purple one.

Before that, we had worn the Star of David. Afterward they gave us a number. I wasn't tattooed. I wasn't the only one who wasn't. They didn't tattoo prisoners in every camp.

16. Why did they shave the heads of the prisoners?
JAKUBOWICZ: Either because of the risk of escape or because of lice. They were afraid that the lice carried various germs, and they live in hair. Our heads were shaved, with a strip the width of two fingers left down the middle to reduce the risk of escape. It enabled people [outside] to see that we were concentration camp internees who had broken out.

17. What prisoner category were you put in?
JAKUBOWICZ: Jews.

18. Can you describe the daily routine in the concentration camp?
JAKUBOWICZ: We were woken early, at half past three, and catapulted out of the barrack onto the street where we had to stand and wait. We were given a bowl of hot water, which sometimes had coffee grounds or the dregs of tea in it, and triangular slices of bread, weighing eight to ten ounces, and a little bit of margarine or imitation honey. Then we had to report for roll call, and that took a long time because sometimes someone was missing. Maybe a prisoner collapsed somewhere en route, or something didn't add up. Sometimes a prisoner would fall into the latrine. They were so weak that they fell asleep there. The prisoner then had to be looked for, and the count went on until he was found. As long as the numbers weren't right, even if only one person was missing, we had to stay standing on the roll-call square. At half past six, we were marched out toward the building site to start work. We were on the building site all day. There was a break at midday, but no food, only your bread from the morning. You either ate it at once or saved it for later.

At the building site, we were all counted again. Every prisoner was assigned to a construction unit working for the various companies that were building the Reichsautobahn, railroad tracks, canals, and other structures for the Germans. There was one man in charge of each unit, and each unit worked for one company. There were a lot of firms, mostly construction companies that were working there in Markstädt and Fünfteichen. They included Wayss & Freytag, Beton—und Monierbau, Grün & Bilfinger, Kreutz & Lesch, and whatever they were all called. I worked for the Austrian roofing firm of Hell & Köhler from Mödling. There were some very good people there. In fact, they saved me. The site manager's name was Hautmann.

We worked from seven o'clock in the morning until seven in the evening. Then we were taken back to the roll-call square, and if we were lucky, we were able to go into the barracks before roll call. If anything was amiss, we had to do exercises on the roll-call square as punishment—knee bends and forward rolls and various other punishments. It lasted one hour, two hours. Then we were dismissed and given a dish of "vegetable soup." That was dried vegetables boiled in water. It wasn't food. That's what we prisoners ate, and then we were herded back into the barracks. That was at around eight or nine o'clock in the evening.

In general, Sundays were free, but a lot of prisoners had to go out. If trucks arrived to be unloaded, we had to work Sundays too.

19. What was the worst thing about the daily routine?
JAKUBOWICZ: Roll call was terrible. We had to stand for hours in tattered clothes and ill-fitting shoes. In winter, in the rain, we had to stand until the roll call was complete. That was the worst thing.

As regards to the work, I was lucky to get into a company like the one from Mödling.

20. Did everyday life lead more to solidarity, or did the prisoners try to cope on their own?
JAKUBOWICZ: Sure, you always stuck together, but what could you do for others? Everyone was in great distress. Everyone had the same problems. The biggest problem was the hunger, and in winter, the cold.

21. Was there anything that helped you take your mind off the horror of daily life for a while (such as music)? What gave you strength?

JAKUBOWICZ: Yes, there was. What gave me strength was that I spent the whole time "organizing." "Organizing" meant trying to get some food or anything else you could swap. That motivated me enormously. I spent a lot of time concentrating on that. I was in such a frenzy of trading, of swapping, that I forgot I was in the camp. I "organized" all kinds of things. In the construction company Hell & Köhler, I also worked with Czechs. The Czechs were forced laborers, but they weren't interned in the concentration camp. Every two to three weeks, they were allowed to go home, and when they came back, they brought schnapps with them. They made plum schnapps, called slivovitz. They supplied me with it, and I smuggled it into the camp to barter with it. Whenever we went back to the camp after work, I hid two bottles round my midriff. But I also had a couple of people who carried the bottles for me. They walked in the same row as me. The camp senior knew this, and because he was the one to whom I supplied most of the schnapps, our line wasn't searched.

I provided the prominent prisoners in the camp, the heavies, the *kapos*, with schnapps, and in return, they left me alone.

22. What were living conditions like in the barracks (prisoner allocation, food supplies, hygiene, clothing, etc.)?

JAKUBOWICZ: We were never in the barracks during the day. We left them at half past three after we were woken up and came back at night after roll call. We only slept there. There were plank beds, one above the other, with a blanket and a pallet. That was all. We went in there to sleep, and in the morning, we were woken up. The toilets were in another building, but we weren't allowed to leave the barrack at night. They put two large buckets in the room so the prisoners could answer the call of nature. There were always two men on night duty. When a bucket was full, they emptied it and put it back. Everyone in the barrack had to do night duty at least once. They always sat by the bucket and made sure it was absolutely full before it was emptied.

In the evening, we were given nothing but a bowl of soup to eat, and in the morning, a piece of bread and a watery brew, a kind of tea or *ersatz* coffee. That was our food. It was nothing whatever.

Each barrack took turns using the shower, each day a different barrack. It wasn't called "showering," it was called "delousing." We had to undress outside the barrack, lay our things on the ground, and go to the road from where we were herded into the barrack. Then they turned on the water, and as we came out, they checked us for lice. They had special people for that. They looked under your armpits, at the genital area, at your head, and so on, to see if you had lice.

23. What jobs did you have to do? How many hours a day did you have to work?

JAKUBOWICZ: I did various jobs. For a time I worked on the Reichsautobahn, the Reich railroad, and then for the Austrian firm of Hell & Köhler. In Fünfteichen, sheds were being built, and the company of Hell & Köhler made the roof. We lined the roof with asbestos tiles. There was no work in Bergen-Belsen. All we did there was haul the dead bodies to be burned.

Normally, the working hours were from seven o'clock in the morning till six in the evening: ten or eleven hours.

24. What effect did the slogan "Work liberates" have on you?

JAKUBOWICZ: I didn't take it very seriously. As far as we were concerned, they had just written it there. What it should have said was, "Work kills!" They simply made the people work and kept them alive for as long as they were able to work. Those who were unfit for work, they killed.

25. What were the guards like in the camp?

JAKUBOWICZ: Most of the guards were sadists. The majority was recruited from penitentiaries. They took the serious offenders and murderers out of the penitentiaries and sent them to Auschwitz to be trained. They were block seniors, in charge of the blocks, and camp *kapos*. Most of them were thugs and many were Germans. They were let out of the penitentiaries into the concentration camps, and they carried out the torture ordered by the SS. The SS were on guard duty in the camp and on the building site outside the camp. I never suffered any harm at the hands of the sentries.

In the camp itself, it was mainly the prisoners themselves who were responsible for supervising the other internees. There was also a camp senior. In Fünfteichen, he was a criminal from Berlin. I knew him very well personally because I traded with him. These people all had enough to eat. In fact they had a lot because they stole everything that the prisoners should have gotten. But they needed alcohol too. And I smuggled alcohol into the camp for them from the building site. As a result, I was highly favored by the camp senior, and he let me off various punishment drills.

One SS man was well-disposed toward me too. He was from Silesia, like me, and had been badly wounded somewhere in the east near Stalingrad. He wasn't sent back to the front, but came to Fünfteichen concentration camp as a guard. He knew about my dealings, shielded me, and even joined in because he himself needed stuff—cigarettes, for instance.

26. Was there any contact between the prisoners and the local population?

JAKUBOWICZ: Only with people who worked on the building site. There was no contact with people who lived in the villages.

The prisoners were assigned to German firms for the work, and I was lucky to be assigned to the company of Hell & Köhler. The firm's site manager was called Hautmann. A certain Josef Weiss and Franz Binder were there too. They were the company's master craftsmen. All three were from Mödling. They were very nice people and treated me well. Compared to other companies, their treatment of the prisoners working for them was exemplary. In the other companies, people were beaten, tortured, and very badly abused. But Herr Hautmann even told me what was in the news and encouraged me to stay strong, saying, "It won't be like this forever." He kept us fully informed and helped us a lot.

27. Were you aware of how the war was proceeding in the outside world?

JAKUBOWICZ: Yes, I had some very good sources. The site manager Hautmann from the firm of Hell & Köhler always kept me informed. He told me he listened to the BBC. Listening to the BBC was punishable by death or internment in a concentration camp.

Hautmann said, "I listen to the BBC every night. The Russians are advancing and are already about seventy-five miles from Fünfteichen camp." That's why we were taken away. I always passed on this information to the other internees to give them the hope that it wouldn't stay like this forever and to encourage them to survive. That was a great help. Courage and hope: without those, survival was impossible.

28. In the concentration camp, were you allowed to receive letters, food parcels, etc.?
JAKUBOWICZ: No, in the concentration, we were not allowed to receive any food or letters. Only in the first year, when I was in Annaberg forced labor camp, was I allowed to receive postcards, and they were censored.

29. What forms of torture did you suffer?
JAKUBOWICZ: I was given a beating once. I don't know how many blows I received, but I was beaten on the backside. They shoved me into a kind of bench and wanted to blackmail me. They wanted me to say where I had gotten some bread I had that wasn't camp bread. Someone had reported me, and on my way home to Markstädt camp after work, I was interrogated about where I got it. I didn't want to tell them who gave it to me. Then they started beating me. Two men, one standing on the right and one on the left, gave me a thrashing. They were camp *kapos*. They whipped me so badly that I couldn't even walk afterward. Every day in the morning, the other internees and my colleagues took me under the arms and hauled me the mile and a half to work. When I arrived at Hell & Köhler to report for work, Hautmann allowed me to stay in the hut, and I wasn't assigned to any tasks, because I couldn't work. Hautmann helped me a lot.

30. What was the most frightening moment for you?
JAKUBOWICZ: The worst moment in a camp was in Bergen-Belsen, before we were liberated. The arrival there was the worst. Before Bergen-Belsen, I had been able to bear it more or less and had been able to save myself in every situation. But conditions in Bergen-Belsen were just indescribable. No water. In the washrooms, there was no water for washing and none for drinking. We broke off icicles from the roof. There were roll calls all day long, and it was dangerous on account of typhoid fever.

People collapsed and died while walking, sitting, and standing. There is nothing more dangerous than that. Thousands of dead bodies in piles they could no longer burn. And we, the prisoners, pushed an empty truck trailer, loaded the bodies on it, and took them to be cremated. But the crematoria could no longer cope, so they dug a big ditch and threw the bodies into it. Then they threw old wood crossties from the railroad in and poured crude oil and gasoline over everything. The fire burned day and night. The whole camp was blackened. A prisoner couldn't recognize another one from a yard away, because the smoke was so thick. It stank to high heaven too.

We loaded these prisoners all day long, from morning to evening, from the women's camp too—dead women, dead men, children who had been born in other camps. It was a motley collection of prisoners from various camps who arrived at the end of the war on death marches and had all died, been killed, or starved to death. They had all died and now lay in front of the barracks, piled up to the third story—heaps of dead people, all skeletons. We had to load them onto the trucks, and fifty or sixty men pushed them. With the last of our strength, we pushed the trailer across the road to the crematorium and unloaded it again.

There's one episode I must tell you about: when we arrived in Flossenbürg, we had to go into the barracks to wash and be deloused. That's what they said. We all had to undress beforehand, outside on the road. We left our clothes lying there. Everyone laid his clothes on a particular spot, and we went in. Then people got scared because they thought it was a gas chamber. They had heard something or other about gas chambers with showers, so they fought against going in. But then the *kapos* arrived and beat them in with sticks and batons. When we were inside, they first turned on ice-cold water, then boiling hot water. When I came out again, my jacket with the number on it was gone. Someone had taken my jacket by mistake. I had to take another jacket, which had a different number on it. So now I had two numbers, the right one and one from a jacket that wasn't mine. Later, when I arrived in Bergen-Belsen, we were unloading the bodies and I found a dead man wearing my jacket. I took the jacket off him and put it on again. I had found my number again while throwing in the corpses. The dead man with my number. What do you say to that?

31. Were there any entertaining or lighthearted incidents that enabled you to forget all the suffering for a moment? Can you describe them?

JAKUBOWICZ: No. People were always under tremendous strain out of fear. All was fear. The fear was so great. The most dangerous thing was the beatings. You didn't survive those. I was lucky that when I was beaten, Hautmann and Weiss and Binder were there. They (*his eyes fill with tears*)—it was terrible, terrible—they saved me.

32. What were your day-to-day thoughts while you were in the concentration camp?

JAKUBOWICZ: For me it wasn't so bad, but the others spent all day wondering where they could find a potato or a potato skin or a morsel of bread. That was it. People didn't wish for more than that. They couldn't wish for any more than that, because their hunger was so great.

I was concerned solely with surviving. I had such a strong character and will to live that I fought hard. I said to myself, I must survive. Since I always heard news from the outside and knew how things stood, I hoped and prayed that we would be liberated as soon as possible because it had become unbearable in Bergen-Belsen.

33. Was it possible for children to be born in a concentration camp? If so, what happened to these babies?

JAKUBOWICZ: Well, there were no women in the camps I was in. I don't know whether they could have babies [in other camps]. There were women in one of the camps, in Markstädt, but they were kept separate and there weren't many, maybe twenty or twenty-five. They were kept completely separate, and they did sewing or worked in the kitchen. But there were no women in the other camps.

34. Was it possible to make friends with prisoners?

JAKUBOWICZ: Yes, the prisoners always formed groups in which they made friends. But what kind of friendship was it? One friend couldn't help the other.

35. Who was your best friend during this dreadful time, and how did he or she help you?

JAKUBOWICZ: That was a certain Leizer Jasny. He died in Bergen-Belsen a few days before liberation.

36. What did you do to relieve the suffering of other inmates?
JAKUBOWICZ: I organized and distributed food. This was possible on the building site, especially with Hautmann. He allowed me to do several things that were prohibited. Every day around noon, I took leftovers to the prisoners and distributed them.

37. Were there particular hierarchies among the inmates?
JAKUBOWICZ: There were in the camp, yes. The prominent prisoners led a different life from us. They were privileged and had access to everything. They didn't have as many difficulties with food as we did. When they were ill, they also received help, but the normal prisoners didn't. They were the camp elite and consisted of the camp *kapos*, block seniors, block leaders, and camp senior 1 and camp senior 2. But they were mostly German-speaking prisoners.

38. Were there any differences in the way the various groups of prisoners (religious, political groups) were treated?
JAKUBOWICZ: No, no differences, only the prominent prisoners. Those were the heavies, *kapos* and block seniors. They were treated better. After all, they treated each other better; no one tortured *them*.

39. What diseases and illnesses were prevalent in the concentration camp?
JAKUBOWICZ: In the concentration camp, there was mostly dysentery. The prisoners had severe colds, work injuries, and so on. We didn't know anything about any other diseases, because we didn't have any contact with the sick people. There was a sickbay from which the people were sent to the gas chambers after three days. If a prisoner was sick, he was taken to the sickbay. He was unfit for work. And if he spent more than three days in sickbay, then the black bus, as it was called, came and took him away; and he was killed. They didn't have eight ounces of bread to waste on people who couldn't work.

40. Did you receive a physical injury?
JAKUBOWICZ: Yes, the beating from the *kapos* meant I couldn't work for a few months. They had battered everything, my whole back, everything was injured. I developed boils where they had beaten me. Hautmann arranged for me to have a plaster jacket for a few months.

Afterward, a Czech cut through it with a saw. I wouldn't have survived if I had had to work, but Hautmann saved me by letting me stay in the hut.

41. How much did you weigh when you were in the concentration camp?

JAKUBOWICZ: I don't know how much it was in the concentration camp, but after my time in Bergen-Belsen, I weighed ninety pounds. There's written proof of that because the English weighed me for the Red Cross certificate—ninety pounds.

42. What did death mean to you?

JAKUBOWICZ: I had gotten so used to seeing dead bodies because I had to deal with them every day. Everywhere, on the way to somewhere, on a march, people collapsed and couldn't walk anymore. They were shot in the neck and then thrown in the ditch. Bodies became quite normal. We dragged them along like a bundle of wood. At first it was dreadful, but later we got so used to it that a dead man was nothing at all—absolutely nothing. It didn't bother us in the slightest.

43. What was the closest you came to death?

JAKUBOWICZ: At the end, when I hid among the dead bodies because I didn't want to go to roll call anymore. I didn't want to go out anymore. In Bergen-Belsen, they rounded up everyone who could still stand and walk and wanted to take them somewhere. And I didn't want to go with them. So I lay down among the dead. I was not only close to them. I came back from the dead.

But I was also close to death when I escaped. If the *Hauptwachtmeister* (sergeant major) had said, "You escaped," he could have shot me. Either he believed me, or he allowed me to live. Normally when a prisoner escaped to a farmhouse, he was asked, "Where have you come from?" or, "How did you get here?" and then he was shot. I was close to death then too.

44. Did you ever build a kind of "wall" to shield yourself from the terrible things that were being done so that the death of a fellow prisoner no longer affected you?

JAKUBOWICZ: That's exactly how it was. At every moment, you had dead bodies around you. All day long—always. On the march, on the death march, and later, at the end, no distinction was made between the living and the dead anymore.

45. What happened to the dead bodies in the concentration camp?

JAKUBOWICZ: They were cremated or thrown into mass graves. That was all.

46. Was there ever a possibility for you to be released from the concentration camp?

JAKUBOWICZ: No, not to be released, no.

47. Were there any escape attempts or opportunities to escape? Did you try to escape?

JAKUBOWICZ: Not many tried, but some did. Very few succeeded. Most were caught, as I was when I tried to escape in the winter of 1944–45. We were on the way from Gross-Rosen to Flossenbürg, partly on foot, partly in cattle cars. The trains could no longer run properly because the bridges had been blown up, or there were other obstacles. The people in the trucks were dying like flies. We had to sit squeezed together on the floor and take off our shoes. There was nothing to eat, no toilets, and the people just wet themselves. The stink was appalling. When the trains stopped, they opened the doors of the cars every day and handed out the dead.

A friend and I talked things over and said to each other that we wouldn't come out of that alive. But we wanted to survive. I had a spoon with me, which had a handle fashioned like a saw. A Czech had made it for me. I sawed two slats out of the car. When the train stopped, I squeezed out of the car and stood on the buffer. That was about three miles from Prague. Now I waited, and when the train started to move, I jumped from the car into the snow. It was the dead of night. It was winter, and I was wandering about in the woods with no shoes. Then I saw a light and made my way to a farmhouse. That was how I came to be among the Czechs.

They looked at me aghast. I was wearing a prisoner's uniform, had no shoes, and my head was shaved with a stripe down the middle. They took me in and gave me something to eat and drink. They asked me where I had come from and I told them. But they began to be frightened, and next morning at ten o'clock, a motorcycle of the German *Feldpolizei* (Secret

Field Police) drove up, and I was taken away. The farmer's family had likely informed on me or reported me out of fear. I was taken to the command post in a village. I can't remember the name. It was in a little house with a courtyard.

I only know that the man who lived next door to this command post was a baker. I was sent into the courtyard to chop wood, and on the other side of the fence was a bakery, which put out some bread especially so that I could take some.

When I was presented to the police officer on duty, he questioned me and asked how I came to be in the farmhouse. I said I had been unloaded from the train onto the siding along with the dead bodies. The train then moved off, leaving me behind. I didn't know where to go. I don't know whether he believed me, but he was very well-disposed toward me. Judging from his dialect, he was from Silesia too. He asked me what town I was from and so on. Then he said a transport would be leaving here tomorrow—a death march with prisoners. He would escort me there and I would have to go on with the transport. That's how I arrived in Flossenbürg.

48. Were there any inmates in the concentration camp who dared to stage a revolt against the camp authorities?
JAKUBOWICZ: I wasn't aware of anything of that nature.

49. Did you think you would ever make it out alive?
JAKUBOWICZ: I hoped very much that I would.

50. Were there any times when you gave up all hope? If so, why?
JAKUBOWICZ: No, there weren't. I always had hope.

51. Did anyone commit suicide?
JAKUBOWICZ: Yes, many people did it on the building site or ran into the electric fence.

52. During the Holocaust, did you ever consider committing suicide out of sheer despair?
JAKUBOWICZ: No, never. I never considered it. That never occurred to me.

53. What thoughts, ideas, hopes, wishes, or religious convictions did you cling to?

JAKUBOWICZ: In the beginning, my faith was still strong, and I often prayed. After I learned that my parents (*his eyes fill with tears*) . . . had been sent to Auschwitz, I lost faith. I could no longer believe. That was in August 1943. I received a message from a member of the Hitler Youth, as it happens, whom I knew well from the building site. He went to my hometown. I sent him to find out what was happening. He came back and said that the inhabitants, including my parents, had been resettled and that the house was empty.

My father, mother, sister, and her four children were killed. They were taken from Auschwitz to other towns, to Sosnowitz and Bendsburg [now Będzin]. The Nazis always took people from small towns to large ones and put them in ghettos. I was already in the camp. But on the building site, I had close contact with a member of the Hitler Youth who hadn't been drafted, because he was born with one foot shorter than the other. He couldn't walk properly and worked with the surveyors. His name was Hans Feil. He was maybe seventeen years old when I asked him to find out about my parents. He said, "I'll have to ask my mother." Next day he came and said his mother had said he should do it. Why? Because his grandfather was a Social Democrat and the Nazis had interned him in Sachsenhausen in 1937.

54. Did you lose your faith in God while you were in the camp?

JAKUBOWICZ: Yes, I did, when I learned that my parents had been taken away. But after the war, I regained my faith.

55. What role did your religion play in how you felt about what was going on? Why?

JAKUBOWICZ: I constantly asked how God could allow such a thing. But no one could tell me. I asked other people in the camp, including scholars and rabbis. They couldn't give me an answer. I don't know.

56. Did you pray during your internment?

JAKUBOWICZ: Yes, during the first years until 1943—until my parents were killed, until they were taken to Auschwitz.

57. Did you ever consider changing your religion (or ideology)? Why?
JAKUBOWICZ: No.

58. What was the date of your liberation from the camp?
JAKUBOWICZ: April 15, 1945, from Bergen-Belsen concentration camp.

59. How were you liberated from the camp, or how did you manage to get out of it?
JAKUBOWICZ: Only a few days earlier, the English had dropped flyers from airplanes. We were told no one was allowed to pick them up, but we did it anyway. The flyers were in several languages and said we [the prisoners] should hold on because we would be freed in the coming hours. Then, in the afternoon, the sentries on the lookout towers, the SS, were suddenly gone. In their place were prisoners wearing white caps. They were German internees from the camp. They [the SS] came down from the towers and the order was given, "Fall in!" All those who could still walk lined up. I said, "I won't go! I've had enough! Transports and marches and death marches. I won't go!"

After I realized what was happening, that it was only a matter of hours, I lay facedown on the main road from the camp, next to a pile of dead bodies. I lay there—it was in the evening, around four, maybe half past four—till the next day. The next day, between three and half past four in the afternoon, the English marched in. They marched in all of a sudden, and I could see, but not identify, the armored cars and the insignia. I couldn't tell whether they were Germans or not. So I was afraid and stayed lying where I was. I only saw them [without recognizing them]. Then, all of a sudden, I saw soldiers running around wearing a different uniform. They had cots, and they were running around with them looking for people who were still alive. They ran past me and I moved. They got a shock because I was in a pile of bodies. They took hold of me straightaway, took everything off me, all my clothes, and threw me naked on the cot. They took me to a vehicle, an ambulance, and drove me away. After a couple of miles, we stopped someplace. There was a field hospital, and they quickly took a blood sample and weighed me.

That's how I got that certificate from the International Red Cross in Bad Arolsen.

60. How were you treated by the people who liberated you?
JAKUBOWICZ: Well, very well. They tried their best and did everything they could.

61. What was the first thing you did after you were liberated?
JAKUBOWICZ: I tried to find out whether any of my relatives or acquaintances were still alive. I tried to get in touch with them and traveled far and wide in search of them.

62. Did you have any problems when you returned home? How did people in your home environment react to you?
JAKUBOWICZ: I couldn't go back, because I was in the English and American zone, and the Poles were in Auschwitz. I had no wish to return to that city. I never wanted to see it again. I didn't want to go back to Auschwitz.

63. Were you able to rejoin your family?
JAKUBOWICZ: No, I have no family. I was left alone. The only one who managed to escape from the Nazis was my brother Samuel. He fled to the Soviet Union on the day the Germans invaded Poland. I don't know what became of him. After the war, I couldn't get in touch with him anymore.

64. Did you have any acquaintances, friends, or relatives in the camps? Did they survive their internment?
JAKUBOWICZ: Yes, some survived. Several relatives, cousins, survived.

65. What happened to your possessions?
JAKUBOWICZ: I myself didn't have any, because I was still too young.

66. To what extent have you received compensation for your internment?
JAKUBOWICZ: As compensation for my internment, I received 150 German marks a month. That's all.

Now I receive a pension for injuries suffered as a result of my persecution, and for which medical examinations have provided confirmation.

67. How did you set about rebuilding your life?
JAKUBOWICZ: Since I didn't finish my school education or learn a trade because of my persecution, I tried going into business and was successful. I earned my livelihood from that. I had a jewelry store.

68. How long did it take you to return to a "normal" life after the Holocaust?

JAKUBOWICZ: I still haven't managed it. It's not possible. You just can't take anymore. The psychological damage is so great that it cannot be healed.

69. What was your life like after the war?

JAKUBOWICZ: How can I describe it to you? It was not pleasant. I was left without any family or friends. I was cut off from everything. I was alone like a solitary tree in the woods. But I had to go on with my life. I got married and have two children. They're certified dental surgeons, my daughter and my son. Thankfully they're doing well and are in good relationships. That kept me alive a little, the fact that I have two children whom I raised with my wife.

During their internment or shortly afterward, many people contracted typhoid fever. I caught it about two weeks after liberation. I was out in the street and I fainted. I was taken to the hospital, and because I wasn't German, I had a so-called DP card, which the English had given me. Do you know what "DP" means? "Displaced person."

28: Josef Jakubowicz and Jente Schwarzberg, his future wife, 1946

They found this card in my pocket and took me to the English who had a department for "DPs." So I was stationed there.

That was in Celle near Bergen-Belsen in the English zone. Hanover, Bergen-Belsen, and Hamburg were the English zone. Everyone said that Holocaust survivors got better treatment in the American zone. And it was true that the Americans treated us better than the English did.

That's why I went to Bamberg and Fürth, and ultimately to Nuremberg. I lived in Fürth to begin with, and in the fall of 1945, I collapsed in the street. Some patrol or other took me to the hospital where they found I had active tuberculosis. They put me in quarantine because it was infectious then sent me to the clinic for pulmonary diseases in Georgensgmünd, where I stayed for about three years.

70. What is your life like today? Do you still often think back to those days?

JAKUBOWICZ: Well, I don't think about them, but the nights are very difficult. Sometimes I have nightmares or dreams about being persecuted and about various events I experienced. They come back to me. It's very difficult. They're wounds that can't be healed.

What do I do today? I'm a dialysis patient. I have to go for dialysis three times a week. I have diseased kidneys, they don't work anymore. That's all I do. My health is very poor. That's down to old age and the persecution I suffered.

71. What physical and mental scars do you carry from that time?

JAKUBOWICZ: The camp has left very deep psychological scars. Physical ones too. I have chronic bronchitis.

72. Did you have any moral support to help your emotional and social recovery?

JAKUBOWICZ: Not much, not much. I don't know whom I was supposed to get it from. Moral support? From a moral standpoint, no one can imagine it. And emotional support? I didn't expect any. After the war, when I was in the hospital with lung disease, I once received psychological treatment. But the whole thing was pointless.

73. Has your view of the world changed since that time?

JAKUBOWICZ: I don't have a different view of the world, no. But there's one thing I do have: no time for current political events. Our present time isn't so wonderful either. When we hear what goes on in the world, it's not so great.

74. Can you think of anything positive that you have gained from your experiences?

JAKUBOWICZ: I have life experience, and one can draw positive conclusions from such experience.

75. Have you ever been back to visit the concentration camp you were held in, and if so, what were your feelings?

JAKUBOWICZ: I visited several: Auschwitz, Flossenbürg, and Annaberg. I haven't visited the others. I was in Bergen-Belsen a couple of times. My feelings were not especially pleasant. My knees were shaking when I went in.

76. Are you still in touch with your fellow internees from the concentration camps?

JAKUBOWICZ: Not anymore, because not many are still alive.

77. What did you tell your family about your internment in the concentration camp? How did your relatives react to what you told them?

JAKUBOWICZ: I didn't tell my relatives anything, because I no longer had any. Later, I didn't want to burden my children with it. One day, when my daughter came home from kindergarten, she asked, "Why does everyone have a grandma except me?" What could I say? My children grew up without uncles, aunts, and grandparents. My children knew that I had been persecuted, that I was in a concentration camp, and that my family had died. But I didn't have the strength to tell them all the details.

78. Do you find it difficult to talk about those days?

JAKUBOWICZ: Yes, very. There are some things I can talk about, but others I'm too sensitive about. I find it very hard to talk about my family. It costs me a lot of effort to talk about all that happened in the past and about surviving. It's very, very, very difficult.

79. Which moment from those days has remained most firmly etched in your memory?

JAKUBOWICZ: What I remember most vividly is when I was in Annaberg, and they brought in all the western Jews. They were Jews from Belgium, Holland, France. They unloaded them at the railroad station. The women stayed in the cars with the children, and the men were brought to us in Annaberg. Annaberg became a transit camp for western Jews. They were registered and then sent to various other camps. Those who had come straight from home had an awful lot of stuff with them: gold, diamonds, all kinds of things. I was a child of fifteen, and it surprised me to see how much people carted around with them. The *Lagerführer* (camp leader) and the SS-*Obersturmbannführer* (lieutenant colonel) told them to throw everything into three drums on the roll-call square: foreign currency in this one, passports in that one, other things in here. The people were afraid to approach the drums, so they threw their things on the ground in front of them and buried them with their feet. They were afraid that the people standing by the drums would see what they had. That made a strong impression on me as an adolescent. It proved very useful to me because I used it to save my life.

Later, after they had all gone, I dug up what they had buried. I managed to get a lot of it out, and with it, I was often able to save myself, by obtaining stuff, for example. I was also able to buy a certain amount of freedom from *Lagerführer* Lehmann. Lehmann was favorably disposed toward me and a compassionate person.

When I learned that my family had been moved into the ghettos in Sosnowitz and Bendsburg in 1941, Lehmann even issued me a three-day permit and gave me money for the train fare. I paid a brief visit to my parents and sisters, and we were overjoyed to see each other again. That was the last time I saw them.

Lehmann also profited from me. I still had various items for another two years and smuggled them into other camps as well. Of course they carried out searches, and you had to be really smart not to get caught, but I managed it. I carried it around my midriff and tied up my trouser legs at the ankle [so it wouldn't fall out]. On arrival in a camp, I worked on the building site as site first-aid attendant. I made the bandages whenever anyone got injured. Later, I filled the bag with gold and other items and took it with me. I smuggled odds and ends from one camp to the next because I bribed the people who searched us. You see? I bribed those people, who were prisoners too. I called it "organizing."

80. Did you ever see or meet Hitler?
JAKUBOWICZ: No.

81. What was your opinion of Hitler in those days, and what is your opinion of him now?
JAKUBOWICZ: I think the same today as I did then: that he was a schizophrenic criminal.

82. Hypothetically, if Adolf Hitler were still alive and you could have five minutes alone with him, what would you say or do?

JAKUBOWICZ: Kill him, I would kill him straightaway with the last of my strength.

83. After the war, did you ever meet any of the people who had tormented you?

JAKUBOWICZ: No, no one.

84. What do you think of the punishments the Nazis received after the war, in the Nuremberg trials, for example?

JAKUBOWICZ: A few times, I myself went to the trials in Nuremberg since I was living there. The death sentences were just. I'm not happy about the acquittals and long prison sentences, because they were the same murderers as the others.

85. Have you forgiven your persecutors?

JAKUBOWICZ: There can be no forgiveness for something like that.

86. What is your opinion of neo-Nazis?

JAKUBOWICZ: My opinion? My opinion is this: they come from families that committed heinous crimes against humanity, and it's been passed on to them. What they now think and do is not normal. In my opinion, they are seriously sick people. They need to be cured.

87. What do you do to explain to people what exactly happened in the Holocaust?

JAKUBOWICZ: For several years, I visited schools with the aim of making sure they aren't infected by these agitators, by this brown plague, because they also try to win over young people. In two years, I visited eighty schools.

88. From today's perspective, how can you explain that "normal people" were capable of such atrocities?

JAKUBOWICZ: I genuinely can't. I cannot imagine that people with a normal intellect would do such things. Only mentally sick people or animals are capable of that; it's not something a normal person would do.

89. What exactly do you feel when you hear that there are still people who claim that the Holocaust never took place?

JAKUBOWICZ: Either they don't want to know it, or they refuse to see it. There's a reason for it. These people are from the type of family or group that participated in all the atrocities.

90. What consequences did the proclamation of the "Nuremberg Laws" on September 15, 1935, have for you?

JAKUBOWICZ: I wasn't on German territory. We had heard about the Nuremberg Laws of 1935 from what the older people said. Even as a child, you were aware of them and knew what the National Socialists were planning: the extermination of the Jews. On German territory, they had to wear the Star of David. But where we were, it didn't all start until 1939, after the German troops had invaded. Then it was immediately stipulated that Jews had to wear a white armband with a blue Star of David. Then they introduced the yellow Star of David. Everything was done in succession. That was the order for a few months, and then we were told, "Do not wear the armbands, wear only the Star of David instead!" We wore that until we were taken over by the SS. Then we were given the striped uniforms and a prisoner's number.

91. What are your personal memories of the "Night of Broken Glass" on November 9/10, 1938?

JAKUBOWICZ: That was only in Germany. There was no Night of Broken Glass where we were; we were not yet occupied by the Germans. But we did hear about it. We learned from newspapers and the radio that they had ransacked the stores, smashed windows, stolen from apartments, thrown out Jews, and arrested them.

92. What are your personal memories of the beginning of the war in 1939?

JAKUBOWICZ: At six o'clock in the morning, the first bombers came. They bombed the railroad station, and the trains stopped running. I was still a child. In the morning, I wanted to go to the station, and there were already Polish troops about, barricading everything off. That was nothing unusual. But we were still frightened. We were very frightened. We knew that if the Germans invaded, it would be over for us. So there was already fear—very great fear.

93. Did you hear that the National Socialists had decided to implement the "final solution to the Jewish question"—the systematic extermination of Jews in Europe—at the Wannsee Conference on January 20, 1942? If so, when and how?

JAKUBOWICZ: Yes, we heard about it. I heard about it. A lot of others knew about it as well because the news spread quickly. I heard it in Annaberg from the *Judenälteste* (elder of the Jews). He said, "They've decided on a final solution!"

94. When you heard that World War II was over, what feelings did you have?

JAKUBOWICZ: I was very glad, and I just hoped I would meet a member of my family. But it was no use. I myself was glad about it.

But I had nothing but health problems. I couldn't walk, couldn't do anything. I had no strength. I first contracted typhoid fever, then tuberculosis.

95. Do you think that humankind has learned something from the Holocaust?

JAKUBOWICZ: I think it hasn't learned anything yet, because terrible things are happening in the world nowadays as well, here in Germany too.

96. Should the atrocities be forgotten and no longer talked about, as some people wish?

JAKUBOWICZ: No, they should not be forgotten. They should be talked about so they're not forgotten and so that it never happens again.

97. What plans do you still have for the future?

JAKUBOWICZ: My future? I have no plans for the future. I only hope that I'm spared any more illness.

98. How would you like to be remembered?

JAKUBOWICZ: That I also did good things. I helped a great many people in those dark days.

99. What else would you like to say to us? Which question was not asked?

JAKUBOWICZ: I think the questions that were asked are sufficient. Whether many people will gain an accurate impression of me or not, I don't know, because this kind of topic can't be covered completely in a matter of hours or days.

Sometimes I'm asked about Anne Frank. She was also in Bergen-Belsen concentration camp at that time. But during my time in the camp, I didn't know anything about Anne Frank and never met her. I didn't hear about her until after we were liberated.

100. After all you have been through, what advice can you give us young people?

JAKUBOWICZ: Accept other people, tolerate them, have sympathy for them, and be helpful. Remember that you cannot always live alone in the world. I wish for a peaceful and happy coexistence of all people.

Simone Liebster: Closed Shutters

Simone Liebster, née Arnold, born August 17, 1930
Grounds for persecution: One of Jehovah's Witnesses (Bible Student)
Length of imprisonment: 1 year, 10 months
Country: France

29: Simone Liebster, 1941   *30: Simone Liebster, 2008*

Simone Liebster, née Arnold, was born into a Catholic family on August 17, 1930, in Hüsseren-Wesserling in Alsace, France. In 1938, the family became Jehovah's Witnesses. Following the German occupation of Alsace in 1940, she and her parents engaged in underground activities, distributing translations of banned literature published by Jehovah's Witnesses. Her parents were arrested and interned in a number of concentration camps and other Nazi camps. Simone Liebster refused to perform the Hitler salute and to support the war in any way whatsoever.

On July 8, 1943, she was separated from her mother and sent to the Wessenberg reform school[7] for girls in Constance, Germany. She remained true to her convictions and was liberated on April 26, 1945. When her mother came to pick her up, Simone Liebster failed to recognize her, so disfigured was she after her time in the camp.

After the war, Liebster was active as a missionary, helping people to get to know the Bible. She married the Jewish Holocaust survivor Max Liebster, who had become one of Jehovah's Witnesses during his imprisonment in the camps. Together with her husband, she traveled to many European and American countries as an eyewitness of history. She still performs this work very actively to this day, regularly holding video conferences on Skype with schools in the United States. She describes her experiences in her autobiography *Facing the Lion*, which has been translated into many languages. Simone Liebster lives in France.

The interviews took place on October 16, 2008; February 6, 2009; August 9, 2011; August 30, 2011; and October 10, 2011.

---

[7]   The Wessenberg reform school is often referred to by the term "home" by Mrs. Liebster. Hereinafter, "home" and "reform school" are used interchangeably in Mrs. Liebster's answers referring to her internment. Questions addressing internment in concentration camps are modified to incorporate the term "[home]."

1. When were you born? What was your father like? What was your mother like?

LIEBSTER: I was born on August 17, 1930, in Hüsseren-Wesserling in Alsace, France. At that time, Alsace was under French rule. I was an only child. My father, Adolphe Arnold, was a gentle man and a painter. He did illustrations for fabrics for a textile printing works. My mother Emma, née Bortot, was a very kind and hardworking lady. When they were first married, my parents were very poor, but they succeeded in working their way up. Our family life was just wonderful. In the evenings, my father would often read aloud to us, Mama would knit, and I would play with my dog, Zita. She was my playmate. Sometimes Papa would also play the violin. We had a loving family life.

2. What is your earliest childhood memory?

LIEBSTER: That was a very strange experience. I was very young, maybe two and a half. It was in springtime. Behind the house there was a grassy bank. At the top of it were beautiful blue flowers, and I wanted to pick them. But I should have gone to the bathroom, because I urgently needed to. I was already potty-trained, but the flowers were more important to me. So I clambered up, and what needed to happen happened. When I came home with my flowers, my mother said to me, "You've become a baby again." She lifted me onto the fountain and washed me down with cold water and a brush. Then she put a diaper on me again, put me to bed, and said in a gentle voice, "Yes, you're a baby now, aren't you?" That preoccupied me for some time. I took the fact that I was a baby again very seriously, and in time, I regretted it. Mother was very kind, but strict too.

3. What kind of childhood did you have?

LIEBSTER: I had a happy childhood. My father was very caring, my mother made me pretty dresses, and we often went to visit my grandparents who lived high up the mountainside. I also played a lot with my dog, Zita. On Sundays, we went to church together. We were strict Catholics, and we lived in Mulhouse in Alsace. But the turning point came when we got a Bible. I was eight years old at the time. Papa didn't like it, but Mama would read me a passage from the Bible every day, and I took it very seriously. That's why I didn't want to go to mass with Papa anymore. He wanted to put a stop to that and did some research of his own. He read the Bible himself and, in the end, came to the conclusion that the Bible would be his guide too. Consequently, all three of us were Jehovah's Witnesses by the time the German army occupied Alsace in 1940.

4. How long did you go to school, and what schools did you attend?

LIEBSTER: First, I went to the French primary school as a six-year-old. At the time, my parents didn't have the money to register me at a secondary school. But after three years of primary school, I passed an examination in 1939 that gave me the opportunity to go to grammar school without having to pay. One year later, we were occupied by the Germans. From that point on, we were only allowed to speak German. French was strictly prohibited. In 1940, I was ten years old. From that time until the end of the war, I had no more school education. Sure, I went to school, but the teachers didn't teach me anymore, because I didn't perform the Hitler salute.

5. What was your adolescence like? What trade did you learn, and what did you do for a living?

LIEBSTER: My adolescence didn't begin until 1945. That was when I came home after the war. I had no school diploma, but at art school I was able to learn the same trade as my father. After working for two years doing illustrations for printed fabrics, I started helping people to get to know the Bible, as a missionary.

6. What can you tell us about your family?

LIEBSTER: In 1950, I went to America. It was there that I met Max Liebster. He was a Jew who became one of Jehovah's Witnesses in the concentration camp. He had spent almost six years in concentration camps. He was in five different camps: Sachsenhausen, Neuengamme, Auschwitz-Birkenau, Buna, and Buchenwald. We got married in Paris in 1956. We have no children. Sadly, Max died on May 28, 2008, at the age of ninety-three. Together we were active as witnesses to the Holocaust. My father died in 1977, my mother, in 1979. My husband and I looked after both of them until the end.

7. Did you use the Nazi greeting "Heil Hitler!" and/or the Nazi salute?

LIEBSTER: I knew that *Heil*, which means "salvation," belonged only to Jesus, and I would never give [ascribe] it to anyone. That was not for political reasons. If *any* person had insisted on being addressed with "*Heil*," I would have refused. And that's what I did.

8. Why were you persecuted by the National Socialists?
LIEBSTER: Because I refused to perform the Hitler salute and refused to have anything to do with any preparations for war.

9. When were you arrested?
LIEBSTER: I was separated from my mother on July 8, 1943.

10. Why were you imprisoned?
LIEBSTER: I was imprisoned because I publicly refused to perform the Hitler salute and refused to go to a [Nazi-run] girls' camp during vacation. I also refused to collect material that could be used for the war. I was supposed to go from door to door and collect four pounds of metal, bones, paper, and rags (old clothing) every week for use in the war effort and take them to school. I refused, and that's why I was brought before the juvenile court.

11. What exactly happened when you were arrested?
LIEBSTER: My mother had to take me to the railroad station. Two matrons took me on the train to the Wessenberg reform school for girls in Constance. Mama got on the same train to see where they were taking me.

12. Did people know right from the start what was happening in the camps? Before you were taken away, did you know what would happen to you?
LIEBSTER: As far as the concentration camps were concerned, we knew what was going on because we had read the book *Kreuzzug gegen das Christentum* (*Crusade Against Christianity*)[8] that was published in 1938. The book contained many reports that had been smuggled out of the camps. We knew exactly what Father was going to have to endure but had no idea what was in store for me. All we were told was that it was a home. The Constance Institution, founded in 1855 for the rescue of decadent children by Mr. von Wessenberg, was a "reform school" and the children were referred to as inmates.

---

[8] Published by Franz Zürcher in 1938 from firsthand reports of Jehovah's Witnesses, which included details exposing to the public the atrocities in the concentration camps. See also Leopold Engleitner, question 12.

13. How many different camps [homes] were you in? How many years did you spend in each one?

LIEBSTER: From July 1943 to April 1945, I was in the Wessenberg reform school. The idea was that I should stay in Constance until I was fourteen. After spending five months in Constance, I was brought before the court again so they could assess my attitude. Again, I refused to back down. Two documents were read out to me. One said that if I stuck to my decision, I would be sent to the concentration camp. The other was a confirmation that I had renounced my faith and was now free to go. The judge said, "There are two stacks of papers on that table over there. Choose one and sign it." I took the document containing my conviction and came back with it to sign it at his desk. Then the judge shouted furiously, "The crafty devil!" That made me look again at the papers lying on the table and I saw that the wording was not the same as on the sheet I was holding. Did that mean it was the renunciation? Would they then have been able to tell my father that his daughter had signed and they had won her over? That might explain why the judge flew into such a rage. In the camp, it was customary for my father to be summoned to the commandant on my account, and it caused him a lot of suffering [since he was punished for my refusal to back down].

After that, I stayed in the same reform school until the end of the war. The [turmoil of] war spared me internment in a concentration camp. They had other things to worry about. I stayed in the home until the French army arrived.

14. Were you the only member of your family in the concentration camp [home], or were family members or friends there as well? If so, did you have any contact with them?

LIEBSTER: I was on my own in the home. For the first nine months, I was completely isolated. I was able to contact my parents only because I had an aunt [Eugenie Walter] who was still free, and she could receive letters.

15. What were the first things that happened immediately following your arrival at the concentration camp [home]?

LIEBSTER: I hardly know how to explain it; I was so miserable that I had no conception at all of what was going on. I was given the name "Maria" and the number 1. All of a sudden I was standing there in a different dress, my hair was tied back, and my shoes were gone because from April through November, we had to go barefoot. All around me I saw nothing but "ghosts" running silently through the rooms because the children were not allowed to speak. It all felt really strange. During the meal, I broke down and started crying and sobbing so hard that I couldn't stop. The three pairs of badly torn socks I had to darn before supper if I wanted any food were no consolation. I cried all afternoon long. My socks were wet from my tears. I went to bed crying and cried all night long.

In the morning, I was shocked to find a bloodstain in my bed. It was my second period. As soon as I saw the first teacher, Fräulein Messinger, I told her about it. She immediately summoned another girl and said, "Show Maria how to wash her sheet." And there I stood, barefoot on the stone floor with severe stomach pains and a tub full of cold water. The stain would not go away. My hand was stinging because my salty tears fell on the torn skin.

When Fräulein Messinger, who was a big, powerfully-built woman, came to check on me, she said scathingly, "Ha ha, you're crying. Why don't you tell your Jehovah to wash your sheet for you!" I looked at her in indignation, wiped away my tears, and never cried in that home again. I said to myself, "I won't allow it that they now hold Jehovah in derision because of my crying!" In the reform school, no one could make me cry again after that.

16. Why did they shave the heads of the prisoners [inmates]?
LIEBSTER: We were all girls with braids that were washed once a year. At night we wore caps, which went totally black because our hair was so greasy. The caps were washed about once every three months. I've never seen such black caps.

17. What prisoner [inmate] category were you put in?
LIEBSTER: They didn't differentiate in the home. We all sat in the same room and received the same treatment. The school was in the same building; the older girls had lessons in the morning, the younger ones in the afternoon. I was one of the older ones, of course. The only difference was in the allocation of chores. I was the only one who was given extra duties. I had to look after a five-year-old, which meant getting up with her in the middle of the night to take her to the bathroom because she was a

bed wetter. If the bed was wet despite that, I was punished: I, and not the child, had to wash the sheets in the morning. I didn't have a clock to get me out of bed. I had to rely on self-discipline. In summer, I was the only one who had to carry water for the tomatoes and beans in the garden.

18. Can you describe the daily routine in the concentration camp [home]?
LIEBSTER: In summer, we had to get up at half past five in the morning; in winter, at six. Everything that went on in the dormitory was precisely regimented. When we undressed or dressed, we were forbidden to look at our bodies. In bed we had to cross our arms over our chests with our hands on our shoulders. In the morning, we were all still in our slips when the windows were opened, even in freezing weather. Still in our slips, we went into a cold washroom. That was also a ritual. We had to wash the back of the girl next to us with cold water. The only parts that couldn't be touched were our private parts. That was forbidden.

Then we went back into the dormitory. The aired bran mattresses had to be smoothed out, completely flat, and our shirts and caps folded as though they were going on shelves in a store. Every girl had a specific cleaning job to do. And when I say cleaning, I really mean cleaning. First, I cleaned one of the toilets, then Fräulein Messinger's private room. At eight o'clock, we were done cleaning the rooms and still hadn't had any breakfast.

Then we were given two bowls of bread soup. Sometimes it had little maggots in it, which we had to eat. In the afternoon, the ten to fourteen-year-olds washed, ironed, and mended all the linen, knitted, and worked in the garden. In the evening, we had another bowl of soup. Before going to bed, we washed our feet because we were barefoot, and we said evening prayers. Then we went to bed in complete silence. Not a single word was heard.

19. What was the worst thing about the daily routine?
LIEBSTER: The work wasn't the worst thing. I loved the work. The worst thing was the way the children took malicious pleasure in telling on each other. Having to watch a child being beaten was also bad. It was always with a stick, with such powerful strokes on the hands that they often swelled up. At supper, a child who was being punished had to say, "Thank you, I'm not allowed to eat, I'm being punished!" in a loud voice

when her bowl was passed along the line and reached the soup pot. At the same time, she had to stand up with her hands behind her back. She had to stay at the table until everyone had finished eating. One stroke of the cane on each hand meant one evening without food, two strokes meant two evenings, and seven strokes meant a whole week with no supper.

The little girl I was looking after was always on the lookout for a chance to get me punished. I had to be on my toes the whole time. For example, one time we had a stocking inspection. Our stockings hung in the storehouse. Her stocking was okay, but then she took a bite out of it, and it was still damp from her saliva. That was plain to see. But Fräulein Annemarie, the seamstress, didn't like me and ordered that I should get no soup because the stocking had not been darned. So in the evening, I had nothing to eat. It was so unfair that I divided the little girl's soup into two portions so that I would get some too. That caused an uproar. The housemother Fräulein Lederle, who was so called because she was the principal, came to see where all the screaming was coming from, but she let it be.

20. Did everyday life lead more to solidarity, or did the prisoners [inmates] try to cope on their own?

LIEBSTER: Solidarity was impossible in that home. We were told, "No talking in the dormitory, no talking when you're working, no talking in the school, and no talking at mealtimes." Well, what else is there? In a home where children can't talk, there can be no solidarity. You live in silence. If a child was caught because she had secretly spoken to another one, she was given a beating and received no food. Only during Christmas week was there any time for play; apart from that—never.

21. Was there anything that helped you take your mind off the horror of daily life for a while (such as music)? What gave you strength?

LIEBSTER: Apart from the school, where we learned only the bare essentials, there were no books in [the home in] Constance, no conversation, no music—nothing. I arrived in Constance with a personal stock of ideas, which came from my father. He always used to say, "Child, in your head, you have the chance to compile your own private library. Whatever you put in it, nobody can take away!" That, together with the prayers that went along with it, became my source of strength. But with the passage of time, I grew so weary and exhausted that I behaved more like a machine.

22. What were living conditions like in the barracks [home] (prisoner [inmate] allocation, food supplies, hygiene, clothing, etc.)?

LIEBSTER: I would say the living conditions in the home had stayed as they were in the Middle Ages. In the Middle Ages, people didn't take a bath very often either. We were then told, "Undress like this! You take your nightshirt, pull your arms out through the sleeves, and hold it fast with your chin. Then you take the other shirt, put it on, and when it covers your body, you let the nightshirt go."

When we went to the washbasin, it all started over again. You lifted the shirt up over the armpit and the person next to you washed your back. The only things that were washed were the back, the face, the hands, the arms, and in the evening, the feet. But the rest was taboo. We were not allowed to see it or touch it. It was taboo.

The living conditions in the home hadn't changed since it was established in 1855. In the past, people didn't take a bath very often, underwear was not changed very often, and the naked body had to be kept out of sight. When taking the annual bath, bodies were washed under the nightshirt. So everything stayed as it had been then. Clothes were only changed once a week. And if anything was dirty, your fruit ration was stopped for a week. For supper, there was a bowl of potato soup, half an apple or a little bowl of berries, and a small piece of bread. Clothes and stockings were very seldom washed. For those who went to church, there was a Sunday dress. Dresses were passed on from one child to the next.

23. What jobs did you have to do? How many hours a day did you have to work?

LIEBSTER: Cleaning the rooms was done on an empty stomach. At first I had to clean Fräulein Messinger's room. That gave me the opportunity to read the Bible a little bit because every day I had to crawl under the bed to clean the bedsprings, and that was where I had hidden the little Bible that I had smuggled in. After a couple of months, I was given the great responsibility of looking after the main office where all the court documents were kept. I was always given the stern warning that, "If we ever catch you with a document in your hand, you'll be put in prison! We will not stand for that!" Three times a day I also had to set the table with fine china crockery for the teachers.

Monday was wash day. About eight or ten of the thirty-six girls had to wash, mend, and iron everyone's laundry for the week. Every day, in the late afternoon, we had to peel potatoes because that's what we had to eat most of the time. That was an ordeal too. If the peelings were thick, the child in question was not given anything to eat in the evening. She was told, "The potato on the skin was your food, and now it's gone!" I was supervisor and had to oversee the children because it would have been my responsibility if thick peelings were found during inspection.

The second winter brought very hard work with it. The home was on the border between Germany and Switzerland, and there were a great many hundred-year-old oak and beech trees on the grounds. Because they offered cover to any "spies" that might be trying to escape, they were chopped down. In the spring, we were to plant potatoes in the newly cleared ground. With three other fourteen-year-olds, we set to work to remove the hundred-year-old tree stumps from the hard ground. That meant hollowing them out, laying the roots bare, sawing through them, and taking them out. After that, we also had to saw through thick branches and pile them up. That was no mean feat. It was quite hard work. But we felt proud because we were "guys" and it gave us the feeling of being strong. We were given an extra piece of bread as a reward. After four hours' work from half past one till half past five in the afternoon, we were exhausted. To this day, I still get a strong feeling whenever I see a tree stump.

24. What effect did the slogan "Work liberates" have on you?
LIEBSTER: In Alsace, when Nazi ideology was the main topic of conversation at school, it was claimed that work liberates. I myself loved working. But this slogan didn't mean that we were supposed to learn to love work. What it meant was if a person worked hard, he couldn't fall prey to false ideologies, because he had no time to do so, and it was through work that he could regain his honor. I had quite a different view. I was always told that work is part and parcel of human life and that it should be honored and not seen as a punishment. So I never regarded work as a punishment.

25. What were the guards [staff] like in the camp [home]?
LIEBSTER: During classes, which were held in the home, we were taught that we were Greater Germany and all the other countries were way

behind us. But of course we, as asocial children, were also inferior. We ought to have been grateful to the state and the municipality for the rare chance of being accepted into this home.

The teacher, Fräulein Messinger, was about thirty-five years old and had allowed herself to be very strongly influenced by National Socialism. The principal, Fräulein Lederle, was about sixty-five, very strict, but impartial and somehow fair. The sewing supervisor, Fräulein Annemarie, who was about the same age and a strict Catholic, was very cold and even treated me unfairly. Fräulein Anna was a mute, withdrawn cook. These four adults ran the home on their own.

On my first Sunday there, I asked Fräulein Lederle for permission to read the Bible that was kept in the school cupboard while some of the Catholic girls went to church and most of them, to the Protestant temple. Permission was granted, but when Fräulein Messinger happened by and saw me, she yelled, "What's she doing? Reading the Bible? Out of the question. From now on, she'll do the cooking!" So from my second Sunday onward, I did the cooking for the thirty-six children and four teachers. Fräulein Anna helped me at the beginning, but later on, she left me on my own and went to church as well. So instead of having a day off, "Maria" became the cook for thirty-six children and the supervisors. I was thirteen years old at the time.

26. Was there any contact between the prisoners [inmates] and the local population?
LIEBSTER: After one year in the home, I was allowed to go to our baker and butcher to pay the monthly bill. The townsfolk would never have spoken to a barefoot "Wessenberg child" in a reform school dress. Nobody wanted to have anything to do with "asocial children" who "stole and lied." So we never talked to people outside the home.

27. Were you aware of how the war was proceeding in the outside world?
LIEBSTER: Yes, a little, as soon as I was allowed to go out and pay the bills. I always had to hurry because I had a fixed time that I was allowed to be out. While outside, I saw people waiting in lines. Sometimes they talked to each other, and I went and stood in the middle of them for a minute or two, straining my ears to hear whether they were talking about

the war. That way I found out how the war was going, especially on the French side. It interested me because I knew it could lead to our release.

28. In the concentration camp [home], were you allowed to receive letters, food parcels, etc.?

LIEBSTER: I was permitted to receive letters after nine months. The letters were read out to me and then taken away. I was never actually given them. My Aunt Eugenie, who was still free, was the person I could write to. She received the few letters my parents wrote from the camps. Now and then she was able to write me some news about my parents and was allowed to visit me many times, though under strict supervision. When my aunt found out that I couldn't receive any parcels, because everything she sent went to the home and not to me, she stopped sending things.

29. What forms of torture did you suffer?

LIEBSTER: There was psychological torture and physical torture. It started when I refused to say "Heil Hitler!" I was summoned by the school principal, Gasser. It was a Saturday and he said he would think of something over the weekend. By Monday he had thought of something. He had prepared a letter to all the classes. It said that there was one girl who refused to submit to the school regulations and that a girl like that could not take part in lessons. This was intended as a warning to the girl in question—without naming names—and if she refused to respect the rules, she would have to leave the school. He read the letter out to me and ordered me to take it to all forty-eight classes to have it read out to them. This meant that I would have to perform the Hitler salute every time I entered a classroom. But I didn't perform it. This confrontation lasted a whole week.

Next Saturday morning, my teacher wasn't there. Suddenly the school superintendent stomped into the classroom accompanied by the principal, Gasser, and my teacher, Herr Zipf. All three went up on the podium. The superintendent went to the desk and gazed round at the girls. He then read out the letter and said, "The girl who knows she is the one referred to will stand up!" I got to my feet. There followed a lecture on National Socialism after which I was summoned up on the podium to stand in front of the picture of Adolf Hitler. Then they said, "Here is Hitler and here you will perform the salute. If you don't, your expulsion papers are here.

Take them and get out of the school! But this is a choice that will decide your whole future, so we're giving you five minutes to think about it." He pulled up his sleeve to look at his wristwatch. Exactly five minutes went by. They dragged dreadfully. I started to be frightened, my head felt swollen, and my feet were tightly tensed. Quietly, I repeated my decision to myself, over and over again: "You want the papers, the papers, the papers . . ." Suddenly his arm shot up and he bellowed "Heil Hitler" three times. On the instant, the entire class and the two teachers followed suit. I just grabbed my papers and ran out of the classroom. On Monday I had to go back to primary school where I was forbidden to say why I was expelled from the grammar school. I was asked, "Why are you here? Did you steal? Did you lie? Were you lazy? What happened?" and I was not allowed to answer. That was very, very hard. So that was psychological pressure.

After that, I was summoned for a psychological examination. Two men in white coats were sitting at an L-shaped table. In the corner, there was a large interrogation lamp and my chair was right in its glare. A long way behind me sat my mother who was not permitted to say anything. Then they bombarded me with questions. Both men spoke at once and demanded that I reply immediately. One of them asked general questions about nature, math, and geography while the other wanted to know something about secret Bible studies and forbidden literature. They even expected me to confirm the names of Jehovah's Witnesses. It was all terribly confusing and went on for a whole hour. Luckily the two men were then called away, and that put an end to the psychological examination that was more like interrogation by the Gestapo. That was a really bad experience. Mother consoled me, saying, "Child, you haven't betrayed anyone or anything."

At that time, every schoolchild had to take four pounds of items to school every week: bones, metal, paper, and rags to support the war effort. I never did this. One day I was told to go to the pile to help sort it, but I refused. "I will not work for the war!" The [primary school] principal, Ehrlich, hit me so hard on the back of the neck with the edge of his large bony hand that I fell unconscious into the stinking pile of bones that was crawling with maggots. Some children then took me home, and I had my first period. Mother took me to the doctor who prescribed three days' rest.

Next day the police came and demanded a five-hundred-mark fine from my mother. She was ordered to send me to school immediately. Mother went back to the doctor. He met her at the door and said, "Please don't come to see me again. I had the Gestapo here and they said, 'If you prescribe anything else for that vermin, you'll be sent to the concentration camp!'" These events are only a part of what I experienced. So there was psychological [pressure], and [there was] physical pressure; and the psychological pressure was constant. It started in 1941, and I felt it continually.

30. What was the most frightening moment for you?

LIEBSTER: There were two. The first one was on September 4, 1941. The doorbell rang at two o'clock in the afternoon. Mama said, "Open the door for your father." I went to open the door, jumped up onto my father to hug him, and then there came a "Heil Hitler!" It was two Gestapo men. And I was clinging to a man who was standing completely stiff and didn't know what was happening, because he had this child round his neck. Then he sent me to my room. He said, "Go to your room." That surprised me; and I thought, "How does he know that I have a room? Lots of children don't have a room of their own." And then I saw the Elberfelder Bible on the shelf. And I thought, if they see that, they'll arrest us. They were violently opposed to the Elberfelder Bible because of the name Jehovah [in it]. So I asked, "Can I go out to buy a notebook? I have to do my homework." The Gestapo man said, "Yes. Go out and come back here again." Mother said, "I'll pay later." I took a bag, put the Bible in [it], and threw the Bible under a tomato plant in our neighbor's garden. I bought my notebook, and when I opened the garage, I saw my father's bicycle. That was a huge relief for me. I went home with a light heart, thinking, "Papa's at home, everything's going to be all right!" I got home, and Papa wasn't there. That was a real shock. I almost fainted. The interrogation of my mother went on for three hours. I could hear it because I was in the next room. In the end, the Gestapo said, "If you want to see your husband, you will have to see things our way. In the end we're going to get you anyway, you and your child." From that day on, the threat of arrest hung over us. Whenever someone came up the stairs, I hid in my mother's apron. That was the most terrible time, those days were just terrible.

Then one day my mother didn't come home. I was in bed with a temperature. She had gone out, missed the tram, and didn't come home until later. When I realized it, I put on my shoes, although I was burning with fever, put on my coat over my nightshirt, and went to the police station. At the police station, I listened at every door to find out whether Mama was being interrogated there. And of course she was not there. When I came down, the tram was just pulling in and Mama got out.

Those two things were the greatest frights of my life. After that, I was willing to take anything upon myself. Those two days—and they weren't very far apart, maybe three months—I had somehow been given a death sentence inside me. "From now on, you're a grown-up; you must stand alone and go forward." That was the turning point. That was 1941, so I was eleven years old.

Afterward we learned that the Gestapo had come to pick my father up from work. He had to cycle all the way home in front of the Gestapo car at exactly the time when my mother was out on her daily errand to collect her milk ration and while I was in school. They searched the house but put everything back as it had been so that Mama wouldn't notice. That's why she never even realized that the Gestapo had been through the house.

31. Were there any entertaining or lighthearted incidents that enabled you to forget all the suffering for a moment? Can you describe them?
LIEBSTER: During recess in the home, we had a "game" where we turned in circles. Sometimes we danced to and fro a little, just to get some exercise. But it was always supervised, and there was no laughing. I don't remember ever hearing children laughing. For Christmas week, they got some toys out. Apart from that, there were no games and no laughter all year long. On Sunday afternoons, we did embroidering. After nine months' imprisonment, my Aunt Eugenie was able to visit me many times. In time she was even granted permission to spend a few hours with me outside the home. That gave me the opportunity to learn something from the Bible or hear news from the camps about my parents.

32. What were your day-to-day thoughts while you were in the concentration camp [home]?
LIEBSTER: Because I knew why I was in the home, I took the advice my mother had given me very much to heart, and her words became my day-to-day thoughts: "Take care that what you do always brings honor to

God and can never be used against Jehovah. Child, you must not say no out of mere contrariness. When you say no, it must be based on religious principles; and only do it when it's a question of obeying God. Always be polite, even when you say no. You'll get much further that way." And mother always used to say, "Never look at anyone through critical eyes because if you do, you will be repaid in kind. You must always behave with humility!" These tips were my day-to-day thoughts. I was hotheaded, so it was only by the grace of God that I succeeded in following this advice. The report that Fräulein Lederle wrote about me, which I obtained a few years ago, ran, "She always behaved irreproachably."

33. Was it possible for children to be born in a concentration camp [home]? If so, what happened to these babies?
LIEBSTER: If one of the girls had gotten pregnant, she would immediately have been sent to a juvenile correction institution. It was impossible for a baby to be born in the home. After the war, I learned that one girl had gotten pregnant when the French came to Constance. Gardening was done outside the wall, and somehow or other something happened there. It was said that the girl was immediately sent to prison and then killed herself and the child, who was black, because the situation was just unbearable for her.

34. Was it possible to make friends with prisoners [other inmates]?
LIEBSTER: When you can't talk, you can't make friends. But one evening, the girl who slept in the next bed, Sophie, put her pillow on the stool that separated our beds and asked me, "Why is it that you are in here? You're so very different from all the others." I was so happy to be able to tell her about the truth of the Bible. Next evening, we wanted to carry on. But Hilde, who lay in the next bed, informed on us. Fräulein Lederle ordered us to come down and explain ourselves. We both told her we were talking about the Gospel. Fräulein Lederle went to fetch her long leather apron and the cane and made Sophie hold out her hand. The cane whistled through the air, smacked into her hand, and cracked against the leather apron. Then came the other hand, and again, and again. Seven strokes on each hand, and that meant seven days without food. Sophie was sent away, her hands stinging dreadfully. Then it was my turn to step forward.

I was scared because you weren't allowed to cry out. If you did, the stroke didn't count. I held out my trembling hand. Fräulein Lederle looked at me. Suddenly the cane disappeared and she said, "You and your religion! You're losing all sense of perspective. I'll let it go this time. But next time the punishment will be double!" I went back to bed feeling sad.

Next evening when the soup was served, Sophie stood up. Her table was the second to be served, mine was the third. Standing to attention, her hands behind her back, she said in a loud voice, "Thank you, I'm not allowed to eat, I'm being punished!" And when my bowl went up, I got to my feet as well, looked at Fräulein Lederle, and said, "Thank you, I'm not allowed to eat, I'm being punished!" Taken aback, she said, "Give the bowl back to me. Sophie, come here. I don't want to hear another word about this." One time when we happened to meet on the stairs, Sophie tried to find out the reason for this turn of events. But I put my finger on my lips, and never again tried to break the talking ban.

35. Who was your best friend during this dreadful time, and how did he or she help you?

LIEBSTER: I had friends, but I wasn't allowed to get in touch with them. My contact with the outside world was limited to my aunt. A few letters from my father in Dachau and my mother in Schirmeck-Vorbruck reached her. My friends were in no position to send me encouraging words, either. I was cut off.

My best friend was always Jehovah God. He guided me as if by the hand. I felt it time and time again whenever I found myself in trouble. And every time I felt something like that, it gave me the strength to carry on. After all, that's how it is when you walk hand in hand with someone. You feel Jehovah much more strongly when you're completely alone, utterly isolated. It was he that I talked to.

36. What did you do to relieve the suffering of other inmates?

LIEBSTER: There weren't many opportunities. But I managed to avoid informing on anyone, although I saw some things that were wrong. The punishments were usually far too severe in relation to what had happened.

There's one particular story I can tell you on this subject: When we went out to pay a bill at the butcher's, we were sometimes given a piece of sausage. We were not allowed to eat it. Instead we had to take it back with us. It was put on a shelf and would replace a meal on the next day. One time the piece of sausage was stolen, and no one owned up to it. The whole class had to sit with our hands over our heads all day long until the culprit came forward. Then Fräulein Messinger said, "Maria is excused; she never steals. She can do some schoolwork instead. We know that you don't steal!" The sitting for hours on end with hands over heads lasted three days. The younger girls were crying in pain. I had deduced almost at once who had done it from the expression on her face, so I asked the teacher for permission to speak to the girl. I then spoke to Erna and advised her to own up because it was pointless, and everyone was suffering on her account. I succeeded in moving her to make a confession. That was a relief to everyone, though it was tough on Erna. We didn't see her for days and days afterward.

37. Were there particular hierarchies among the inmates?

LIEBSTER: The hierarchy was based on age. There was a difference between the six to ten-year-olds and the ten to fourteen-year-olds. Both groups were treated the same, but the jobs they were allocated were different. We had one large room to sleep in with twenty-five iron beds with bran mattresses. I was in the smaller dormitory, which had ten beds. I was the only one who was responsible for taking a five-year-old bed wetter to the bathroom in the middle of the night. But the unruly, rebellious Hanna was always plotting ways to pay me back for getting her out of bed. She often quickly urinated in bed on purpose when she saw me coming in. Afterward I always had to wash her sheet. That was a real chore. The pallet was wet and had to be dried. One time I got so fed up with her: I was the one who had to wash the sheets; I was the one who got punished. I took hold of Hanna, gripped her between my knees, forced her against the washbasin, put her hands in the cold water, and washed the sheet over them.

She screamed as if I had been trying to kill her. Then Fräulein Lederle came along and asked, "What in the world is going on here?" I said, "She wet the bed on purpose. And now I'm being punished. She must be punished too. It's just not fair!" In the end, Fräulein Lederle sided with me. That was no small matter. I was held accountable for everything that child did. I was the only one who had the job of raising a child.

38. Were there any differences in the way the various groups of prisoners [inmates] (religious, political groups) were treated?

LIEBSTER: It's possible, but I didn't know enough about such matters. If you don't talk, you don't know much.

39. What diseases and illnesses were prevalent in the concentration camp [home]?

LIEBSTER: Speaking for myself, passing water caused me great pain, but that was due to the emotional strain. One time I had to look after little Zila. She had a nasty abscess in her throat and a raging fever. I had to treat her with hot potato poultices and was responsible for making sure she got well again.

40. Did you receive a physical injury?

LIEBSTER: No, never.

41. How much did you weigh when you were in the concentration camp [home]?

LIEBSTER: I don't know anymore how many pounds I weighed, but one thing I do know: during those two years, I didn't grow one single centimeter, and if anything, I was smaller when I came out than when I went in. When I came out at age fifteen, I was still wearing the same dresses I wore at thirteen. There had been absolutely no change—a standstill.

42. What did death mean to you?

LIEBSTER: To me, death would have meant that I had stayed faithful. Death on account of steadfastness would have been a victory. I was well aware that death might separate us. During the last night I spent with my mother in Meersburg, we went to a vineyard to pray and softly sang a resurrection song. We knew there was a chance that we would never meet again. I had that in my mind when I went into the home.

43. What was the closest you came to death?

LIEBSTER: Fortunately, Constance was not bombed, and the turn of events meant that I didn't end up in a concentration camp. However, Marcel Sutter, a childhood friend who refused to do military service, was beheaded in Torgau in November 1943. Fräulein Messinger told me that piece of news with evident satisfaction. But the effect it had on me was quite the opposite. Not fear, but pride in his faith. For me, Marcel's death proved his loyalty, and he became an example for me to follow.

44. Did you ever build a kind of "wall" to shield yourself from the terrible things that were being done so that the death of a fellow prisoner [of one of the inmates] no longer affected you?

LIEBSTER: Not really, because I wasn't in a situation where dead bodies were lying around me. But I myself was prepared for death.

45. What happened to the dead bodies in the concentration camp [home]?

LIEBSTER: I didn't see any. I don't know.

46. Was there ever a possibility for you to be released from the concentration camp [home]?

LIEBSTER: Yes, for me personally there was. It was when I was brought before the judge for the second time, and he asked me the same question again, [namely], whether I wanted to stay a Bible Student and would refuse to say "Heil Hitler!" or not. One reply would have meant freedom; the other, a concentration camp. So of course I had the chance to sign, but I didn't do it.

47. Were there any escape attempts or opportunities to escape? Did you try to escape?

LIEBSTER: I never thought of escaping. It was clear to me that the state had put me there and that, as a Christian, I had to submit to the law. But we did have one instance of a girl who tried to escape. She was caught and sent to prison.

48. Were there any inmates in the concentration camp [home] who dared to stage a revolt against the camp [home] authorities?

LIEBSTER: The only thing I saw was that the supervisors sometimes had difficulties with problem children—children who refused to back down. But why they behaved like they did, I can't say.

49. Did you think you would ever make it out alive?

LIEBSTER: Not really. My feelings were mixed. I had no idea where my family was and came to the conclusion that they may have died. This uncertainty made me feel that I was already an orphan, and I thought I would have to stay a prisoner for the rest of my life. I didn't expect anything to change during the last days of the war.

50. Were there any times when you gave up all hope? If so, why?
LIEBSTER: I never gave up hope in the earthly paradise. As a Christian, I never gave up that hope. But the hope of being able to go back to a normal life began to fade because we were so far away from real life and completely cut off from the outside world.

51. Did anyone commit suicide?
LIEBSTER: I don't think so.

52. During the Holocaust, did you ever consider committing suicide out of sheer despair?
LIEBSTER: I was never in despair. Never. Although I cried all through the first night, I was never in despair. The tears only came because it hurt so much to lose my dear mama. It was awful, and I felt so heartbroken until Fräulein Messinger made fun of Jehovah. That was what I needed, and it snapped me completely out of my self-pity.

53. What thoughts, ideas, hopes, wishes, or religious convictions did you cling to?
LIEBSTER: My strong conviction that one day the earth will be a paradise was very clear in my mind. I made plans for how it would look if I had a beautiful garden and children who would play and for what I would teach them. There was a fine park in front of the home. It was absolutely forbidden for us to go into it. But it so happened that my bed was by the window, which I had to open. So every day I took a brief glance at the park. That reawakened my imagination and nourished my hopes. I made very, very many plans for the house I would build: it would have a lot of rooms and big windows and a farm. I still have these plans in my head today. Sometimes it happened that my hands stopped moving altogether when I was sewing or darning because I was so wrapped up in my dreams. Then the teacher Fräulein Annemarie would come and shout, "Maria, wake up!" Then I started sewing again. But I also knew that this life in paradise might only come about through death and resurrection.

54. Did you lose your faith in God while you were in the camp [home]?
LIEBSTER: Quite the opposite: I felt God everywhere. It was he who had saved me. My thoughts were focused on him, and what I had in my heart came from him. That's why my faith got stronger. When people ask me that question, I often use this comparison: there is wheat that is sown in autumn. Then it does nothing. All winter long, it's only this (*indicates with fingers*)—about an inch—high. But then its roots begin to grow. And that is what happened to my faith. It was a small belief like that of a twelve-year-old child, but it took root during those two years, and the roots were very deep, and I came out of it much stronger than I went in—exactly the opposite of what the Nazis had expected.

55. What role did your religion play in how you felt about what was going on? Why?
LIEBSTER: Somehow I had a feeling of satisfaction when I saw that God was giving me the chance to remain faithful in different circumstances. I was no giant. This had nothing to do with strength of character, but only with obedience and loyalty to God. On every occasion, I was able to find the strength I needed even though I felt small and weak. It could only have been the strength of God that came to my aid again and again. I could pour out my heart to God at any time, and I wanted to be loyal to him.

56. Did you pray during your internment?
LIEBSTER: Yes, God was the only person I could talk to. They weren't long prayers. But I kept praying that I would be able to obey God and that my parents might be protected.

57. Did you ever consider changing your religion (or ideology)? Why?
LIEBSTER: Definitely not. On the contrary, I wanted to spread my faith. But change it, never. How could I do something like that when I had felt the hand of God so many times?

58. What was the date of your liberation from the camp [home]?
LIEBSTER: April 26, 1945. The French army arrived in Constance at the end of April 1945, and I was thrown out of the home. I went across the border to a refugee camp in Switzerland and then through Switzerland.

59. How were you liberated from the camp [home], or how did you manage to get out of it?

LIEBSTER: My mother was arrested after me and sent to a camp. Her camp was liberated before mine. She made it as far as Constance, but had a serious accident that left her with a badly battered face. I was completely confused. This woman couldn't possibly be my mother. She didn't look at all like her and just sat there, motionless, wearing a man's jacket. Her injured face was blue and red, gaunt, and surrounded by shaggy hair. I didn't recognize her at all and didn't even say hello to her. I was told it was my mother, but I thought to myself, "That's impossible; she looks terrible and has men's clothes on!" Then they said, "Maria cannot leave the home. You'll have to go to the courthouse and obtain a document for her to be free because she's in the home by order of the court. Maria can take you there." We walked next to one another, my mother and I. We didn't talk. She didn't give me her hand, and I didn't take it. We just went along to the courthouse. We were out of luck because none of the judges was there. My mother asked someone at the office there but was told, "There's nothing I can do. They've all gone. The army is at the gates." Then this woman put up such a fight to secure my release that I realized it was my mother. Up to then I hadn't recognized her as my mother. And I started to cry. All the tears I had kept bottled up inside for two years came pouring out. I cried and cried and cried. But she didn't get the necessary papers and had to take me back to the home.

Then she said to me, "Child, don't worry. When the French come, they'll throw you out. They won't want a French girl in there when the French army arrives!" And she was right. When the French army arrived in Constance, I was the only girl they threw out; all the others were German. My mother was asked to take me away from the home without delay so that I, as the only French national, should not be a problem to the governess of the home.

60. How were you treated by the people who liberated you?

LIEBSTER: In the refugee camp, the Swiss treated us like royalty. That was vastly different to the way other people were treated who were sent elsewhere. We were even given chocolate, Swiss chocolate, of course. We traveled all through Switzerland in clean, warm trains as far as Evian in France. From Evian, we went to Lyon on a freight train. During this journey, I fell out of the cattle truck. The steps were a little icy, and we wanted to get out and relieve ourselves in the woods. I sprained both my feet in the fall. But I fought tooth and nail against being kept at the Red Cross office. I had found my mother again. No one was going to separate me from my mother. I fought like a tigress. My mother said, "Incredible!" I grabbed hold of the mother I had found again and stuck to her like glue.

61. What was the first thing you did after you were liberated?
LIEBSTER: The very first thing I did when we opened the door at home was to say a prayer of thanks with Mama. We found the apartment just as we left it. The Gestapo had sealed it, and the youth welfare department had sealed it as well. The apartment belonged to the factory where Papa worked, and they sealed it too. One group couldn't get in because of the other group, and we found everything still there. That's why we first gave thanks. But then came a heavy blow: my father was on the list of the dead, and we realized that Mother might have to go out to work. But she was very weak.

62. Did you have any problems when you returned home? How did people in your home environment react to you?
LIEBSTER: Everyone had problems with the return home. The townsfolk didn't want to hear anything about it at all. They all said, "We suffered too! There was a war on!" And in a way, it was true to a certain extent that they had suffered. There were some violent battles, after all. But of course that had nothing to do with what our family had gone through. That was hushed up. It was quite simply not talked about anymore.

63. Were you able to rejoin your family?
LIEBSTER: Yes, my mother came to fetch me. Finally, one day, a friend of mine came. The doorbell rang, I opened the door, and she said, "Simone, Papa is here!" He had been on the Red Cross list of missing prisoners, and that came about like this: he was in Ebensee and was dying, so he was not put on the list of survivors [according to the Red Cross]. The American Red Cross had taken him to Bad Ischl where he was nursed back to health somehow or other, and then he made his way home alone from Bad Ischl via Strasbourg. Of course that took a while because the train connections were very bad or nonexistent.

And then he came up. That was another very upsetting moment. He went straight past me without recognizing me. Four years had passed. Then he fell into Mama's arms. We wanted to talk to him but he couldn't hear us anymore. The SS had beaten his ears so much that he was deaf. His teeth were all gone. The SS had knocked his teeth out. He had been a [medical] guinea pig in Dachau and was nearer death than life. That was an appalling time. For a whole year, he screamed at night because there had been cannibalism in Ebensee. They had cut pieces out of living people—people who were dying—and eaten them. And because he was dying, he was constantly

31. Simone flanked by her parents, Emma and Adolphe Arnold, 1948

afraid that he would be killed and eaten. He was in an appalling state. It was nearly two years before he was able to recover to some extent.

64. Did you have any acquaintances, friends, or relatives in the camps? Did they survive their internment?

LIEBSTER: My father was arrested on September 4, 1941, and was initially interned for four months in Mulhouse prison. After that, he spent a few weeks in the Schirmeck-Vorbruck high-security camp before being transferred to Dachau concentration camp in January 1942, where he was used as a guinea pig in medical experiments. Following that, he was sent to the infamous quarry in Mauthausen concentration camp and finally, in the fall of 1944, to Ebensee concentration camp where, by May 1945, he had wasted away to become a "*Muselmann*," a prisoner too emaciated to stand on his own two feet. He was liberated by the Americans and taken to the hospital in Bad Ischl. He came home at the end of May.

In August 1943, after a day in prison, Mama was sent to the Schirmeck-Vorbruck high-security camp in Alsace. Later on, the entire camp was moved to Gaggenau. She was supposed to be sent to Ravensbrück, but the course of the war prevented it. That's how it was that she was liberated from Villingen camp in April 1945. Mother had been through terrible things. She came very close to starving to death.

Twice she was incarcerated in the bunker and given only bread and water. She had refused to repair a soldier's clothing. The second time it was because she had talked to some young girls about the Bible. This bunker was next to the SS interrogation center. She always heard the screams and saw the blood. One day, a highly-decorated personage came to see why a prisoner had been locked in the bunker a second time. Most prisoners of this type were shot on his orders. Mother stood to attention and had to tell him why she was in the camp. She said, "Bible Student!" "Ah, you've read the Jewish book," he said. She didn't know what his decorations meant and replied, "Yes, Admiral!" [He burst out,] "Ha ha! I'm an admiral! Ah, I'm an admiral!" and he went away laughing loudly. Some time later, the guard came to her and said, "You were lucky. All the prisoners who are locked up in the bunker a second time are shot! But he found the business with the 'admiral' so amusing that he passed you over. Don't you know who it was you were talking to?" "No, how should I know?" said Mother. Then he said, "That was Himmler!"

In Mulhouse, we had a lot of acquaintances, Jehovah's Witnesses, who were sent to concentration camps or displaced to southern France. Four of them were imprisoned with my father, five with my mother. Of those, an older man by the name of Huber never came back. My childhood friend Marcel Sutter was beheaded for refusing to do military service.

In 1956, I married Max Liebster, a Shoah survivor. He had been arrested as a Jew in Pforzheim in Germany on September 11, 1939, and spent four months in solitary confinement in the prison in that town. He was transported in a train divided into cells, manacled to another prisoner. This prisoner was one of Jehovah's Witnesses. During this transport, which lasted many days, Max found out a lot about the Bible. They were interned in Sachsenhausen concentration camp where, in the separate barracks for Jews, he discovered his father who was dying. Bernhard Liebster died a short time later. Max had to carry his own father into the crematorium. All his life he "carried" the weight of his father on his shoulders. That was some burden to bear. After that, he was sent to Neuengamme where Jehovah's Witnesses were sometimes able to share rabbit food[9] with him and continued to share the Bible's teachings with him. In the end, in 1943, all the Jews had to go to Auschwitz-Birkenau. He was put in Buna camp and had to help establish the Buna Werke (Buna Works). After the death march from Buna in January 1945, his internment, which lasted nearly six years, ended in Buchenwald. There he met another Jew, Fritz Heikorn, who was also studying the Bible with Jehovah's Witnesses. The two of them were baptized as Jehovah's Witnesses in Buchenwald during liberation by the Americans.

65. What happened to your possessions?
LIEBSTER: Thanks to the threefold sealing of our apartment by the factory, the Gestapo, and the youth welfare department, our possessions were protected.

66. To what extent have you received compensation for your internment?
LIEBSTER: None at all because Constance was not on the Red Cross list. The authorities drew up a list. No home for juveniles was on it. That's why I never received any compensation. The French government awarded me the minimum pension for the physical injuries I received as a French national deported by the Germans. It scarcely covers my medication.

67. How did you set about rebuilding your life?
LIEBSTER: It was very difficult because I had completed no apprenticeship and could not go back to school either. Luckily, thanks to my particular aptitude, I was able to attend art school for two years; and afterward, I worked in the same factory my father worked in. In 1952, I fulfilled my wish to become a missionary when I was able to attend "Gilead School" in the United States. I still carry out this activity today.

---

9   The SS officers raised rabbits for food, and Jehovah's Witnesses were assigned to look after the animals. They sometimes smuggled rabbit feed to give to starving fellow prisoners.

68. How long did it take you to return to a "normal" life after the Holocaust?

LIEBSTER: It took the family two to three years to regain our equilibrium. When Papa was arrested, I was a vivacious, happy eleven-year-old. When he came back, he was so weak that he was close to dying. He found a withdrawn fifteen-year-old daughter who showed no initiative. We didn't talk to each other about what we had suffered and experienced. It was too hard. We would not have been able to bear knowing exactly what the others had been through. We kept it to ourselves in our respective corners. Why cause the others moral anguish after the event? In addition, we needed of a lot of time-consuming nursing to regain our strength. What helped us to reestablish a happy family life was the religious activities we undertook together: reading and studying the Bible, attending conventions, and visiting people with the Bible.

69. What was your life like after the war?

LIEBSTER: As soon as I was back home, I started carrying out Christian activities with my family. Through them, the wish to attend missionary school took shape. I valiantly learned English because the school was in the United States. In the meantime, I worked part-time as a fabric designer. At the age of twenty, I went to New York, and in 1952, I was invited to attend "Gilead School." I had met Max Liebster for the first time in 1950, and he was working at the Jehovah's Witnesses' headquarters in New York as a typesetter. Six years later, we met each other again. At that time, he was attending the missionary school. We got married in 1956 in Paris. We devoted our entire lives to missionary work in France and helped people to get to know the Bible. In France, the association CETJAD [Cercle Européen des Témoins de Jéhovah Anciens Deportés et Internés, foundation of formerly deported and interned Jehovah's Witnesses] was founded. I was its representative, and in the 1990s, we began examining the Holocaust. As trilingual witnesses of history, Max and I visited many exhibitions and schools in France, Germany, Italy, Belgium, England, Spain, Canada, Russia, the United States, and Switzerland and spoke about our experiences. When Max was ninety-one years old and no longer able to travel, we learned to hold video conferences on Skype with schools in the United States. We both published our biographies too. Max's is called *Crucible of Terror: A Story of Survival through the Nazi Storm*; mine, *Facing the Lion*.

70. What is your life like today? Do you still often think back to those days?

LIEBSTER: Max passed away at the age of ninety-three. I'm now in the process of reorganizing my life and would like to start visiting schools again.

32: Simone and Max Liebster, 1979

It depends on how my health develops. I'm not as young as I used to be and not as fit as I was twenty years ago. Sometimes I have very vivid dreams that make me feel that I'm back in the home. There was a time when my dreams of Constance were extremely vivid: "Now you've been arrested for the third time." And recently I dreamed, "Now you've been arrested for the fourth time and are back in the home for the fourth time." But in the morning, I wake up and say to myself, "Oh good, it was only a dream!" So it doesn't bother me.

71. What physical and mental scars do you carry from that time?

LIEBSTER: I'm pretty sure that much of the pain I have in my joints and back is the result of sawing wood, digging out roots, and carrying heavy loads. I was only fourteen at the time. Now and again I need silence and don't want to talk. I am sometimes affected by negative feelings about my self-worth, and now and then I have another nightmare about Constance. This shows that the past has also left mental scars.

72. Did you have any moral support to help your emotional and social recovery?

LIEBSTER: I had no support from any individual because most people had absolutely no idea what lay behind us. Reading the Bible gave us moral support. The feeling of having done the right thing was very valuable too. We very much appreciated our victory over those who persecuted us, which was only possible through God's strength. We always spoke of that with gratitude. Max suffered a lot more and saw far worse things than I did. Although the only time we ever spoke about it was when we attended events, we understood each other's feelings and bad moods. We were able to help each other, understand each other well, and give each other support. If he saw I was uncommunicative, he didn't say, "Now what's the matter? Why don't you say something?" He knew exactly why it was. If he was very restless at night or suddenly said, "I'm worthless!" which, especially with Max, happened often because he was a Jew and the Nazis had drilled it into him, repeatedly saying, "You're worthless!" I knew exactly where it came from and was able to offer him support. So we encouraged each other a great deal. There were some nights when Max suffered greatly from epileptic fits.

73. Has your view of the world changed since that time?

LIEBSTER: It has become deeper. Not different, but deeper. What I learned as a child has, for me, proved true. In the course of the years it has become deeper, or bigger, or broader, or [something like that]. It has become much clearer how God's laws help imperfect human beings to live in peace.

74. Can you think of anything positive that you have gained from your experiences?

LIEBSTER: Everything you go through has a lesson that can teach you something worthwhile. The great lesson I learned is the absolute necessity of searching for fundamental principles before following an ideology. Again and again people chase an ideal for the sole reason that someone has a strong personality and charisma. But they don't look for the motive, and even less often do they ask whether the proposed ideology is compatible with God's law. But when a person follows a human ideology, then that's all it is: a human one. It has limits and can never evolve into an entirely positive set of principles. Every person has only his or her own perception, and the perspective it opens up is necessarily limited. Through my personal experiences, I have seen and felt how people can be misled. These experiences helped me again and again to make decisions in the light of Bible principles, and that brings peace and joy.

When I went to Constance, my mother said to me, "Child, now you are going to a greater school. It will educate you for life. What you experience there will be of use to you for the rest of your life." Once I was in Constance, I always thought, "My goodness, what on earth is all this now? Now I have to cook for thirty-six children. What good will this be in my life?" Somehow I didn't understand. But afterward, I thought, "Yes, it really was a lesson: a lesson in taking care how you do things, staying polite under pressure, remaining flexible without giving in, and putting strong convictions into practice in a peaceful way." I learned all of that, and those are values I have benefited from all my life. It really was a valuable education.

75. Have you ever been back to visit the concentration camp [home] you were held in, and if so, what were your feelings?

LIEBSTER: Yes, I visited the home twice. One time I visited it with my husband after the war, and I met the teacher Fräulein Messinger again. Fräulein Lederle had died; the others had left. My heart was thumping a little the first time. Fräulein Messinger was so edgy that I felt sorry for her. She thought I had come for revenge, which of course I hadn't.

76. Are you still in touch with your fellow inmates from the concentration camps [home]?

LIEBSTER: After the war, I was in touch with Sophie, who had the bed next to mine. But it didn't last long. Sophie told me that her father was a customs officer and her mother was Jewish. When the law against Jews came into force, the customs officer no longer wanted to raise his child because she had Jewish blood. Sophie had blond hair, but dark brown eyes. It was thought possible to make a Teuton out of her, so she was sent to Constance. Once the war had ended, when she was sixteen, her father came to pick her up and told her why she had been put in the home. It was such a shock to her that she contracted diabetes and died in the 1950s.

77. What did you tell your family about your internment in the concentration camp [home]? How did your relatives react to what you told them?

LIEBSTER: My relatives wanted nothing to do with the three of us, and I never said anything to Papa and Mama out of consideration for them. So they didn't know the full story. My biography had not yet been written. Initially I wanted to call my book *Closed Shutters* because I never spoke about it, but in the end, the title *Facing the Lion* was chosen.

78. Do you find it difficult to talk about those days?

LIEBSTER: I could say yes, I could say no. "No" when my intention is to communicate something that can help other people. "Yes" when I think of myself. So I have to be aware of myself and the standpoint I'm speaking from.

79. Which moment from those days has remained most firmly etched in your memory?

LIEBSTER: None from the time in Constance. What has remained most firmly etched in my memory is my father's arrest and the threat of my own arrest that came with it. All three of us were engaged in underground activities. All the publications of the Watch Tower Society were strictly forbidden. We had a French courier who met us at a secret location in a cave near a lake in the Vosges Mountains. *The Watchtower* was in French and had to be translated. I knew where the translations were done and under what conditions. Copies were distributed further afield, reaching as far as Freiburg. It was very dangerous to have this kind of literature at home. It meant constant vigilance: making sure no informers were tailing us and the Gestapo was not watching us. Those are the experiences I remember most clearly.

80. Did you ever see or meet Hitler?

LIEBSTER: I saw him once, just glimpsed him. I was cycling with a friend of mine in woods near Mulhouse in Alsace. And then the distinguished visitor, Hitler, came by. He was driving very slowly because he was driving through [surveying potassium] mines—Alsace is a very wealthy region [in natural resources]. We hid ourselves under a bush. Straightaway I said, "Listen, we will not salute him. That could be really dangerous." So we hid under a bush, and to make matters worse, it was a thorn bush, and we really felt it. And then I saw him. He passed, between twenty and thirty feet from us, standing in the usual way and gazing around, enjoying being master of all these mines. "Demon eyes," that's what I always remember. Every time I saw a high-ranking officer, I always saw the "demon's eyes" beneath the cap, even though the man may not have had them. But these "demon's eyes" went right through me. There was something in his eyes. Although, he didn't see me, much to our good fortune.

81. What was your opinion of Hitler in those days, and what is your opinion of him now?

LIEBSTER: My feeling is the same now as it was then. I saw, and still see, an arrogant man who committed crimes and claimed to be a messiah, a savior. His ideals cost millions of people their lives because he was not the savior he claimed to be.

82. Hypothetically, if Adolf Hitler were still alive and you could have five minutes alone with him, what would you say or do?

LIEBSTER: I would do nothing and say nothing and look at him the way he looked at the world: in the eye. It's God who passes judgment, not me. Say something to that man? For me he is nothing. I would remain silent.

83. After the war, did you ever meet any of the people who had tormented you?

LIEBSTER: I never met the Gestapo men or my teachers. Except for the teacher Fräulein Messinger, who made my life "a little" miserable in Constance, whom I saw three times. I discovered that there were documents in the archives in Constance, and I was given them. I asked someone to make inquiries and was sent Fräulein Messinger's address. My friends visited her, and after she had read my account of my life in the magazine *Awake!,* she said, "But you must be on your guard, the child talks nonsense. Maria was just a child then." When I heard that, I straightaway wrote her a detailed account, without accusing anyone of anything. I recounted to her the exact details of the time she cross-examined me to try to find out the names of Jehovah's Witnesses in Mulhouse.

In Constance I never mentioned Mulhouse to avoid accidentally revealing any names. Suddenly, she started mentioning names that I was supposed to verify. I was able to get around it without lying. She asked about a man whose name was Arzt, which means "doctor," and I answered, "I know a lot of doctors." After a while, she said, "But you surely know Graf!" That was the name of the meeting overseer and underground *Watchtower* translator, and it means "count," as in nobleman. So I said to her, "Well, my acquaintances don't extend to counts!" That, of course, made her angry and nervous. I knew the Gestapo was looking for him. Most likely she asked this question on the orders of the Gestapo. That then proved to me that she was a snake. I realized that I would never be able to speak openly to her, and I thought, "Watch out what you say to her!"

In 1997, when I wrote that long letter, I told her that I was unable to confirm those two names back then because otherwise I would have been to blame for their arrest. When I met Fräulein Messinger the following year, 1998, she recognized me at once, although she was ninety years old. "Maria, it's you. Did you write that letter? Can you still write such good German?" she asked. "It's not that good," I replied. "But *you* didn't finish it, did you?" she said. "Yes, it's possible that I forgot to send you the last page," I answered, "It was seven pages in all. But I can tell you exactly what was on the last page." Then I recited the last part of this seven-page letter to her. She realized that it really was I who had written the letter, and that made her very nervous. She said, "Do you need money? I can give you money, if that's what you need." I naturally declined and said, "That's not why I came. I came to give you this." I offered her a book for Bible study. Later, I met her again when we had an exhibition in Constance and took her another book on Bible subjects. I knew that she was deeply Catholic, and I thought she may want to open the Bible one day.

84. What do you think of the punishments the Nazis received after the war, in the Nuremberg trials, for example?
LIEBSTER: From a human point of view, they got what they deserved. But it is not the place of a Christian to judge. But, after all, the principle exists that says we reap what we sow.

85. Have you forgiven your persecutors?
LIEBSTER: A Christian must not bear hatred toward any other human being. He does not know what lies deep in another's heart. He doesn't know whether his persecutors were misled or got carried away. So a Christian must not take revenge. The Bible says explicitly that vengeance is God's and God's alone, not man's.

86. What is your opinion of neo-Nazis?

LIEBSTER: The Nazis prided themselves on discipline, loyalty to the fatherland, and devotion to the Führer. I can understand why this kind of ideology becomes popular again. It has always been that way. Throughout history, there have repeatedly been people who revived a past ideology and found something good about it because they didn't judge it according to the fundamental principles of the Bible, but rather according to emotions and personal feelings. What's the good of discipline if there is no love or justice? Is someone who demands unconditional obedience as a leader and places himself over others really worth emulating?

87. What do you do to explain to people what exactly happened in the Holocaust?

LIEBSTER: We already did a lot. We were involved in many exhibitions. We set up a website [www.alst.org] and established a foundation, the Arnold-Liebster Foundation. Its purpose is to continue to remember victims of dictatorships and religious persecution. This should help young people see clearly what leads to good and what can lead to evil. The website has already been used in schools in the United States and will continue to be used. I'm gradually getting older and won't be able to speak in person for much longer, but with the site, we have made sure that the life stories are documented and passed on.

88. From today's perspective, how can you explain that "normal people" were capable of such atrocities?

LIEBSTER: We need to ask ourselves where atrocities come from. Atrocities appear when a person develops character traits such as hatred, pride, or discrimination without self-control. If such feelings exist in a heart, wicked deeds and damage will result. People just have to learn to examine themselves to see whether they have any tendencies of this kind. If they have, they must fight them with all their might so that they can control themselves under pressure. That is a real challenge for every one of us.

89. What exactly do you feel when you hear that there are still people who claim that the Holocaust never took place?

LIEBSTER: It's not easy to hear such things, but I can understand it because there will always be people who refuse to accept reality. There have always been people like that throughout history. All kinds of things that happened in the past have been denied: "That didn't exist and that's not true!" because they simply don't investigate. They are biased, they don't want to admit it, and then they shout all the more. They are quite convinced and want to convince others too. We find them not only in relation to the Holocaust, but in every context: people who do not search for the truth and just rigidly and stubbornly follow their own ideas without checking them. They categorically reject anything that doesn't fit in with their ideology. It makes me sad that there are people who are misled in this way.

90. What consequences did the proclamation of the "Nuremberg Laws" on September 15, 1935, have for you?

LIEBSTER: The Nuremberg Laws had no consequences for me personally because we were accepted as "Imperial Germans." Alsatians were so-called "Imperial Germans" who came home again. But that wasn't the case for my husband, Max, who was a German-born Jew.

91. What are your personal memories of the "Night of Broken Glass" on November 9/10, 1938?

LIEBSTER: I was eight years old and didn't hear much about it, because we were French. When we became German in 1940, the synagogue was set on fire. For Max, the Night of Broken Glass was the start of the terror. The textile store where Max worked was plundered of its entire stock during the Night of Broken Glass. The proprietor and Max guessed what was coming and managed to hide in the woods before it happened. When they returned, everything was smashed, stolen, gone. Max then went into hiding in someone's house. Ten months later, he was found there and arrested.

His two sisters, Ida and Hannah, and his mother, Babette, were able to flee the country in 1938, but his father could not. He was sent to Sachsenhausen concentration camp.

92. What are your personal memories of the beginning of the war in 1939?

LIEBSTER: I was still young, nine years old, but the shock in Alsace was very great because we were in the border zone. The Alsatians thought the troops would come over the Rhine. In the end, the Germans came via Paris, round the back way. But the fear of war had gripped Alsace because it had been through two wars in the space of seventy years: from 1914 to

1918 and in 1870. In the same area, in one generation, there was now a third major war. So there was a lot happening: anxieties, people fleeing, the black market, and concealing [hoarding], all amid great fear.

93. Did you hear that the National Socialists had decided to implement the "final solution to the Jewish question"—the systematic extermination of Jews in Europe—at the Wannsee Conference on January 20, 1942? If so, when and how?

LIEBSTER: I didn't hear about that until after the war. During the war, we were battling our own difficult situation, the persecution of Jehovah's Witnesses.

94. When you heard that World War II was over, what feelings did you have?

LIEBSTER: The end of World War II was a release. But in Alsace, there was a period of bitter retribution. Those who had collaborated with the Nazis paid a very high price for it. In some cases, they were stripped, driven around naked on hay wagons, their heads were shaved, and they were jeered and insulted. Shortly after the war, there was still a lot of unrest in Alsace. It took some time to calm those waves of malice and for the situation to die down. There were still hard times afterward. Apart from that, there was a lot of bomb damage. People had nothing to eat. The war may have been over, but the aftermath was terrible.

95. Do you think that humankind has learned something from the Holocaust?

LIEBSTER: People have learned something, humankind has not. Individuals, and even groups of people, have definitely learned something, but humankind has not. What is required is a change of heart, and humankind, as a whole, can't accomplish that so easily. There will be no miracle in this case. It requires teaching, persuasion, and consequently, time. It would be utopian to say that humankind now has a set of principles and that a transformation is in progress. That kind of thing is simply impossible. The Bible has another answer, and people must look for it.

96. Should the atrocities be forgotten and no longer talked about, as some people wish?

LIEBSTER: What's the use of talking about atrocities? Or what do we achieve when we don't talk about them? Those are two different questions. It depends what you wish to learn. If you want to know how these atrocities were perpetrated, you'll leave well alone. But if you want to know why people commit atrocities, you'll find a useful lesson. Unfortunately, past and recent history show that deeds of this kind keep surfacing and are sometimes performed by those of whom we would least expect it. Let's take the Inquisition as an example. How did that come about? Through false teachings. So teachings are the foundation of atrocities, and these false teachings must be remembered as a warning.

97. What plans do you still have for the future?

LIEBSTER: What plans? Well, to carry on as I have been doing since I was liberated: helping as many people as possible to find inner peace through a sound understanding of God's word so that they see where human values are to be found, how they can promote peace—peace with themselves, peace with their neighbors, peace with God—real peace. And as long as I can still talk, I will continue to do so. I want to help people to be happy, as I am, because I'm very content. All in all, I have lived a positive life that I don't regret. It's a good path. I can recommend it to everyone.

98. How would you like to be remembered?

LIEBSTER: As a meek, simple woman who tried to give her fellow men and women something of value. That's all.

99. What else would you like to say to us? Which question was not asked?

LIEBSTER: There isn't much left that wasn't asked. I would say this is a good summary. Maybe one could ask, "Who has the best ideals, and what about human rights? Where can they be found?" Human rights have their roots in the moral values we find in the Bible: "Love your neighbor as yourself." Every one of us is invited to take a deeper look.

100. After all you have been through, what advice can you give us young people?

LIEBSTER: That's a very nice question. Well, I would say, "Make sure you know what you are standing on." That's why you must know exactly what the ground is made up of. The ground is the past; it's the lessons, values, human values. What do they stand for? Are they just? Are they right? Do they contain love? Do they contain positive effects for the people around us? Does it bring peace? Does it bring solidarity between people? Does it unite them?

If so, your conscience is trained, and then you must try to follow your conscience. Because there is nothing worse, nothing more evil, than a bad conscience. You have to carry it around with you all your life. But if you see beforehand which path is the right path, and if you stay on it, you get through life and can always say, "I have a clear conscience and did what I should." That's what I wish you, because that's what counts: that your life is a good life. [Having] good relationships and a happy life depends on the decisions you make now. Decide according to good principles.

Hermine Liska:
An Eight-Year-Old Stands Her Ground

Hermine Liska, née Obweger, born April 12, 1930
Grounds for persecution: One of Jehovah's Witnesses (Bible Student)
Length of imprisonment: 4 years, 3 months
Country: Austria

33. Hermine Liska, 1940   *34. Hermine Liska, 2008*

Hermine Liska, née Obweger, was born on April 12, 1930, on her parents' farm in St. Walburgen in Carinthia, Austria. As a child of Bible Students, as Jehovah's Witnesses were then known, she was raised in accordance with the principles of the Bible. She refused to join the Hitler Youth and use the greeting "Heil Hitler!" Because her father did not sign the order issued by the Nazi juvenile court that obliged him to bring Hermine up in the Nazi ideology, her parents' right to raise their children was revoked. In February 1941, Hermine Liska was taken away from her parents.

She was sent to the Waiern home for juveniles[10] in Carinthia and the Adelgunden institute[11] in Munich. Hermine Liska remained true to her principles, and after completing the mandatory year of community service for girls at an inn with a small farm in Carinthia, she was able to return home on May 8, 1945. After the war, she married, had three children, and became a housewife. Since 1999, she has visited schools all over Austria as a witness of history and every year tells as many as thirteen thousand students her story. Hermine Liska lives in Austria.

The interviews took place on October 26, 2008; June 19, 2011; June 23, 2011; August 12, 2011; August 19, 2011; and October 10, 2011.

---

[10] The Waiern home is often referred to by the term "reform school" by Mrs. Liska. Questions addressing internment in concentration camps are modified to incorporate the term "[home]."

[11] The Adelgunden institute was a youth welfare home administered by an order of Catholic nuns and is sometimes referred to by Mrs. Liska as a "convent." In question 13, Mrs. Liska explains why this institution was a "reeducation center" in her case. In answers referring to her internment, in addition to the terms "convent" and "reform school," Mrs. Liska uses the term "home" to refer to either institution, and the context will clarify which institution is referred to—the Waiern home or the Adelgunden institute.

1. When were you born? What was your father like? What was your mother like?

LISKA: I was born on April 12, 1930, on my parents' farm in St. Walburgen in the Görtschitztal valley in Carinthia, Austria. I had four brothers: Hansl [Johann], born in 1914; Peppi [Josef], born in 1920; Michael, born in 1925; and Franz, born in 1926. I was the youngest. Another brother died in infancy before World War I. Michael died on December 31, 1939, of a burst appendix. My parents weren't exactly young when I was born. My mother, Elisabeth Obweger [née Peitler, born 1888], was forty-two, and my father, Johann Obweger [born 1886], was two years older.

35. *Hermine's mother, Elisabeth Obweger, ca. 1950*

My father was extremely good-natured. He didn't say much, but what he said always hit the nail on the head. I remember that he read a lot, an awful lot. Sitting at the table, he would either read the Bible, Bible literature, or magazines about bees or agriculture. He had a great many beehives. Yes, I have happy memories of my father. He never hit us. He was a very peaceable man. I never saw him angry.

36. *Hermine's father, Johann Obweger, ca. 1950*

My mama was the opposite, but I never saw them quarrel. They never argued. I'm sure they had differences of opinion, but they never let them show in front of us children. I was very close to my mother. Yet she never mollycoddled me. I only had brothers, and I was always with them, up every tree, and today I know that she was afraid for me.

2. What is your earliest childhood memory?

LISKA: I hadn't started school yet, though I must have already been five years old, when my grandmother died. She was my father's mother. We lived in Lower Carinthia. For the funeral, I went with my father to Upper Carinthia for the first time, to his parents' farm high up the mountain in Kleblach-Lind in Siflitz in the Drautal [valley]. In the farmhouse parlor, there was a tiled stove that took up nearly half the room. A fire was burning in this stove, and I slept on top of it. So I can remember that, that's my earliest childhood memory. I can't remember the funeral at all.

3. What kind of childhood did you have?

LISKA: I have only vague memories of the time before I started school. I only know that it was great fun at home because at that time a lot of people lived on the farm. It was a large family. My mother took in three nieces who had lost one of their parents; we had our grandmother living there too, and she always told us stories. By the way, whenever Mama came for us with a switch, we ran to our grandmother. She had a long skirt and hid us under it, protecting us from the switch. Those are things I still recall. There was no machinery on the farm in those days, so we had farmhands and maids. Right from the start, we had to help our parents with the work. My mama did most of the cooking and fed the pigs too. I always wanted to do something to help her.

4. How long did you go to school, and what schools did you attend?

LISKA: I completed eight years of primary school, and after the war, I attended the home economics school in Klagenfurt for two years. There's one incident from my first grade at primary school that I still remember. I wasn't Catholic, and the parish priest used to come and teach our class a couple of times a week. When he came, I either left the room or didn't go in. But one time I forgot. He was already in the room, and I didn't dare stand up anymore. He started talking, then all at once, he noticed me and said, "Get out, heathen child!" Nonetheless, at that time I got on really well with the other children.

5. What was your adolescence like? What trade did you learn, and what did you do for a living?

LISKA: Originally I wanted to be a teacher, but because I didn't use the "Heil Hitler!" greeting, I was barred from any higher education. After the war, I wanted to be a kindergarten teacher, but I couldn't do that either.

The training would have taken three years, but because my mother had fallen ill, I had to return home in 1948. I stayed at home until 1952, the year my brother Franz got married, and I got married that year too. From then on, I was a housewife. So I never learned a trade.

6. What can you tell us about your family?

LISKA: Maybe I had better start with World War I. My father was called up in 1914 and was sent to the front. Two years later, he was wounded and, owing to this injury, was captured by the Russians. He was held captive by the Russians for six years and still had a piece of shrapnel in his back. He was in constant pain. He came home in 1922.

In Russia, he was given a German Bible to read while he was with German farmers in Siberia, and he realized that the teachings of the Catholic Church were wrong. When he came home, he started telling others that hell and purgatory didn't exist. Then he came into contact with Bible Students, because there was a postman who was a Bible Student in Upper Carinthia. His name was Richard Heide. Having gained more knowledge of the Bible, he immediately resigned his membership in the Catholic Church and didn't have my two brothers baptized, who were born in 1925 and 1926. Nowadays we can scarcely imagine what a serious matter it was back then to leave the church and tell people what was in the Bible. He had enormous difficulties. Today, I must say that I have nothing but admiration for my father because it really required tremendous courage. Because of these difficulties and problems, which were caused by his brothers and sisters and other relatives who lived round about, he decided to sell the farm in Upper Carinthia, and in 1928, he moved to Lower Carinthia. There he bought the "Lassnig" farm in St. Walburgen. It was probably a little easier for him that way.

And my mother? There's one story I've never told before. I don't even know whether I should. It's such a tragedy. When my father joined the army in 1914, my brother Hansl was four months old. In 1916, Father was wounded, and my mother didn't receive any more letters from him. He was declared missing, and she had a mountain farm to look after, with alpine pastures as well. Then she met another man and, in 1920, had a son with him. That was Peppi. She wanted to marry this man because, officially, Father was missing. My mother had to declare my father dead, which she did in 1922. And then, having been missing for eight years, he came home again. He went to pick up his own declaration of death from the post office. Just imagine how tragic it all was. We never spoke about it. My sister-in-law told me about it after my mother died, though my father was still alive at the time.

I married Erich Liska in 1952 and had three children: Margit in 1953, Angelina in 1958, and Andreas in 1963. My husband found work in Styria, near Graz. He worked for the firm of Payer-Lux, at first repairing electric razors, and later becoming the plant manager. Sadly, Erich died in February 2002.

7. Did you use the Nazi greeting "Heil Hitler!" and/or the Nazi salute?
LISKA: Although it was compulsory, I never used the greeting "Heil Hitler!" and that's why my problems started.

8. Why were you persecuted by the National Socialists?
LISKA: My parents were Bible Students, as Jehovah's Witnesses were then called, and we were all raised according to the teachings of Christianity. They really set us an example of a Christian way of life and lived entirely in accordance with their faith. When Hitler invaded on March 12, 1938, my problems started the very next day. All the pupils were in the yard; the flag with the swastika was already flying. The principal took up his position in front of the flag and held a speech to the effect that the dark days of unemployment were now over. "Everyone will be given work. No one will have to go hungry anymore; the farmers will truly flourish. In short," he said, "a golden age is ahead of us, and we owe it all to the Führer, Adolf Hitler." He finished by stressing that, "Now, when we arrive in school, we will no longer say 'Good morning' or 'Good afternoon.' From now on, the only proper greeting is 'Heil Hitler!' with the arm extended." But our parents had told us not to use this greeting. Why not? Because the Bible says that salvation, which is what *Heil* means in German, comes from Christ alone and not from any person. But this greeting—"Heil Hitler!"—meant a great deal more than merely wishing someone a "Good morning." In practice, using this greeting meant you had joined the body of National Socialists. It was their visible trademark.

Afterward, when I went into the school building—the classrooms were upstairs on the second floor—the principal was standing by the stairs, and I said, "Good morning, sir!" He said, "Hermine, go back out again, then come in and greet me properly, with the Hitler salute." So I obediently went out, came back in, and said, "Good morning," again. Well, in time I did get a little smarter. I just waited until the bell had rung and went in at the last moment hoping the principal wouldn't be standing there anymore. That was a bit easier, but it soon got worse again because some of the pupils began to make fun of me. One girl, for example, said to me, "Oh, you're a Bible Student," in a very disparaging tone. Another one said, "You're a Jew." At that time, if someone said to you, "You're a Jew or a Jewess," that was absolutely the worst thing they could say. One boy said, "Your brother Hansl ought to be hanged because he refused to train for military service."

37. *Hermine Liska, 1940*

That was very, very hurtful to me because it was a very small school. Everyone knew everyone else. In the winter, we small ones would go sledding with the bigger kids, and now they didn't let me do that anymore. At the end of each gym class, we were allowed to play dodgeball. Now I was excluded from that too. On the first report card I got after that—I was in second grade, I was eight years old—I got a six in conduct. Up to that time, we had only had four grades; under Hitler, there were six, and I had gotten the lowest one on my report card. When we turned ten, we all automatically had to join the Hitler Youth; but I didn't do that either.

When I began fifth grade—that was the class taught by the principal—he said, "Hermine, pack your things and go back to first grade. I don't need a hardhead like you in this class." So he sent me back down. The first-graders were in the same room. The school in St. Walburgen only had two classrooms: we spent four years in the first one, and four years in the second one. So in reality, he moved me down to the fourth grade again.

In January 1941, my father had to appear before the juvenile court. He was presented with a document prepared by the Nazis for Bible Students. It was intended to make them renounce their faith, and my father was supposed to sign it. But the document prepared for him included a rider stipulating that he had to raise his children according to Nazi ideas. He didn't sign it. As a result, he was told that he and my mother had forfeited the right to raise children and I would be taken away and put in a Nazi reform school for reeducation.

9. When were you arrested?
LISKA: I wasn't arrested; I was a child of eleven. But I was taken away at the beginning of February 1941 by a woman from the welfare services in St. Veit.

10. Why were you imprisoned?
LISKA: I was taken away from my parents' house because my parents were Bible Students and had given me a Christian upbringing. Also, I did not use the greeting "Heil Hitler!" and did not join the Hitler Youth. My father didn't sign the document saying that he had given up his faith and would raise his children the Nazi way. That's why I was taken away from my parents.

11. What exactly happened when you were arrested?
LISKA: You can't call it an arrest, but at the beginning of February 1941, I was taken away at the crack of dawn by a woman. This woman was a welfare worker. We took the train to St. Veit, changed trains, and went on to Feldkirchen. There, at the top of a hill, was the Waiern reform school.

12. Did people know right from the start what was happening in the camps? Before you were taken away, did you know what would happen to you?
LISKA: My parents already knew there were concentration camps, and Dachau was very well-known in Carinthia. For example, if someone made a joke about the Nazi system, a neighbor would say, "Hey, watch out, or you'll end up in Dachau!" So it was well-known as a labor camp. I'm sure that my parents knew more than other people did, having read the literature of Jehovah's Witnesses.

I knew there was an extremely strict regime at the reform school I was being sent to, because while I was still at home, I had to learn to fold my underwear and sweaters nicely. We had a locker at the school, and everything had to be folded up very neat and tidy. But my mother had already taught me that at home.

13. How many different camps [homes] were you in? How many years did you spend in each one?

LISKA: In February 1941, I arrived in Waiern, in Feldkirchen in Carinthia. For me, it was a "reform school" because I was supposed to be reeducated there. For the others, it was a home for young people. In September 1941, I was sent to the Adelgunden institute in Munich. I regarded it as a "convent" because it was run by Catholic nuns, and the man in charge was a priest. Officially it was an orphanage run by the Catholic youth welfare department of the archdiocese of Munich and Freising. For me, it was a "reeducation center" like Waiern, since I had been sent there to be educated according to the ideology of the National Socialists. I stayed there until the summer of 1943. Because Munich was frequently bombed at that time, and we often had to go to the air-raid shelter as a result, all the children up to the age of fourteen were evacuated from Munich during vacation in 1943. I went back there at the end of March 1944.

Our beds were in the basement shelter, and every night there were terrible air raids. When my parents heard that Munich was being bombed so often, they wrote endless petitions to have me sent back to Carinthia. Before I was allowed to go home again, on April 29, 1944, I personally experienced a terrifying raid.

In those days, when a girl left school, she had to do a mandatory year of community service. Farmers' daughters were allowed to do the year at home, and my mother applied so that I could do mine at home too. The application was rejected. In May 1944, I was taken away again and placed with an older married couple by the name of Langsteger. They ran an inn and a small farm in Lambichl in the municipality of Köttmannsdorf near Klagenfurt. That's where I spent the last year of the war, until May 8, 1945, when the war ended, and I was able to return home again at last.

14. Were you the only member of your family in the concentration camp [home], or were family members or friends there as well? If so, did you have any contact with them?

LISKA: I was alone in the institutions, and visiting was not allowed. Despite that, my father secretly visited me several times on my way to school, cheering me up each time. Then, because I hadn't changed, or "improved," so to speak, they sent me further away, to Munich. They said that the influence of my parents was still too strong. I have no doubt that they had noticed those visits.

But in Munich, I had visits too, this time from my brother Hansl. He visited me once with "Aunt" Julie. We were even allowed to go to the zoo. That I was allowed to go was really something exceptional.

15. What were the first things that happened immediately following your arrival at the concentration camp [home]?

LISKA: Following my arrival in Waiern, they sat me down in the large common room where the ten to fourteen-year-old girls were assembled. So I just sat there and cried. Then a girl came up to me, comforted me, and said, "Don't cry. It's fun here, you'll see." Her name was Judith.

In front of the home, there was the roll-call square. Every Sunday, we had to line up there and salute the flag. But I didn't join in; I hid in the toilet because I didn't want to be noticed and didn't want to line up. I wanted to make sure they didn't see me not saluting the flag. But then two girls came looking for me. They found me and said, "Hermine, you have to come out and line up!" So I had no choice but to go out, and I lined up with the girls, in the back row. There were three or four rows of girls, and facing us were the boys; there were boys in Waiern as well. The woman in charge of the home was standing on the left between these two groups, and on the right was the flagpole. The girls pushed me forward into the front row. Then someone called, "*Achtung!*" There was dead silence. Everyone raised their right hands except me. Then the woman in charge of the home yelled, "Hermine, raise your hand!" And because I didn't do it, the girl on my right, and the one behind me, tried to push my hand up, which didn't really work. I was punished for that. At midday I had to go without dessert, and it was pudding. Today we might say, "What's so great about pudding?" But in those days, we really looked forward to such a delicious dessert all week long, so it was a punishment that hit home.

Also, being exposed like that in front of all those children, whom I didn't really know yet, was a distressing experience.

16. Why did they shave the heads of the prisoners [inmates]?
LISKA: I can't answer that; I don't know. But when I went to the "convent" in Munich, they immediately cut off my braids, and really short too. I think that was to punish me, because the other girls were allowed to keep theirs. Normally, the Germans were proud of braids, especially if you were blonde.

17. What prisoner [inmate] category were you put in?
LISKA: I was one of those who were persecuted. Of course, there were various different groups, but at the time, I didn't really know what they were.

18. Can you describe the daily routine in the concentration camp [home]?
LISKA: We were woken up early in the morning: "Get out of bed, wash, get dressed, make your beds!" After breakfast, we practically "marched" to school. That was strictly regimented too. We all had to keep together. You couldn't go just anytime or anywhere. After school, we all had to go home again together. Then we had our meal and had to do our homework. After that, we might be allowed to play for a little while or go into the yard. We had to go to bed very early after our evening meal. Once we were in bed, we weren't allowed to talk anymore. There had to be silence. Talking was not permitted while we were eating, either. We could talk on the way to school, but in the "convent," very little talking was allowed.

19. What was the worst thing about the daily routine?
LISKA: In Waiern, bedtime was the worst thing. It was in Waiern that I missed my mama most, because I went there in February 1941, and it was the coldest winter for many years. We ten to fourteen-year-olds slept together in a dormitory. Everything was spotless and tidy. We had to clean the room ourselves, and every week we had to go under the beds as well. The bedstead had iron springs, and we had to dust them and wipe them. Although there was a stove in the corner, a tall tiled stove, I don't know if it was ever lit because it was dreadfully cold. Sure, we had a blanket and a pillow, but the bed was very cold compared to the one at home. What made matters worse was that up to the age of eleven, I slept in Mama's

bed. Until I was taken away from my parents, I had slept with my mama in her bed. She was a little plump, and it was just so warm and cozy in bed with her. I did get my own bed when I started school, though. At the foot of my parents' bed, there was a divan, and I was put to bed there. But I kept sneaking into Mama's bed because she was so soft and warm. I didn't even need a pillow; her right hand was my pillow. In fact, I really slept in her arms.

When I think about it now, it was actually very hard on her because she was the first to get up: at half past four. She never took an afternoon nap, was the last one to go to bed, and at night I was with her. And an eleven-year-old is quite big. But she never made me get out. Probably because she feared that I would be taken away from her. That's why it was so hard for me in Waiern.

20. Did everyday life lead more to solidarity, or did the prisoners [inmates] try to cope on their own?
LISKA: I really only had one friend in Munich and one in Waiern. Somehow I coped on my own. But I was isolated anyway because of my views. The others couldn't understand why I wouldn't say "Heil Hitler!"

21. Was there anything that helped you take your mind off the horror of daily life for a while (such as music)? What gave you strength?
LISKA: In Waiern, I wasn't allowed to have any visitors. Father secretly visited me several times as I was going to school, and he always brought me something that I would then smuggle into the home. One time, he brought me a little Luther Bible. I hid it in my bed, and whenever an opportunity arose for me to read, I always read that Bible.

When I went to Munich, they didn't give me my Bible when I unpacked. In Munich, the girls in the "convent" had to go to church every Sunday. There was a chapel in the "convent," and the man in charge of the institution was a priest. He said mass, and because I didn't go to church, I had to wait with the sister in the porter's lodge. She asked me, "Why don't you go to church?" I replied, "I'm not Catholic." "Aha. What are you then?" "One of Jehovah's Witnesses." "One of Jehovah's Witnesses? Don't you have any churches?" "No." "What kind of religion is that, if it doesn't even have a church?" "As a family, we used to read the Bible together at home every Sunday." "I see. And why aren't you reading it now? Today is Sunday!" "They didn't give it to me." Then she said she would see if she could get the Bible for me. And sure enough, next day, she beckoned to me from the cubicle and handed me the Bible through the peephole. I was overjoyed to have my Bible again. Even in those days, it meant a great deal to me. But that was not all. Every Sunday I was able to read passages from the Bible to her.

Just imagine that! I read chapters 4 and 5 of the Acts of the Apostles to her, where the apostles were persecuted and defended [testified for] themselves. After that, I read Psalm 23 and Psalm 91. Of course, that gave me renewed strength. I always had the feeling that Jehovah had come to my aid. But of course I had been very well prepared by my parents. I knew where those passages were located in the Bible, and they gave me a tremendous amount of strength. Besides, I must say that I always had someone somewhere who was nice to me, even among the supervisors.

22. What were living conditions like in the barracks [home] (prisoner [inmate] allocation, food supplies, hygiene, clothing, etc.)?

LISKA: We always had enough to wear, but there weren't any uniforms or institution clothing. There was always enough food—potatoes and vegetables—as well. In winter, we usually had sauerkraut and cabbage, and every day there were potatoes in some form or other. It was simple fare, but we didn't go hungry.

23. What jobs did you have to do? How many hours a day did you have to work?

LISKA: We did have to work in Waiern. There was a large farm called Staberhof that belonged to the reform school in Waiern. There, for example, we had to weed the cornfield. On school days, after doing our homework, we went to work until the evening. During vacation, we had to work in the field all day. And of course, indoors we had to make the beds and wash the dishes. That's stayed in my memory.

We also had to keep our dormitory clean. Every week we had to crawl under the bed. The bedstead had iron springs. We had to dust them and sweep the floor under the bed. We had to make our own beds. But these days you just can't imagine how neat the bed had to be. The blanket and pillow had to look like a box. No creases were allowed anywhere, and the sheet had to be perfectly smooth. If you couldn't do it—and as an eleven-year-old, I couldn't, of course—you just had to keep practicing until you could. Then you went to the nun and said, "I've finished!" She came with you into the dormitory, inspected the bed, and said, "You call that finished? There's a bump, and there's a crease!" All the bedclothes were torn off the bed, and I had to do it all over again from the beginning until I managed to do it to the nun's satisfaction. In your locker, a narrow cupboard, you had to tidy your things away end to end.

24. What effect did the slogan "Work liberates" have on you?

LISKA: We didn't have that slogan in the reform school like they did in the concentration camps. I didn't find out until afterward how hard the people in the concentration camps had to work.

25. What were the guards [staff] like in the camp [home]?

LISKA: In general, things were very strict. We were taught to be clean and appreciate tidiness. But I must say that I always had someone somewhere who was very nice to me. In Munich, for example, there was a novice who worked in the office. She didn't sleep in the home, and we met each other on the way to school. We greeted one another, and she said, "Hermine, come and see me in the office this afternoon; I need your help with something. You must go shopping for me!" We weren't really allowed to leave the home on our own, but I was allowed to go shopping for her, unsupervised. A square called Rosenheimer Platz was nearby; that's where the store was where I went shopping for her, and it was always very pleasant. She always gave me some candy or a piece of chocolate. That was a real treat. She told me, "I just wrote a good report about you." She also said that my parents kept sending petitions. When she knew that I would be going home soon, she told me she thought it wouldn't be long before I was allowed home. So she was really very kind to me.

26. Was there any contact between the prisoners [inmates] and the local population?

LISKA: Hardly any, although in 1943, we were taken to the country, to a farm near Nandlstadt in the Hallertau region. There was some contact there, of course, while we were digging out potatoes. A classroom had been cleared in a school, and that's where we slept.

There was a farm opposite, and we got our meals in the farmhouse. We spent the days on the farm and even had lessons in the parlor, taught by a teacher who had come with us from Munich. The interesting thing was that we weren't allowed out alone at night there either. We went to our lessons together and came back again together. But I really wanted to go out on my own. So I thought, "What can I do to be allowed to go out alone at night when it's dark?" Then it occurred to me that if I volunteered to work in the stables, which was work I knew from home, it might be possible.

And so it proved: I was allowed to go out. There was a French prisoner of war working there too. I was given strict instructions not to talk to him. But they needn't have bothered, because he didn't speak German and I didn't speak French. He was a very nice man. He had a twirled-up mustache and was very kind to me. Maybe he was also pleased with my work. At any rate, I always got a piece of chocolate from him, which was a real treat in those days. Nowadays it's impossible to imagine what a treat it was.

27. Were you aware of how the war was proceeding in the outside world?

LISKA: Not in Munich, but when I did my year's community service at the Langstegers' in Lambichl near Klagenfurt during the last year of the war, I heard something. My room was next to the kitchen, and my bed was against the wall adjoining the kitchen. At night, when I was in bed, the family used to listen to the "enemy station," the BBC. They had two sons at the front, so of course they were interested in how the war was going, and listened to the BBC. It always started with "Boom, boom, boom, boom; Boom, boom, boom, boom." Then I knew it was the BBC. I didn't understand anything, but from what the family said, I discovered where the Allies were, and that they were getting nearer and nearer.

28. In the concentration camp [home], were you allowed to receive letters, food parcels, etc.?

LISKA: Yes, my parents always sent me encouraging words in their letters. Mama wrote them. Other families that were friends with ours also cheered me up by signing as "Uncle" or "Aunty." One day, the head of the "convent" summoned me and asked, "Who exactly are this aunt and this uncle?" "One is Mama's brother and the other is Father's sister." Then he said, "I don't care who they are! From now on, only your parents will be allowed to write to you. But there mustn't be anything in their letters that strengthens your views. If there is, you won't get the letter! You are allowed to receive one letter a week, and to write one a week, and to receive two parcels a month." I had to write home and tell them that. Then he threatened to have me put in a mental home if they didn't comply. I received the letters regularly as long as I was in Munich.

29. What forms of torture did you suffer?
LISKA: I didn't have to suffer any torture. I was never beaten and I never went hungry. I can't compare myself to the people in the concentration camps. I didn't have to go through those terrible things.

30. What was the most frightening moment for you?
LISKA: The worst thing was being torn from my home and my family circle. The homesickness I felt in Waiern was really dreadful. The air raids in Munich were very frightening too. We had our bunk beds—three beds one above the other—in the basement shelter, and there were air raids every night. Whenever a bomb landed anywhere nearby, making the whole shelter shake, we were naturally terribly frightened. The nun would then comfort us, saying, "There's no need to be afraid, our shelter is bombproof."

I remember a particularly severe raid in the night of April 19/20, 1944. The area surrounding the institution was targeted for particularly heavy bombing. Reconnaissance aircraft flew over first and marked the area to be bombed with flares. These flares were known colloquially as "Christmas trees" because when they were dropped, they looked like a giant burning tree. Outside it was bright as daylight. The reconnaissance planes dropped flares on four corners of the target area and then flew off. Then the bombers arrived with their bombs. And it's almost impossible to imagine how many bombs they dropped in the area they had marked. Ninety-three firebombs and nine white phosphorus bombs fell on the site of the Adelgunden institute alone, and it was by no means a huge complex. There were fires everywhere. At the front, on the street, was the main building with apartments and the kitchen. At the rear, in the yard, were the tailor's shop and the laundry, and the shoemaker lived there. The shoemaker was also the janitor. He ran across the yard. The coal bunker was in the yard, and the lid had been ripped off by an explosion, with the result that the shoemaker fell into the coal bunker, dying a few days later. In the midst of this firestorm, we had to run down to a stream. We filled buckets with water from the stream and passed them back from one person to the next. That's how the fire was extinguished.

31. Were there any entertaining or lighthearted incidents that enabled you to forget all the suffering for a moment? Can you describe them?

LISKA: Yes, in the "convent," we ten to fourteen-year-olds were looked after by Sister Elradina. She even told us a joke about the Nazis. When I think about that now, she was taking a huge risk, because if we had told anyone about it, she could have been arrested. She could either have been sent to prison or even to a concentration camp for telling a joke like that. It was about "Weiss Ferdl." He was a very well-known cabaret artist in Munich. The joke went like this: Weiss Ferdl is standing at the food market. He's selling fish and yelling at the top of his voice, "Folks, get your herring, as fat and plump as Gering." The joke was that Göring, the second-highest ranking man after Hitler, was very corpulent, and in the local dialect, he was known as "Gering" [*gering* means: slight, slim, small]. So then they arrested Weiss Ferdl and told him that if he did it again, he would be sent to Dachau, which isn't far from Munich. After subjecting him to indoctrination, they let him go again. Next day, he's standing at the food market again, selling fish and yelling at the top of his voice, "Folks, get your herring, as fat and plump as the day before yesterday." She told us a joke like that.

32. What were your day-to-day thoughts while you were in the concentration camp [home]?

LISKA: When will I go home again? Sometimes the homesickness just kept coming back, mainly at night, though, not so much during the day.

33. Was it possible for children to be born in a concentration camp [home]? If so, what happened to these babies?

LISKA: I don't know anything about that. There were girls there as old as eighteen, but I'm sure they didn't have any babies in the reform school.

34. Was it possible to make friends with prisoners [other inmates]?

LISKA: Yes, I had a friend everywhere. In Carinthia, it was a certain Judith, and in the "convent," it was Trude Künstner.

35. Who was your best friend during this dreadful time, and how did he or she help you?
LISKA: That was really Jehovah God. He always helped me when I was faced with adversity and prayed to him.

36. What did you do to relieve the suffering of other inmates?
LISKA: I can't recall anything in particular.

37. Were there particular hierarchies among the inmates?
LISKA: Well, I don't know of any. I wasn't aware of anything like that.

38. Were there any differences in the way the various groups of prisoners [inmates] (religious, political groups) were treated?
LISKA: Not in the "convent" itself, but outside, in the school, the blue-eyed blondes were treated better. Because that [stereotype] was Hitler's obsession.

In the 1990s, a Jewish survivor of Auschwitz told me that he survived because he had blond hair and blue eyes. They had to disembark from a train and line up. An SS man stood in front of them and carried out a selection. He started with those he was going to send to the right [to the gas chambers]: "You—to the right! You—to the right! You—to the right! You—to the right!" Then he came to the blond blue-eyed youth, who was sixteen, and said to him, "You're a German, you go to the left!" That's how he was the only one from his entire family to survive Auschwitz. All his relatives were dark-haired and they were killed.

39. What diseases and illnesses were prevalent in the concentration camp [home]?
LISKA: I contracted jaundice one time. In the morning, one of the girls said to me, "Look at you! Your eyes are all yellow." So I had to go back to bed, and all I remember is that I was given a huge amount of stewed rhubarb. They didn't take me to a doctor, even though there was a hospital next door.

40. Did you receive a physical injury?
LISKA: Yes. Although I was never beaten severely enough to sustain an injury, there was one occasion when I received a serious wound. That was in Waiern. In summer, we were allowed to go swimming in the Flatschacher pond. There was a bathing hut there with steps leading down

into the water. I couldn't swim very well yet, so I always went in down the steps. But one day, a boy from the home grabbed me and tried to throw me in. I held on to the bathing hut. Around the hut, there was rusty barbed wire and it cut my right hand, leaving a long, deep gash. There was an awful lot of blood. They poured something on it that stung like mad. Then my hand was bandaged, and the next day, I had blood poisoning. I had a red stripe running up to the elbow. In those days, it was said that blood poisoning was fatal. I asked a supervisor, "I have blood poisoning, am I going to die?" She said, "Of course not! It's in your right hand; if you had it in your left hand, it would be dangerous because [the blood] goes straight to the heart." So I didn't die, and it all cleared up again.

41. How much did you weigh when you were in the concentration camp [home]?

LISKA: No idea. We were all weighed, sure, but I can't remember how heavy I was. I was away for quite a few years, after all. When I came home again, I was taller and heavier, but I certainly wasn't fat.

42. What did death mean to you?

LISKA: Well, I didn't see or hear of anyone's dying in the reform school or the "convent."

43. What was the closest you came to death?

LISKA: During the bombing raids, it was very close. When I left the Adelgunden institute, I went to say goodbye to the head, and he said, "Hermine, write me that you've arrived home safely, and stay the way you are." I wrote him as requested, and a few weeks later, I received a reply saying that the institute had been badly damaged by bombs. In the part of the basement where I had sat with the fourteen to eighteen-year-old girls, nine girls and one of the nuns had been killed. The basement was regarded as very safe, it's true, because a lot of people from outside the school had taken refuge there. But it wasn't bombproof. If I had still been there, I would have surely died.

44. Did you ever build a kind of "wall" to shield yourself from the terrible things that were being done so that the death of a fellow prisoner [of one of the inmates] no longer affected you?

LISKA: It would surely have been terrible if I had been obliged to go through something like that. But fortunately that wasn't the case.

45. What happened to the dead bodies in the concentration camp [home]?

LISKA: While I was there, I wasn't aware that there were any dead bodies. Later on, I discovered that wood coffins were made for the nine girls who were killed by the bombs in Munich to avoid having to bury them in mass graves.

46. Was there ever a possibility for you to be released from the concentration camp [home]?

LISKA: There would have been a possibility if I had used the greeting "Heil Hitler!" though I still wouldn't have been able to go home. The head summoned me one time and asked, "Hermine, are you afraid your parents might disown you if you used the Nazi salute?" I replied, "No." "Well, did they say that to you?" "No, they didn't say it." "So how can you be so sure? Maybe you *are* afraid of that!" Then I said, "No, definitely not, because one of my brothers, Peppi, is not one of Jehovah's Witnesses, and he joined the army. Mama sent him parcels and letters too, just like the ones I get now." I knew that, because I was the one who had to take them to the post office in Brückl. Then I argued, "I'm sure my parents find it much harder to accept the fact that Peppi joined up than if I were to say 'Heil Hitler!' because my father always spoke out against the war. He fought in World War I and went through a lot. He was wounded, captured by the Russians, and he always maintained that war is the worst thing that can happen to a nation and that a Christian must not support any war. That's why I'm sure that they wouldn't disown me."

Following that, the head sent me to a mental home in Munich to frighten me. I was accompanied by a nun. That was really frightening for me. I then asked him, "Will I be allowed to go home if I use the greeting 'Heil Hitler!'?" And he said, "No, I don't think so." "Well, why should I say 'Heil Hitler!' if I won't be allowed home anyway?" But I don't believe I would have done it, because I was absolutely determined not to.

47. Were there any escape attempts or opportunities to escape? Did you try to escape?

LISKA: I had plenty of opportunities to escape. I was allowed out on my own. But it would never have entered my head, I wouldn't have dared. Where could I have gone? Besides, somehow I knew that if I escaped, my parents would be locked up too.

48. Were there any inmates in the concentration camp [home] who dared to stage a revolt against the camp [home] authorities?

LISKA: No. We ten to fourteen-year-olds had no contact with the fourteen to eighteen-year-olds, for example, even though we were in the same building. We didn't have any contact with the little ones, either. I would have very much enjoyed being with the little ones.

49. Did you think you would ever make it out alive?

LISKA: Yes, I was convinced that I would go home again.

50. Were there any times when you gave up all hope? If so, why?

LISKA: No, I never gave up hope. I was always convinced that Jehovah God was helping me and that I would get out again safe and sound. Before my internment, we had talked about the stories of Daniel and the fiery furnace and the lions' den, and the fact that Daniel always prayed, although he knew it would have terrible consequences for him. So that's how my mother prepared me, and she said I should pray often. And I always did so whenever I had particular reason to, such as when I was supposed to salute the flag, or when the head summoned me and threatened me with the mental home.

51. Did anyone commit suicide?

LISKA: I don't know anything about that.

52. During the Holocaust, did you ever consider committing suicide out of sheer despair?

LISKA: No, never.

53. What thoughts, ideas, hopes, wishes, or religious convictions did you cling to?

LISKA: Well, prayer was one thing that was very important to me, and my mama had prepared me very well for that time. She started explaining Creation to me, the flowers and the stars, when I was still very little. She loved the stars and showed me the Little Dipper and the Big Dipper. On clear nights in summer, we would sit on the bench in front of the house, and she would explain the constellations to me, including the Pleiades. Then she said, if ever I were to be taken away from home and didn't receive any more letters, I should look up at the Pleiades. It might happen that she wouldn't get any more mail from me, and I none from her. Then

I should look up at the Pleiades, and she would do the same. Then we would be together again in our thoughts. She added, "Minnerle, you need never feel abandoned, because Jehovah God and Jesus will always be with you!" In Munich, I regularly received letters; that was no problem. Nevertheless, one night when we had to go down into the basement shelter, I pulled aside the blinds a little on a high-up window on the stairs to see if the stars were shining. But one of the nuns immediately pulled me away.

But outside the home, in the country—that was in 1944—it was likely true that no more mail arrived for us, so I asked to be allowed out. That's when I went to work in the stable. I stood in the yard between the house and the stable and looked up at the stars, thinking of my mama sitting at home and looking up as well. So then I was with her again. That was simply wonderful.

Standing in the yard and looking up gave me strength and, more than anything, so did prayer. I really always felt that Jehovah God was helping me.

54. Did you lose your faith in God while you were in the camp [home]?
LISKA: No, definitely not. In fact I emerged stronger from every type of adversity that I overcame: for instance, when I had to appear before the supervisors, the head, or all those youngsters in front of the flag.

55. What role did your religion play in how you felt about what was going on? Why?
LISKA: Religion played the biggest role because it was on account of my religion that I was there. I understood why it was so, and that meant in particular that I didn't have to ask myself, "Why is God allowing this?" I know why, and I knew it then as well. Of course, through religion I had the hope that it would end one day, that I would go home again, and that I would see my loved ones again. I always had that hope.

56. Did you pray during your internment?
LISKA: Yes, of course, I prayed a great deal. I never went to sleep without saying my prayer. In the morning, I always said thank you for being able to get up again in good health. I prayed especially when particular incidents occurred, such as when I was supposed to salute the

flag, or when the supervisor wanted to put the uniform jacket on me. Then I prayed to Jehovah to help me, and he really did always help me. So I really did have the feeling that he was helping me, and that made everything easier to bear.

57. Did you ever consider changing your religion (or ideology)? Why?
LISKA: That thought never entered my head, because I knew that what I had was right.

58. What was the date of your liberation from the camp [home]?
LISKA: I was released from the "convent" in Munich on April 29, 1944. But then I was taken to a husband and wife near Klagenfurt where I had to do my compulsory year of community service. The war ended on May 8, 1945, and I went home again at long last.

59. How were you liberated from the camp [home], or how did you manage to get out of it?
LISKA: Munich was already being very heavily bombed. There were raids every night. My parents were afraid that something would happen to me and kept writing petitions, asking that I be allowed to be sent back to Carinthia. In the end, permission was granted, probably because the situation was extremely dangerous. So I was released on April 29, 1944, and went home on my own by train.

60. How were you treated by the people who liberated you?
LISKA: Where we lived in Carinthia, the English came and liberated us. The first soldiers rode to our home in St. Walburgen on horseback. They tethered the horses on the garden fence, and we children were even allowed to ride them. We had a wall in front of our front door. The English soldiers sat on this wall, and Mama gave them unfermented fruit wine to drink. When they came back again, they brought Mama ten pounds of sugar. In those days, that was worth a lot. The first Englishmen who came as the occupying army were very approachable and friendly.

61. What was the first thing you did after you were liberated?
LISKA: I thanked Jehovah that I was able to go home and that we had survived. Then I went to see some brothers in the faith in Klagenfurt. A sister in the faith lent me a bicycle. I used it to cycle home to St. Walburgen, which was nearly nineteen miles. It was really funny. I

held on to the back of a truck so I wouldn't have to pedal so much. But the truck drove into a pothole because the gravel road was in such a state of disrepair. Then I lost my grip and fell into a ditch. But I didn't hurt myself, apart from a bit of a bang on the knee.

62. Did you have any problems when you returned home? How did people in your home environment react to you?

LISKA: Although I had been taken away from my parent as an eleven-year-old child, and didn't return home until more than four years later, there was no loss of familiarity. My mama had written to me regularly, and she was very shrewd. She always kept me up to date with what was going on. For example, she wrote about the work they were currently doing: bringing in the hay, harvesting the crops, picking apples. We children had each been allotted a cow, which was "ours," and mine was called Alma. Of course, she was the prettiest cow, and she was easy to milk as well. She had brown and light-colored markings. And Mama wrote me, "Your Alma had a calf! It's a female and looks exactly like Alma. When you come home, the calf will belong to you." That's how she always prepared me and gave me hope. She was convinced that I would come home again. Of course, that gave me a lot of strength. When I came home, I saw the calf. Of course, it wasn't so small anymore, but it really did look exactly like Alma.

63. Were you able to rejoin your family?

LISKA: Yes, we all came home again and were reunited. Naturally, we were all very, very happy.

64. Did you have any acquaintances, friends, or relatives in the camps? Did they survive their internment?

LISKA: My oldest brother, Hansl, was called up to do his military training in Austria in 1937. He refused to do it and was sentenced to a year in prison. However, he was allowed to serve the sentence over two winters in Klagenfurt. In summer, he was allowed to work at home. As a result, his release was delayed, and when he came out, Hitler was already in Austria. Hansl was sent a certificate of exclusion from the German Wehrmacht since he was regarded as unworthy to fight for the German fatherland because he had a criminal record. That saved his life because if he had been drafted, he would have refused to comply for sure. In that case, he would have been sent to Berlin and sentenced to death. He would have been hanged, beheaded, or shot. Around fifty young men between the ages of nineteen and thirty—Austrian Jehovah's Witnesses—were killed that way. But Hansl was sentenced to forced labor in Eisenerz am Erzberg.

In the fall of 1944, the so-called *Volkssturm* (a militia) was introduced, and my father, who was nearly sixty, and Hansl, who was in Eisenerz, were conscripted at the same time, Christmas 1944. They didn't go. On January 2, 1945, they were taken away to the prison in Klagenfurt. Two men came to the house to pick them up, and they all went down [the hill]. In those days, there was no road leading up to the house; the car was probably down below someplace. As they were on the way down, they met a neighbor coming the other way. The neighbor asked, "Lassnig,[12] where are you all off to today, then?" My father said, "To Dachau!" The neighbor said, "That's nothing to joke about." My father replied, "No, but it won't be a joke. We've been called up into the *Volkssturm*, and as you know, we won't join up." My father was convinced he would be sent to Dachau. At any rate, he was brought before the Gestapo captain, who asked him why he didn't report for duty. My father said, "I'm a Christian, and the commandment says, 'You must not murder.'" "But," said the Gestapo captain, "you won't have to kill anybody. Maybe you won't even need to touch a rifle. Go down into the yard and take the oath. If you don't, I'll have to send you to Dachau. You don't know what Dachau means. You're too old, you wouldn't survive that." My father answered, "I know exactly what Dachau means, but I cannot take the oath, because my life was not given to me by a human being."

His argument was that he always gave the state what he owed it, which would normally have been taxes. But in those days, it wasn't a matter of money; farmers had been given precise instructions about what they had to contribute. My father said to the Gestapo captain, "I've always contributed exactly what was required of me. That means I've done my duty toward the state." The Gestapo captain replied, "And it's lucky for you that you did, because during the past few years, we've been receiving reports from the local farmers, asking us to remove your entire family

---

[12] Families were often known by the name of the farm they owned. See Hermine Liska, question 6.

from the farm." That was because we were said to hold opinions hostile to the state. "That gave me a reason to say, 'Let's make the farmer work for us. What good would it do us if we locked them all up?'" He then tried again to persuade my father to take the oath. Then my father said, "You know what? I had enough from World War I to last a lifetime!"

In World War I, he was at the Russian front. Two years later, he was wounded and still had a piece of shrapnel in his back. He was really in constant pain. He was held captive by the Russians for six years and then went across the whole of Siberia as far as the Chinese border. The last town was Vladivostok. Then he said to the Gestapo captain, "When I was in Russia, I swore never to join the army again. Since then, I have gotten to know the Bible and now have justification for my refusal." The Gestapo captain replied, "You're in pain? I'll send you to the prison doctor; maybe he can declare you unfit for imprisonment." And so it proved: three weeks later, he was allowed to go home.

My brother, Hansl, was sent to Dachau. By then it was the end of January 1945, so the war was to last only a few more months. At the end of January, he was transferred to a subcamp where he had to do hard labor in a quarry. Afterward, he told us that the worst thing was not the work, not the cold, not even the hunger. The worst thing there was the sanitary conditions. They couldn't even change their striped working clothes anymore, couldn't even wash properly. Because of the dirt, they got lice, and the lice carried typhoid. He contracted typhoid, so he was taken back to Dachau and put in the isolation ward. For three weeks, he was more unconscious than conscious. On April 25, 1945, the camp inmates had to line up. The camp commandant held a speech to the effect that the camp was to be evacuated, and they had a long and arduous march ahead of them. Anyone who didn't feel strong enough could stay in the camp. A friend of Hansl's, who was also one of Jehovah's Witnesses, Valentin Thaler, came and told him that. Hansl said, "I can't get up anyway." The other said, "I'll stay too." So when the Americans liberated Dachau concentration camp four days later on April 29, 1945, there were still many people left alive there. He was taken to the American military hospital and spent exactly two months there. On June 29, 1945, he came home. He weighed only ninety pounds, even though he was five foot nine inches tall. But at least he had survived.

One Sunday, a friend of his came and asked him, among other things, "Hansl, was it really so bad in Dachau?" In Carinthia, Dachau had been known as a concentration camp, a labor camp, from the very beginning. But what was really there—gas chambers, crematoriums, starvation, beatings, appalling things—most people probably genuinely didn't know. When the Allies liberated concentration camps like that one, they filmed everything. The films were then shown in movie theaters. Maybe the friend had seen one and afterward asked Hansl, "Was it really that bad?" And Hansl replied, "It was much worse! I cannot describe it to you, because anyone who didn't see it or experience it himself can't believe it." So he never really talked about it.

My mother was never taken away; she was allowed to stay at home. In 1944, my youngest brother, Franz, was called to the *Reichsarbeitsdienst* (Reich Labor Service). But because the Service provided training with a view to joining the military, and he would have had to swear the oath, he refused to join and was sentenced to three weeks' imprisonment in a bunker. The bunker was a little room in a cellar, created specifically for this purpose. There was only a slit in the ceiling, which let a little light in, and as a special punishment, he was only given a hot meal twice a week; the rest of the time he got only bread and water. After three weeks, they took him out and asked him whether he was now willing to join. No, he still refused. So then he was taken to the prison in Klagenfurt. The head of the Labor Service wrote a letter to the head of the Gestapo. About ten years ago, I obtained his file from the archives in Klagenfurt and read the letter. It said that he recommended the immediate internment of Franz Obweger in a concentration camp. They had tried everything to make him change his mind, but he would not give in. Consequently, he was to be interned in a concentration camp without delay. But the head of the Gestapo gave permission for him to stand trial, at the end of which Franz was sentenced to one year in a reform school. He was sent to the reform school in Kaiser-Ebersdorf in Vienna and was released from there on April 4, 1945. When he came home, his call-up papers were waiting for him. Of course, he didn't report for duty and went into hiding at home. Once, they came to pick him up, but luckily they didn't find him, so he survived. My half-brother, Peppi, joined up. He came home as well, in October 1945. So all my relatives survived.

But many of our friends didn't: people from Carinthia, close friends of my parents. Among them was the Dorner family. Anton was interned in Dachau concentration camp in 1944 and died there in December of that year. His son, also called Anton, was called up for military service in 1939 and didn't go. He was taken to Berlin, where he was sentenced to death and executed in January 1940.

The brother of Anton Dorner Sr., whose name was Franz, hid in the woods at home. Anton's wife disapproved of Jehovah's Witnesses. She informed on him, and he was sent to Dachau concentration camp, also in 1944. Although he lived long enough to be liberated, he was in such bad shape that he died only one day before the surviving Carinthian Jehovah's Witnesses came home on a special train on June 29, 1945.

65. What happened to your possessions?
LISKA: They stayed with my parents. After the war, we heard that our property had already been divided up among the villagers round the table in the local inn. They said, "That field suits that neighbor, that meadow suits this one." So they evidently firmly believed that we would all be taken away. And there was something else we heard afterward too: we were told, "You're lucky the war was lost because if Hitler had won, he would have carted all you Bible Students off to Russia!" Later on, I read a book by Dr. Detlef Garbe who wrote that this wasn't Hitler's intention, but Himmler's.

66. To what extent have you received compensation for your internment?
LISKA: In 1997, I was awarded compensation from the Austrian state fund. I wasn't recognized as a victim until 2010, when I received official certification from the government of the province of Styria.

67. How did you set about rebuilding your life?
LISKA: Well, I missed a lot of schooling. I wasn't allowed to go to high school, because I didn't use the greeting "Heil Hitler!" After the war, I went to school in Klagenfurt. Then, my dream was to be a kindergarten teacher. But that wasn't possible either, because my mother fell sick, and I had to abandon my schooling after two years to work on my parents' farm. After I got married, I moved to Styria with my husband, into a house in Reiteregg in the municipality of St. Bartholomä.

68. How long did it take you to return to a "normal" life after the Holocaust?

LISKA: It took some time, naturally—definitely five to ten years. That's not something you can get over very quickly. As long as the occupying armies were still here in all of Austria, we weren't completely free. For instance, there was a border crossing on Semmering Mountain, where the Russians were. Then, in early 1950, I wanted to go to a convention of Jehovah's Witnesses in Frankfurt, Germany. It wasn't possible, because I hadn't received my travel documents.

69. What was your life like after the war?

LISKA: Sadly, Mama died pretty soon after, on April 19, 1956, and Father on March 27, 1970. Hansl died on April 22, 1993, Franz, in April 2006, and Peppi, on October 20, 2006.

I attended a home economics school in Klagenfurt. It was a three-year course, but I had to return home after two years because Mama had fallen sick. I married in 1952. Then my husband found work near Graz and was manager of a factory until his retirement in 1987. Sadly, he died on February 22, 2002. I had three children and stayed at home as a housewife. I never learned or practiced a trade.

70. What is your life like today? Do you still often think back to those days?

LISKA: Today I live in Reiteregg, in the municipality of St. Bartholomä. I lead a pleasant life in the country. To be honest, during the past decades, I didn't think back to those days at all. But in 1980, first steps were taken to come to terms with that period by going to schools and telling the students about it. In 1995, historians approached Jehovah's Witnesses and said we ought to review our history and tell people about it. I now have the privilege of going to schools. I've been doing so since 1999, and in 2002, I was accredited as a witness of history by the Federal Ministry for Education, Arts and Culture. I'm able to visit so many schools that I'm in one on virtually every school day, all over Austria. I couldn't manage all that alone. I'm always accompanied by good friends who are a great help to me. And it gives me such pleasure. It keeps me fit, and I'm grateful that I'm able to carry out this activity. In the fall of 2009, I was invited to the [United States] Holocaust Memorial Museum in Washington, D.C., and was able to tell my story there.

38. Hermine Liska as a witness of history in a school, 2009

71. What physical and mental scars do you carry from that time?

LISKA: All my life I've had problems with my gallbladder, possibly stemming from my bout of jaundice. And mentally? The worst thing for me was being taken away from home. After I had married and was living in Styria, I sometimes took the train to visit my parents at home. When I said goodbye to Mama, we would both cry, and I would cry all the way from home to the train. I scolded myself, saying, "What are you crying for? You're glad to be going back to your husband, aren't you?" I didn't realize it at the time, but now I know that being taken away from home by the welfare worker was a cause of recurring subconscious distress. As soon as we had a car and I didn't have to take that walk to the train anymore, it was gone.

72. Did you have any moral support to help your emotional and social recovery?

LISKA: Not so much, really, but faith always helped me to overcome those things.

73. Has your view of the world changed since that time?

LISKA: My view of the world has not changed. After all, the Bible prophesied long ago what is now happening. That's why we were able to cope with that time more easily and get over it, because the Bible has shown us the meaning of life.

74. Can you think of anything positive that you have gained from your experiences?

LISKA: For me, there really were positive effects because [my] steadfastness helped me to cope with life more easily. God always helped me. Life gives me pleasure, and I appreciate everything, even small things. It's important to enjoy life, even when bad things happen—for example, when my husband died. He had already suffered heart attacks and minor strokes, so I was very much afraid of how things would be when he was no longer there. Exactly a month before he died, I received my accreditation as a witness of history from the ministry and was so busy afterward that I didn't have time to feel lonesome. I always told myself, "You were married for fifty years and it was a good life. Be glad about that. There's no use crying over spilled milk." And the hope that the Bible gives me for the future is really bright.

75. Have you ever been back to visit the concentration camp [home] you were held in, and if so, what were your feelings?

LISKA: I went back to the Adelgunden institute for the first time in 2001, with my husband. In 2004 I returned again, with a friend. Everything had changed, and I didn't have any particular feelings.

During my visit in 2001, I was given a diary to read that one of the nuns had written during the war. She wrote that in the fall of 1941, six girls from institutions in Carinthia were transferred there. But they were not at all happy with these girls, because one of them committed forty-six thefts, one ran away seventeen times, and one had been brought up in a completely different religion. That was me, of course. Then she wrote, "In general, these girls were lazy, sloppy, and dishonest." Then a secretary showed us around the whole building. We ten to fourteen-year-olds had all slept together in one single dormitory. Now there were only double rooms. We saw three cleaning ladies. We had to do all the cleaning ourselves.

As we went around, the secretary said, "Although we aren't a 'convent' anymore, we still celebrate the Christmas and Easter holidays just as we did then." I asked her, "Do Krampus and Saint Nicholas[13] still come as well?" "Of course they do! Why?" I told her that when Saint Nicholas came with his companion Krampus, every girl was given a poem to recite, and I still remember mine perfectly. It went, "Hermine's from Carinthia, which makes us glad to know and see her. She's thorough, full of fun and zest, at mealtimes she's a welcome guest. The only thing that I find foolish: she's often just a little mulish!"

Why did I recite that? Because I didn't want the secretary to think I had been lazy, dishonest, or sloppy in those days. After all, my mother had prepared me very well for that time. At home she had made me practice folding up sweaters and underwear. She said that when I was given a job to do, I shouldn't talk back, but do it, and do it properly. She said I should do everything my conscience would allow. "But that decision is up to you," she said.

76. Are you still in touch with your fellow inmates from the concentration camps [home]?

LISKA: Yes, I'm still in touch with Judith, at least by telephone. We've never visited each other. Several years ago, I received a letter from a lady in Zeltweg. She had read in the newspaper that I was visiting schools as a witness of history. She wrote me that she had been in the Adelgunden institute as well. I went to see her, we talked for two hours, and I learned a lot from her.

77. What did you tell your family about your internment in the concentration camp [home]? How did your relatives react to what you told them?

LISKA: We didn't talk about it much. I told them that I hadn't had such a hard time. I was never beaten and never went hungry, because there were always potatoes and cabbage to eat. Mama said she was proud of me all the same.

---

[13] In Alpine countries, Saint Nicholas visits children on December 6 with his companion Krampus. Traditionally, Saint Nicholas rewards good children with small gifts, while Krampus punishes the naughty ones.

78. Do you find it difficult to talk about those days?

LISKA: Actually, I never really talked about it for decades. When I started my talks in the schools about those days, it was very difficult to begin with. Sometimes I did wonder whether I should do it or not. It wasn't so bad when I was actually talking, but at night, when I couldn't sleep, I started thinking, the memories returned, and everything that Mama said came back to me. That has been tough. But I enjoy it so much when the students are listening to me that I forget all that. Their comments and the things they write in the guest book are so nice that sometimes I just can't believe it. What I'm able to experience today makes up for everything I went through then.

79. Which moment from those days has remained most firmly etched in your memory?

LISKA: That was without doubt the moment I was practically torn from my parents' home and taken away. A welfare worker came early in the morning on the first train from St. Veit. Then we had to say goodbye. I can still see Mama standing by the front door. Yes, that was definitely terrible (*cries*).

80. Did you ever see or meet Hitler?

LISKA: No. Hitler did come to Klagenfurt, though, and there was great excitement all over Carinthia, but I wasn't there.

81. What was your opinion of Hitler in those days, and what is your opinion of him now?

LISKA: In those days, I already thought Hitler was a monster. I had heard about the concentration camps from my parents, and about the way Jehovah's Witnesses were being persecuted. So for me, Hitler was always an appalling dictator, and nothing has changed to this day.

82. Hypothetically, if Adolf Hitler were still alive and you could have five minutes alone with him, what would you say or do?

LISKA: That's a tough one. First of all, I wouldn't do anything, because I have no right to do anything to him. I think I would get such a fright that I wouldn't get a word out. If I did, I would tell him about the hope that the Bible gives us. But I guess he would probably have heard about that someplace already.

83. After the war, did you ever meet any of the people who had tormented you?

LISKA: I never ran into the principal of my home village's primary school. But I did see him once. My brother Peppi was in the hospital in St. Veit, and in the ward, Peppi said to me, "Look who's sitting over there!" It was the wife of the principal of my primary school. The principal was in bed. I went over, said "Hello" to her, and she then said to her husband, "Look who's here, Papa, it's Lassnig Hermine!" "Oh, yes," he said. I took his hand and gave it a squeeze. He was pretty well out of it; he was practically at death's door and died the next day. So I saw him once again right at the end.

84. What do you think of the punishments the Nazis received after the war, in the Nuremberg trials, for example?

LISKA: I never heard enough about them to be able to say much. But what is interesting is that these people argued in their defense that they were only obeying orders. But they should have acted on their consciences. Their consciences were evidently unmoved because they did terrible things.

85. Have you forgiven your persecutors?

LISKA: Yes, and again my mother played a central role because she told me from the outset, "Minnerle, if someone hurts you, you must not hate the person. You must not plot revenge, because that harms you even more. Vengeful thoughts are the worst you can have; they do *you* more harm." Then she said, "You must just remember that these people have been blinded by these policies, this propaganda, this National Socialism. People don't realize what it will lead to."

After the war, in early June of 1945, a man from the village, who had been a political prisoner in Dachau, came to us. He was a socialist, and he said, "Frau Obweger, I want you to tell me the names of the people who did that to us." Mama said, "Herr Lesniak, you won't get any names from me!" "Why not? They must be made to pay!" Mama replied, "We will not avenge ourselves, we'll leave that to one greater than ourselves; he will do it fittingly. Besides, it's the responsibility of the secular courts. We will not avenge ourselves." None of Jehovah's Witnesses ever took personal revenge on anyone.

86. What is your opinion of neo-Nazis?
LISKA: That's really bad. Those young people should stop and think. If someone yells a lot, then it cannot possibly be right. If you're right, you don't need to yell.

87. What do you do to explain to people what exactly happened in the Holocaust?
LISKA: I have the privilege of telling students in schools what I experienced, and of talking about the Holocaust. I enjoy it tremendously because they listen attentively and show enormous interest.

88. From today's perspective, how can you explain that "normal people" were capable of such atrocities?
LISKA: They were brainwashed by Hitler: they weren't supposed to think at all. All they had to do was what he told them to do. He took responsibility; they had no need to justify anything. That's how something like that can happen, when people don't think and only believe what another person promises them.

89. What exactly do you feel when you hear that there are still people who claim that the Holocaust never took place?
LISKA: I cannot understand that at all. I can understand that the people who were blinded by the propaganda at the time joined the party and were enthusiastic. They were genuinely blinded by the propaganda. But today, to deny what is so well-known—I find that incredible. I even experienced that once myself. In the late 1990s, Jehovah's Witnesses staged the exhibition "The Forgotten Victims of the Nazi Era" in every provincial and district capital in Austria. There was a reconstruction of a concentration camp barrack, talks were given by people who had been there, videos were played, and display boards put up.

In Feldbach in Styria, one man came over and said, "In Fürstenfeld, there's a former SS man who was a guard in Mauthausen concentration camp. He says there were no gas chambers and no crematoriums in Mauthausen." I said, "You can go there and see for yourself. I was there once. You go down into the gas chamber. I'm not going down there again, it's really horrifying!" And he said, "Yes, they're there now." I said, "What do you mean, they're there now?" He told me that this SS man claimed that the

Americans built the gas chambers when they came to Mauthausen. That kind of thing is just unbelievable.

90. What consequences did the proclamation of the "Nuremberg Laws" on September 15, 1935, have for you?
LISKA: None. I was a child of five at the time and didn't really understand why the Jews were being persecuted the way they were.

91. What are your personal memories of the "Night of Broken Glass" on November 9/10, 1938?
LISKA: I don't know anything about that, I can't remember anything.

92. What are your personal memories of the beginning of the war in 1939?
LISKA: I don't recall the actual beginning of the war exactly. I only remember that something awful happened at home in that week. Six of our twelve cows died of bloat. In the evening, Mama had wept and said, "Now war's broken out and there's nothing left to buy! Where are we going to get cows from, now?" Father comforted her, saying, "We'll get them back." And in fact, it wasn't long before he had replaced them. At any rate, that was a catastrophe, and that was how I experienced the beginning of the war.

93. Did you hear that the National Socialists had decided to implement the "final solution to the Jewish question"—the systematic extermination of Jews in Europe—at the Wannsee Conference on January 20, 1942? If so, when and how?
LISKA: Not during the war, because I was still a child and was unaware of such things. I heard about it after the war, of course, but the bulk of it, only in the last fifteen years.

94. When you heard that World War II was over, what feelings did you have?
LISKA: It was a huge relief, naturally. There were already signs of it in the BBC news that the family listened to during my year of community service. Whole platoons of German troops had already been withdrawn from Yugoslavia and had passed us by. They looked very disheartened. When the English soldiers arrived, scenes of jubilation broke out. They were cheered when they arrived.

95. Do you think that humankind has learned something from the Holocaust?

LISKA: If I look at the world, not really. Since 1945, hardly a day has passed without a war being waged somewhere in the world. It's incredible that people still allow themselves to be led astray by propaganda.

96. Should the atrocities be forgotten and no longer talked about, as some people wish?

LISKA: Hubert Mattischek, who survived many years in Mauthausen concentration camp, often quoted the saying, "Anyone who forgets the past, deserves to live through it again." We should forgive, yes, but never forget! Such times must never return.

97. What plans do you still have for the future?

LISKA: I hope to remain active and healthy enough so that I can continue visiting schools and telling students about those days for a long time to come. It's something that really gives me a lot of pleasure.

98. How would you like to be remembered?

LISKA: As someone who remained true to her faith, who didn't succumb to peer pressure, and who genuinely enjoyed life.

99. What else would you like to say to us? Which question was not asked?

LISKA: One day in Waiern, a supervisor came up to me holding a brown velvet jacket and said, "Hermine, put this jacket on!" I replied, "I'm not putting that on, it's a Hitler Youth jacket, and I am not in the Hitler Youth." "All right," she said, "we'll soon see whether you put it on or not!" She took my left hand and pulled the sleeve up over it, but only got as far as the elbow before I slipped out of it again. She put my arm back in, I pulled it out, in, out, in, out. So then she kept hold of my hand and it developed into a real fight, it must be said, until we were both sweating.

Then she gave it up and was a little angry. She said, "There will be no swimming for you today! Today you're in detention and will write a report as a punishment." Well, I accepted that she had to punish me; that didn't bother me. What really bothered me was that she ignored me from that moment on. She had been really nice to me before, and I always felt that she treated me better than she treated the others. But then she just shunned me completely, and that was really very hurtful.

100. After all you have been through, what advice can you give us young people?

LISKA: I would advise you to uphold human values such as tolerance, not to give in to peer pressure, and to show respect for every human being. Live in peace with everyone, and always genuinely appreciate and respect life. Thank you!

Richard Rudolph[14]:
A Victim of Double Persecution

Richard Rudolph, born June 11, 1911
Grounds for persecution: One of Jehovah's Witnesses (Bible Student), conscientious objector
Length of imprisonment: 18 years, 11 months
Country: Germany

39. Richard Rudolph, 1930

40. Richard Rudolph, 2008

[14] Although according to his birth certificate the correct spelling is "Rudolf," most of the documents, certificates, prison records, and Stasi files were issued in the name of "Rudolph." Because Richard Rudolf spelled his name "Rudolph" until 2006, that is the spelling that is used in this book.

Richard Rudolph was born on June 11, 1911, in Rothenbach, Silesia, Germany [now Boguszów-Gorce, Poland]. World War I caused him to develop a deep revulsion of war and shattered his trust in the established churches. Following a long search for answers to the problems of humankind, he began an intensive study of the Bible and became one of Jehovah's Witnesses in 1935. On July 2, 1936, Rudolph was arrested by the Gestapo for smuggling banned publications and imprisoned in the municipal prison in Hirschberg [now Jelenia Góra].

After two and a half years in the Hirschberg prison and the penitentiary and juvenile prison in Breslau [now Wrocław], and short terms of imprisonment in the Breslau police prison and Alexanderplatz police prison in Berlin, he was interned in Sachsenhausen concentration camp on January 26, 1939. There, on September 15, 1939, he witnessed the execution of August Dickmann, the first conscientious objector to be executed in World War II. After four years in Neuengamme concentration camp, during which he spent several weeks in its subcamps Darß-Wieck and Darß-Zingst, he was permanently transferred to another of Neuengamme's subcamps—Salzgitter-Watenstedt/Leinde near Braunschweig. After that, he was briefly held in Ravensbrück concentration camp. He was liberated in May 1945 while on the death march to the ocean liner *Cap Arcona*, anchored off Lübeck. Richard Rudolph spent a total of nine years in Nazi prisons and concentration camps.

After the war, he again found himself persecuted because of his beliefs, this time by the communist regime in the German Democratic Republic. In 1950, he was sentenced to fifteen years' imprisonment. After this sentence had been reduced, he was held in communist prisons for ten years, until September 21, 1960. In January 1961, he succeeded in escaping to West Berlin in the Federal Republic of Germany. In the course of nearly nineteen years' imprisonment, Rudolph was interned in six concentration camps and subcamps and nine prisons. As one of the last surviving victims of double persecution under two German dictatorships, he was, and still is, active as a witness of history. In 2004, his lectures even took him as far afield as universities in Japan. Richard Rudolph lives in Germany.

The interviews took place on August 30, 2008; September 15, 2011; and October 11, 2011.

1. When were you born? What was your father like? What was your mother like?

RUDOLPH: I was born on June 11, 1911, in Rothenbach, Silesia, Germany. I was born out of wedlock, which is why I was raised by my grandparents. My mother [Martha Mathilde Rudolph, married name Nagel, but later divorced] and I were Protestants. My father [Johann Strauch] was Catholic, and I never met him until much later, and then only by chance. After I was born, my mother had to work for pastors as a domestic. In Protestant circles, it was customary for girls in particular to work in pastors' houses. She worked in Thuringia, a long way from Rothenbach and Silesia, and traveling was very difficult during World War I. As a result, I was seven years old before I got to know my mother, but I only knew her as "Aunty." As a little boy, I called my grandfather [Heinrich Rudolph] "father" and my grandmother [Mathilde Rudolph, née Künzel] "mother" and thought they were my real parents. My grandparents were very hardworking, kindly folk; but they were old.

2. What is your earliest childhood memory?

RUDOLPH: I had an uncle [Gustav Rudolph], my mother's brother, who did a lot for me. Of course, he was a staunch supporter of the emperor, as was the custom at the time. He took a great interest in me and my education. He taught me many things when I was a little boy. He meant everything to me. But in 1916, he was drafted and, soon after, was killed in Russia. That was a great loss for me. After that, all I had were my elderly grandparents. That caused me great distress in my early childhood.

3. What kind of childhood did you have?

RUDOLPH: I was always surprised that the other boys had such young fathers and mothers. My "father" was a very old man, you see, and my grandmother, who was my "mother," was an old lady. World War I had left her with a severe nervous disorder, because her son, my uncle, was killed in the war. Of course, it also affected me very badly, and during my first years at school, I couldn't concentrate enough to learn. All I could think of was the misery we found ourselves in, and above all else, I always wondered at the peculiar situation we lived in. Instead of happiness, kindness, and peace, we had hatred and chaos. Family ties were strained too as a result of World War I. I asked my grandmother one time why everything was so strange. She said, "But, my boy, in the future, everything will be much better when we're in heaven!" I said to her, "But

I don't want to go to heaven!" I liked it better on earth than in heaven. Besides, as a boy, I got dizzy very easily, and I was always afraid of heaven because I thought I would never stop being dizzy up there. Well, that's how I grew up, anyway.

4. How long did you go to school, and what schools did you attend?
RUDOLPH: Primary school. In those days, during World War I, primary education was of a very poor standard. Why? Because the male teachers had been drafted, and we had female teachers. And most of them were, in plain language, stupid. They taught us things that weren't correct, also about religious matters. They told us lots of stuff that wasn't true, and as children, we believed it. But in fact, what we learned was all nonsense.

During our last school years, the children in my home region had to work really hard. In springtime, we had to gather coal. Why? Because the miners were on strike and the bakers had no coal. So we gathered coal from the coal heaps, risking our lives if truth be told. It was a very dangerous business. When the dump trucks were emptied up at the top, great lumps of rock would roll down the pile. We had to be extremely careful not to get injured while we were gathering coal. It was back-breaking work too. But we had no choice; we had to gather coal to get bread from the bakery. In the fall, I tended goats. That was the best job. Of course, I also did my homework while I looked after the goats, and it showed.

In winter, my grandfather bound birch-twig brooms. Ten of them would be loaded on a sled, and I took them to the villages and sold them. However, most folk made their own brooms because they were poor. Where I lived, it was a deprived area. So those were my school days.

5. What was your adolescence like? What trade did you learn and what did you do for a living?
RUDOLPH: The following thing happened to me when I was selling the brooms: I was going round all the villages with the brooms, when I came to one village where a wonderful smell of freshly baked bread was coming from a bakery. So I went into the bakery with a broom. The baker's wife came out, and I asked her, "Wouldn't you like to buy a broom?" She said, "You're selling brooms, are you? Who are you, then?" She asked me all about myself, then opened a door and called, "Johann, come into the shop

310

for a moment!" The baker came lumbering out and said, "So it's brooms you're selling?" I said, "Yes." He then asked, "Now, where do you live? What's your name?" I told him, then he said to his wife, "Make some coffee for the boy." I went inside, into the kitchen, and drank the coffee. At home, we didn't have any cake, but in the bakery, they sure had some. They placed a heap of cake in front of me, and I ate it all up. Then a little boy appeared, and I just started playing with him. The boy was so happy that I played with him. Then the old baker said I ought to come by more often and play with the boy.

So then I took some coal in to them as well, and the baker bought every single one of my brooms. He gave me a bag of flour, some bread, and some rolls to take home. In those days, we had never even seen rolls, but as I say, the bakers had such things.

So I went home with all that stuff like Hans in Luck. I had sold all the brooms and had the money for them. I had bread and a bag of flour. When I got home to my grandfather's house, the whole family had congregated there. My mother's sister was there with her husband and his son; his younger brother was there, an aunt, my grandmother and grandfather. I came home beaming with happiness because I had sold all the brooms. That didn't happen very often. So, of course, they were all curious to know where I had been, where I had gotten the bread and the flour; and I told them. Then one of the aunts shrieked, "The boy must never go there again!" My mother started to cry, my stepfather [Alwin Nagel] was laughing, my grandmother was looking very pensive, and so was my grandfather. All in all, confusion reigned in the family. The other aunt said, "He ought to go there again. He ought to take advantage of the baker's family." I had no idea what was going on. In the end, it turned out that the baker was my real father. And the little boy was really my nephew, whom I had known nothing about. The boy's father was my half-brother. Finding my father in that way was a terrible experience for me to have to come to terms with as a child. But he was very kind to me, and after that, I regularly took him coal.

When I left school, my grandfather asked me, "What do you want to do for a living?" I answered, "I want to be a baker." He said, "You won't be a baker, you'll be a carpenter!" Because my grandfather was a carpenter, he naturally wanted me to be one too. But I got my way. How? Because I was very interested in how bread is made, how rolls are made, and later, how cake is made. I found it all very interesting, and that's why I learned the baker's trade in my father's bakery. I addressed the master baker, my father, as "Herr" or "Mr." and called my half-brother Georg, who taught me the trade, "Herr" as well. After all, they were like strangers to me. Then I trained as a baker, and once I had finished my apprenticeship, I obtained my first position as a journeyman baker.

I held several positions as a journeyman baker, the last one in Petersdorf [now Piechowice] in the Giant Mountains [now Krkonoše]. In Petersdorf, I became acquainted with a family whose womenfolk were highly intelligent. They were already advanced in years, worked in a big glass grinding works, and were very well-read. They encouraged me and took great interest in me. They introduced me to world literature, and I began to think seriously about the meaning of life. At all events, the big question arose in my mind of who would solve the problems facing humankind. In our part of the world, we only had the so-called Social Democrats, of course. I found their politics interesting, but it was Karl Liebknecht and Rosa Luxemburg who interested me most. So my education began to focus more and more on the international perspective. The national perspective didn't interest me at all. Why not? Because I had a fundamental hatred of war and revolutions. The situation in Germany was utterly unbearable for me. At any rate, I found Rosa Luxemburg and Karl Liebknecht, the archetypal Communists, appealing, if only because I liked what they thought about religious matters. Although I was a Protestant, the Protestant faith—and the Catholic one too—had been badly tarnished by World War I. For that reason, I started searching in other religions for the solutions to the problems. And I was dreadfully disappointed by what I heard about the immortal soul, hellfire, and all that stuff. So I moved away from Christianity, although Jesus was a very important person to me. What interested me about him was the fact that he was a humane person.

I had a notable encounter with Walter Ulbricht. A family called Ulbricht lived near us and they told me, "Uncle Walter's holding a big speech." I met Uncle Walter, had a discussion with him, and naturally, quarreled with him. Why? Because he rejected everything—Schiller, Goethe, and Jesus—seeing them all as slaves to capitalism. As a result, I lost interest in him. Later on, I learned about Lenin; he was very interesting too. But when Stalin got hold of it, communism was dead and buried as far as I was concerned.

So once more, I had no clear orientation; I wanted nothing to do with religion. Wherever I went, I talked to many different people about the solution to humankind's problems. I was given various pieces of advice. From some people came a variety of political views and suchlike that I couldn't completely accept, but I had to live with them because there weren't any others. Early in the 1930s, I was discussing the solution to the problems with a woman, and she said, "Oh, I have something marvelous here!" It was the brochure *Prosperity Sure* that the Bible Students had published in 1928. I read it and thought, "If that's really true; if that's really true; if that's really true—if what it says here is *really* true, then I believe in God again." That's how I became interested in the Bible Students. I went to talk with them, studied with them, and attended meetings. I also went along when they were out preaching. It all went very well, all very pleasant, although not everything squared with my views.

Anyway, when I left the Church, I visited my father once in a while. I addressed him as "Herr Strauch," since he was the master. He said, "I heard that you've left the Protestant Church." He was Catholic, super-Catholic; I never saw anyone as fanatically Catholic as he, and despite that, he had fathered an illegitimate child: me (*laughs*). Well anyway, when I left the Church, he went to his father confessor—a prior, a Catholic clergyman—and told him he had a wayward child and so on. He confessed that to him. The Catholic prior said to him, "Leave the boy be; the Bible Students are the only ones who really believe in God." At that moment, he made his peace with me again. I wasn't baptized as one of Jehovah's Witnesses, as the Bible Students were now calling themselves, until May 10, 1935. At the time, baptisms only took place at major conventions, and during the Nazi era, I couldn't go to any of them. But then a brother in the faith who had a small farm took a tin bathtub up into his hayloft, and five or six of us were baptized in the bathtub in the hayloft.

6. What can you tell us about your family?

RUDOLPH: My mother no longer worked after 1918 and suffered from a serious lung disease. Then she met the brother of a friend of hers and married him some time later. That was Alwin Nagel, and he became my stepfather. My mother subsequently had two girls and a boy with him. So I had a half-brother, Gustav, and two half-sisters, Hildegard and Eli. I also had two other half-brothers, Max and Georg, sons of my father. My father died in 1945 in a rest home, and my mother died in the 1970s. My grandparents, who were in effect my parents, died before World War II: my grandfather in 1929, and my grandmother in early 1939 shortly after I was interned in Sachsenhausen concentration camp.

On June 16, 1961, I married my wife, Frieda Junge, née Manig. We were married for thirty-two years. She died in 1993. In 2006, I married again. My second wife is Irmgard Kriebel. I was ninety-five years old when we married.

7. Did you use the Nazi greeting "Heil Hitler!" and/or the Nazi salute?
RUDOLPH: No. I opposed Hitler right from the start. Why? Because I opposed every form of nationalism. Not just National Socialism; I hated nationalist thinking, the international perspective appealed to me more. That's why I was originally interested in communism. And because communism was a total failure, I naturally turned my attention elsewhere.

8. Why were you persecuted by the National Socialists?
RUDOLPH: Because I was a Bible Student and Jehovah's Witnesses [Bible Students] were banned. They were banned in 1933, and we had no more literature and received no more copies of the *Watchtower*. So of course we had to try to obtain literature from abroad one way or another. The opportunity arose to get it from Czechoslovakia. The publications were sent from Bern via Prague to Hohenelbe [now Vrchlabí] and brought from Hohenelbe to Spindlermühle [now Špindlerův Mlýn] by a farmer. We then carried them in backpacks from Spindlermühle over the mountains in the evening and at night. This smuggling was, of course, a dangerous business because the Sudeten police force patrolled in Czechoslovakia and cooperated with the Nazis. But the guys who were really in charge were the Czech police, and we had a very good relationship with them. They tacitly helped us by sometimes showing us the best way to cross the border.

9. When were you arrested?
RUDOLPH: I was arrested on July 2, 1936, for smuggling literature.

10. Why were you imprisoned?
RUDOLPH: We had brought a lot of literature to Hirschberg [now Jelenia Góra] in the Giant Mountains. From Hirschberg, the literature was distributed to the various towns, Halle, Leipzig, Berlin, and so on. There was a brother in the faith in Berlin who rented a garage, and he was being watched. When the Gestapo searched the garage, they found the literature and saw that it came from Hirschberg. It could only have come from Bible Students. Because our brother in the faith Mischok, who was chiefly responsible for organizing the smuggling, was already known to the Gestapo, he was arrested. Then they arrested me and our brother in the faith Sterz. We told them we were the only ones responsible, although several people had been involved in smuggling literature. Sisters in the faith were also involved. They always went on ahead of us, and whenever a border patrol appeared, they would jump up and down and fool around. That meant we could see from a long way off that something was amiss, so we disappeared into the woods. In that way, the smuggling went on successfully for several years.

11. What exactly happened when you were arrested?
RUDOLPH: The Gestapo came into the bakery where we were working and arrested me there. They locked me up in the municipal prison in Hirschberg. I was held there pending my trial. I spent ten months in detention awaiting trial and was then sentenced to two and a half years' imprisonment by a special court. I served most of that sentence, less the ten months already served, in solitary confinement in the penitentiary and juvenile prison in Breslau.

12. Did people know right from the start what was happening in the camps? Before you were taken away, did you know what would happen to you?
RUDOLPH: Yes, we knew precisely what was going on in the concentration camps. And we also knew that some of us would be in mortal danger. That was well-known.

13. How many different camps were you in? How many years did you spend in each camp?

RUDOLPH: Let me think. First of all, I was placed in detention awaiting trial on July 2, 1936, in Hirschberg. Then I was held in Breslau prison until December 31, 1938. Once I had served that sentence, the Gestapo was waiting at the gate and escorted me away at once. I was immediately placed in protective custody in the police prison in Breslau. Following that, and a brief period spent in the Alexanderplatz police prison in Berlin, I arrived in Sachsenhausen concentration camp on January 26, 1939. On March 1, 1940, I was interned in Neuengamme concentration camp, and in 1944 in the subcamp Salzgitter-Watenstedt/Leinde near Braunschweig. In April 1945, I was sent on the evacuation march to the Cap Arcona, which we never actually reached. During the course of the march, I was also briefly in Ravensbrück concentration camp. I was liberated in early May. If I add to that the years I spent in prison, it was nine years in all. In East Germany, I was sentenced to fifteen years in prison, but served ten.

14. Were you the only member of your family in the concentration camp, or were family members or friends there as well? If so, did you have any contact with them?

RUDOLPH: No family members were in the concentration camp, but many brothers in the faith, by which I mean Jehovah's Witnesses.

15. What were the first things that happened immediately following your arrival at the concentration camp?

RUDOLPH: The first thing was that the SS made fun of us and told us we wouldn't get out of there alive. They ridiculed the name of Jehovah in the most offensive way. Never before had I heard such blasphemy and contemptuous remarks. Preparations were immediately made for "sending us through the chimney" as soon as possible. These included isolating us, exposing us to hunger by not giving us any food for the first five days, forcing us to perform heavy manual labor in the bitter cold in inadequate clothing, and other forms of intimidation. We were "branded" as Jehovah's Witnesses by the purple triangle. The camp commandant, Hermann Baranowksi, issued the following threat to us: "I am the camp commandant. They call me 'Foursquare,' and you, you dog, will be given a thrashing." With that, he struck a weakened prisoner so hard that he sailed through the air. The "bone men," in other words, the SS, carried black boxes—coffins—through the camp. Foursquare warned us, "Look at those boxes: you'll all end up in one if you don't sign [the declaration renouncing affiliation with Jehovah's Witnesses]."

16. Why did they shave the heads of the prisoners?
RUDOLPH: Because of the risk of escape. They cut our hair off, leaving us bald. Because of the risk of escape, our clothes were also marked: a large cross on your back, and yellow and red stripes on the jacket in oil-based paint, with more stripes down the trousers. They didn't make a big deal out of it, and if a prisoner was likely to try to escape, he was given a black dot as well. The procedure varied from one camp to another.

17. What prisoner category were you put in?
RUDOLPH: In the Bible Students'. We weren't called Jehovah's Witnesses. The SS was "afraid" to use the name Jehovah, so they called us Bible Students.

18. Can you describe the daily routine in the concentration camp?
RUDOLPH: The daily routine was extermination through labor. It included every kind of work, whether excavation or other work. The central purpose was extermination through labor.

19. What was the worst thing about the daily routine?
RUDOLPH: Intimidation, intimidation. Of course, it depended where you worked, but you were always required to fulfill a huge quota.

20. Did everyday life lead more to solidarity, or did the prisoners try to cope on their own?
RUDOLPH: Oh, you had to stick together. There was no other option. It was completely impossible to work on your own because we were organized in groups.

21. Was there anything that helped you take your mind off the horror of daily life for a while (such as music)? What gave you strength?
RUDOLPH: There was a band in the camp, and it played especially when prisoners were being particularly badly tormented or executed. That was the "variety" provided by the band. Of course, the various groups of prisoners, the political prisoners, habitual criminals, and so on, used their "leisure time," if you could call it that, as they saw fit. We tried to study

the Bible, illicitly of course. And without a Bible, naturally. But most of us had the Bible in our heads.

22. What were living conditions like in the barracks (prisoner allocation, food supplies, hygiene, clothing, etc.)?

RUDOLPH: Before the war, a great deal of importance was attached to personal hygiene in Sachsenhausen. Specifically, they placed a lot of importance on the prisoners' brushing their teeth. They used to inspect our toothbrushes, and if there was tartar in them, our rations were stopped. If you hadn't made your bed properly, it was pulled apart, and the SS man who handed out the rations gave them to the others. That was a major problem in Sachsenhausen in particular. In Neuengamme, things were different. We lay two men to a pallet, and most of us had lice. The lice were introduced by criminal elements, and they got so bad—there were so many little lice—that when you put your jacket down, it moved because there were suddenly so many lice. After that, we got fleas. The sanitary conditions in Neuengamme were catastrophic. Our clothes were wet through and through every day, and we couldn't dry them, so in the morning, we had to put our wet clothes back on. We had one single toilet for over one hundred people. It was so full that it overflowed, and the whole passage was full of excrement. Then the prisoners contracted diarrhea. That was a disaster of the utmost seriousness, and of course, many prisoners died as a result.

23. What jobs did you have to do? How many hours a day did you have to work?

RUDOLPH: In Sachsenhausen, we had to push iron trucks. Our clothing was way too flimsy, we were undernourished, and our hands froze to the trucks. We got frostbite, which of course stank when it blistered, and were given no treatment for it, [not] even in the sickbay. They told us Jehovah would help us. When we set out to go to work, the commandant would ride his mare next to us and say to the horse, "Liese, do you notice how they stink?" And the horse would always snort, which delighted him. And one year later, he himself perished in his own stench.

He had a stroke, and after his death, one of our brothers in the faith, Stefan Urbanzig, who was from Upper Silesia, had to redecorate his [the deceased commandant's] entire house with a gang of painters. While he was there, the commandant's daughter came up to him and said, "Do you

318

know what my father died of? The Bible Students prayed him to death." He replied, "The Bible Students do not pray anyone to health, neither do they pray anyone to death."

In Neuengamme, I started off in the railway station detail. This was a work detail that had to unload from the train all the material necessary for building the camp. We loaded cement, lime, and all the building material. After that, I worked on barrack construction and was also in a penal company. I worked as a janitor too and in the SS kitchen. In Neuengamme and Sachsenhausen, I also worked as a carpenter in the carpentry detail.

41: Richard Rudolph (right) and Karl Junge (second from the right) building the kitchen barracks in the carpentry detail in Neuengamme concentration camp, 1940

And the working hours? Well, the morning started with roll call. It made no difference if it was raining or the sun was shining. We had to go out in the pouring rain. It rained often in Neuengamme and Sachsenhausen. We had to stand on the roll-call square for hours on end, and then we went to work. Work was assigned according to blocks and groups. It depended on the type of work to be done. Excavating was the job the prisoners liked least, because that's where there was the most intimidation. For the other jobs the *kapos* determined how the work was done. If you were doing a job and the *kapo* was one of Jehovah's Witnesses, it was easier. But you still had to work very hard. We worked until six in the evening. That was the general rule, but there were also situations in which we prisoners had to work longer. It varied from case to case.

24. What effect did the slogan "Work liberates" have on you?

RUDOLPH: Well, to be frank, that slogan was a mockery. No person was ever liberated by work. I don't know of a single instance in which someone was liberated by work. It was nothing but a mockery of people in general, as if all the people who were interned were lazy. In reality, most of them were taken away from their work by being locked up.

25. What were the guards like in the camp?

RUDOLPH: In the first years, the SS men were very, very bad. They acted arbitrarily, doled out punishments arbitrarily, canceled meals arbitrarily, and so on. Later on, there were, of course, SS men who were very well disposed toward us—I mean toward Jehovah's Witnesses. But they were just one or two, and those one or two couldn't offer the camp command any resistance, of course. Apart from that, prisoners were used as *kapos*. These included various types of character. There were some who tried to ingratiate themselves with the SS and were their helpers, so to speak. There were others who were totally neutral. So you can't generalize and say all the *kapos* were bad. But there were some who were extremely bad.

The commandant of the protective custody camp, *Hauptsturmführer* (Captain) Anton Thumann, the hangman, was particularly strange. At first, he was skeptical and kept wanting to hang me for my refusal to do military service. Although I was already in the concentration camp, they still kept wanting to send me to war. After he had watched me working, and assessed my character, he became better disposed toward me. Then he said I could be released if I signed [the declaration renouncing my faith]. I explained why I wouldn't sign: because I believe in Jehovah God and the coming of his kingdom, and that only God's kingdom will bring genuine peace, security, and health. He was very impressed by that and said he believed in the same thing, but couldn't live that way because he felt he was imperfect.

Hauptsturmführer Thumann didn't have me executed; instead I was sent to Watenstedt, near Braunschweig, to take up a post as a *kapo* in the bomb foundry there. But because I rejected this appointment on the grounds of my Christian conscience, I was to be hanged there. When the hangman came to take me for execution, he first had to report to the commandant's office with me. There, I happened to meet *SS-Rottenführer* (Section Leader) Gustav Arndt. He had been very good to me and had taught me to cook in Neuengamme. He had been a cook in the navy and subsequently was assigned to the concentration camp. He was a good cook and gave me many a tip about how I could do things better, especially sauces. He had been transferred to Watenstedt as well and was the chef there. The commandant said to him, "Stay away from that guy, he's really dangerous!" Gustav Arndt said, "He's not dangerous, I know him very well." Then he used all his powers of persuasion to convince the commandant to let me work in the kitchen with him.

In the spring of 1945, an executioner came into the kitchen again. I was standing next to the *Rottenführer*. The executioner said to *Rottenführer* Arndt, "Gustav, is a prisoner 333 with you?" "What about him?" asked Arndt. "He's to be hanged," said the executioner. Luckily, I was wearing my normal shirt and not my prisoner's jacket. Then *Rottenführer* Arndt told him I was on a transport, even though I was standing right next to him. So they looked for me in the transport that had just departed, but didn't find me. And that SS man, Gustav Arndt, hid me until we were taken away from there. He saved my life.

26. Was there any contact between the prisoners and the local population?
RUDOLPH: None. On the contrary, most of the population had been whipped up into a state of animosity against us prisoners. If they had met one of us, they would have immediately informed on us. Escaping from a concentration camp meant putting your life at risk.

27. Were you aware of how the war was proceeding in the outside world?
RUDOLPH: In general, we didn't know. We had no newspapers, heard no news. All we heard was the propaganda, but we had no way of checking whether this propaganda was accurate or not. When we were in Neuengamme, we could see the "Christmas trees,"[15] the

---

[15]   See Hermine Liska, question 30, for a description of "Christmas trees," or phosphorous bombs.

phosphorus bombs, coming down over Hamburg. And in Watenstedt near Braunschweig, we could see how Hanover and Braunschweig were reduced to ashes.

28. In the concentration camp, were you allowed to receive letters, food parcels, etc.?

RUDOLPH: We were allowed to write a letter once a month. If the letter didn't pass the censors, it came back. There were no two ways about that. We received letters too, but they were censored as well. Letter writers on the outside ran an enormous risk of ending up in a concentration camp themselves. Many husbands and wives were each interned in a concentration camp. Jehovah's Witnesses in Sachsenhausen even received letters in which their wives bemoaned their fate. As a result, their husbands were given a beating.

In regard to food: when starvation had reached catastrophic levels, prisoners were allowed to receive parcels. The Polish prisoners in particular got good parcels. We Germans only got what our relatives had been able to save up with their coupons. But in Neuengamme, there was a "parcel collective" and a "commodity collective" among Jehovah's Witnesses. All the parcels that arrived belonged to everyone. Because many of their wives were also in concentration camps, many brothers in the faith were unable to receive any parcels. Jehovah's Witnesses were the only ones who did that. We even made a pair of scales with a piece of string and a beam to weigh everything so that the portions were the same size and no one went short. There was a group of brothers in the faith that were responsible for distribution. That was a great help. None of our parcels could be stolen, and every evening, everyone had an extra helping. That was a twofold blessing, because among the other prisoner groups, any parcel sent to a prisoner was generally stolen. There was nowhere to store things, except in your own bed. It was very common for a prisoner to find his parcel had been stolen when he came back from work in the evening.

29. What forms of torture did you suffer?

RUDOLPH: Being hung on a stake. The prisoner was manacled with a chain on his back and hung up. We hung on the stake for an hour—that's how long they left us hanging there. Afterward, you couldn't use your hands, of course. They swelled up like balloons, but we still had to go back to work again immediately. We had to dig and could only move the shovel by putting it under our arms. We Jehovah's Witnesses were bullied more than the others; the SS would pull on our feet to stretch us. That was extremely painful.

30. What was the most frightening moment for you?

RUDOLPH: That was in Sachsenhausen. It was early September [19]39, when the war had started. We all had to go into the camp, and from a long way off, we could already see a heap of gravel piled up to stop bullets. In front of the pile of gravel was a wooden wall, roughly nine feet long and seven feet high. We lined up by this wooden wall, about two hundred of Jehovah's Witnesses on the right, and two hundred on the left. On the right, by the wall, there was a black box. Then our brother in the faith August Dickmann was brought forward. The commandant said that he was to be executed because he refused to defend the German fatherland. Dickmann was asked whether he stood by his statement, and he said yes, he stood by it. Then he was ordered to turn around. The firing squad was given the order to shoot, and our brother in the faith August Dickmann fell to the ground.

42. August Dickmann, ca. 1935

He was tossed into the box. His own brother [Heinrich Dickmann] had to nail it shut. The box was carried away, and the commandant asked us, "Which of you will sign?" Two men who had already signed stepped forward. They announced to the commandant that they retracted their signatures. Not a single one of Jehovah's Witnesses signed. They were all of the same mind as our brother in the faith August Dickmann.

Then those born in the years 1911 and 1910 were targeted. After August Dickmann had been shot, they were picked out one by one after work in the evening and shot dead in the *Industriehof*, the workshop area. Then there were only about ten of us left. We were told that prisoners such and such would be shot that evening after the last roll call. We had already said our last goodbyes to our brothers in the faith, Jehovah's Witnesses. I had done so too. After that, we were not in the least afraid of being shot. When it was time for evening roll call, it was so short and over so quickly that we thought something must have happened. And in fact something had happened: the commandant who had ordered the shootings had had a stroke and perished in his own stench.

31. Were there any entertaining or lighthearted incidents that enabled you to forget all the suffering for a moment? Can you describe them?
RUDOLPH: There were no lighthearted incidents initially, at least not for Jehovah's Witnesses. There may have been lighthearted incidents for others, but not for Jehovah's Witnesses.

32. What were your day-to-day thoughts while you were in the concentration camp?
RUDOLPH: The political prisoners and the others had a lot of slogans. They drew strength from those slogans. We Jehovah's Witnesses concentrated on the Bible, the word of God. That was our relaxation, our leisure, so to speak. Of course, if anyone caught us doing it, they informed on us. That once happened to me too. We were talking about Schiller while we worked: about his marvelous thoughts, for example, where he says, "Brothers—over the canopy of stars a loving father must live. Brothers—over the canopy of stars, God judges as we judge." And just because I recited that, a prisoner informed on me. He said I had quoted from the Bible. As a result, the political prisoners, the Communists, wanted to beat me up.

33. Was it possible for children to be born in a concentration camp? If so, what happened to these babies?
RUDOLPH: I don't know. Our concentration camps were all male.

34. Was it possible to make friends with prisoners?
RUDOLPH: Yes, we were friends. We were a community of brothers and, as Jehovah's Witnesses, had close ties with one another.

35. Who was your best friend during this dreadful time, and how did he or she help you?

RUDOLPH: He couldn't help me much; we had to help each other. That was Karl Junge, one of Jehovah's Witnesses. He went down with the *Cap Arcona*, and I later married his widow.

36. What did you do to relieve the suffering of other inmates?

RUDOLPH: We helped each other within the bounds of our possibilities. I gave my parcels to the "parcel collective" like the others did. We depended on mutual support. We Jehovah's Witnesses took particular care to make everyone else's life easier. But opportunities to do so were few.

37. Were there particular hierarchies among the inmates?

RUDOLPH: Of course there were hierarchies. There were also fights for supremacy in the camp between the political prisoners—the Communists—and the habitual criminals. But we Jehovah's Witnesses weren't involved in that. We weren't interested in obtaining any particular positions in the camp.

38. Were there any differences in the way the various groups of prisoners (religious, political groups) were treated?

RUDOLPH: Jehovah's Witnesses were treated particularly badly in Sachsenhausen concentration camp. In other camps, it wasn't as bad, but in Sachsenhausen, it was terrible.

Not all, but a lot of the political prisoners were very spiteful toward us and collaborated with the SS. Of course, there were some sensible ones among them too who helped us.

In Sachsenhausen, within the camp, there was a separate enclosure, which was surrounded by barbed wire. That's where we Jehovah's Witnesses were isolated. The political prisoners were our block seniors, and of course, they harassed us and informed on us to the SS. We also had a Bible. Our brother in the faith Schurstein had smuggled it into the camp inside his wooden leg. The political prisoners got wind of the fact that we had a Bible and naturally reported it to the SS. The SS then searched the block from top to bottom, but didn't find anything. A political prisoner had taken the Bible, and that's why they couldn't find it. He gave it back to us afterwards. His name was Albin Lüdke. He was well disposed toward us.

In Neuengamme, I was supposed to be hanged. Until the time came for my execution, I was put in the penal company. All the sewage from the SS camp and the prisoners' camp flowed into a large basin in our [the penal company's] camp. Prisoners in the penal company whose names were on a blacklist were pushed into the cesspool. Of course, they couldn't get out again, and died in it. I was also one of those at risk. Then the *kapos* who were favorably disposed toward me said to the penal company's *kapo*, "If that little Bible Student in your gang dies in the penal company, that's the day you'll hang from the truss beam!" That frightened the *kapo*, so he took me out of that detail and hid me in the cement bunker.

While the commandant of the protective custody camp, SS-*Obersturmführer* (First Lieutenant) Albert Lütkemeyer, was on leave, I was released from the penal company. It is interesting to note that the wives of Bible Students had to work on the estate in Schleswig-Holstein that belonged to Lütkemeyer's mother. Himmler had sent them there to help Frau Lütkemeyer, and she said to her son, "Just you leave the Bible Students alone, they're the best people I've ever come across." That made him change his mind. Later, it was through him that I got a job in the SS kitchen, away from the worst of the dirt and in the best position in the camp.

39. What diseases and illnesses were prevalent in the concentration camp?

RUDOLPH: There were so many diseases that we didn't even know what they were all called. So many died, and a large number were killed. The order was given one time that all the *"Muselmänner"*—a prisoner who was too weak to work was called a *"Muselmann"*—were to be put in the "sanatorium." There was an express train car in a siding, and we Jehovah's Witnesses were in the station detail at the time. We had to carry the *Muselmänner* into the car. There was a brother in the faith who was blind among them, and we really believed they were taking them somewhere where they would be better off and wouldn't have to work, because they were unfit. But a few days later, a pile of naked corpses lay on the path where we had been working. That was the "sanatorium" they had been put in. They were killed there. That was in Neuengamme.

Then *Muselmänner* were sent to Neuengamme from all the other camps because Neuengamme was a reception camp. But in Neuengamme, they had no idea what to do with them. So they were summoned to the "sickbay." There was a large room there, where a man dressed as a doctor was sitting. He then injected something into their hearts. They were given a lethal injection. Even though they were still half alive, they were immediately thrown onto the flatcar and burned in the field. That was the second extermination. For the third extermination, they gassed them. They put all the *Muselmänner* in a cell and piped gas into it. You cannot imagine how that stank—the whole camp stank; it was unbearable, appalling.

40. Did you receive a physical injury?
RUDOLPH: I was never seriously injured as such. The only injury came from being manacled and hung from a stake by the hands.

41. How much did you weigh when you were in the concentration camp?
RUDOLPH: Maybe around ninety pounds. We had no scales and weren't weighed. We were nothing but skin and bones. When we showered, you could almost see into our stomachs from behind. Nothing but skin and bones.

42. What did death mean to you?
RUDOLPH: Release. There were times when I longed for nothing more than dying. It would have been a release.

43. What was the closest you came to death?
RUDOLPH: I was often very close. Especially every time I received an inquiry from the district Wehrmacht command. They could have come and hung me at any time. I didn't know when I would be hanged. The camp commander said, "When the time is ripe." So when is the time ripe? It would have been ripe if a revolt had broken out in the camp. They would have hung me first, even though I would have had nothing to do with the revolt.

44. Did you ever build a kind of "wall" to shield yourself from the terrible things that were being done so that the death of a fellow prisoner no longer affected you?
RUDOLPH: We all became desensitized. Death didn't matter to us anymore. There were corpses lying around every day, and you had to say to yourself, "One day you'll be lying there too; one day you'll be on that pile."

45. What happened to the dead bodies in the concentration camp?

RUDOLPH: Oil was poured over them and they were burned. The stench was appalling; it must have stunk for miles around. The most horrible thing was that Russian prisoners of war always wanted to work outside in the crematorium, cremating the bodies. We wondered why. One time, one of our brothers in the faith had to work there. He saw two Russians dragging a dead body across the field. One of them was holding a roasted hand and eating it; the other was holding a foot and biting into it. He said to me, "Richard, I can hardly begin to tell you what I saw today." Then he told me what the Russian prisoners had done. The way they were treated was dreadful. They were given rutabagas boiled in dirt. One of them was given the rutabaga, the other the water, and they would fight over the rutabaga. The crimes perpetrated against the Russian prisoners of war were horrendous. It's indescribable. They were so hungry that they even ate parts of dead bodies. They tore open their comrades' dead bodies and ate their livers. It's simply unimaginable. That was in Neuengamme.

46. Was there ever a possibility for you to be released from the concentration camp?

RUDOLPH: Only if I had signed the statement renouncing my faith, and that was a scam too. We were told we would be released, but that was a lie—unless you joined the army.

47. Were there any escape attempts or opportunities to escape? Did you try to escape?

RUDOLPH: We had the opportunity, but we didn't escape. Where could we have run to? We would have been reported at once if we had been running around outside the camp. But there was one escape attempt. It was in 1939, shortly before Christmas in Sachsenhausen. It was cold, and it was even snowing.

We were working on the group command. The group command was a large building intended as the functions building for the SS. It was a splendid building, and I worked as a roofer. When the building was finished, a habitual criminal was appointed as janitor. We were on our way to work when, suddenly, the siren went off. We had to go back. A prisoner had disappeared, and they didn't know which one. They were too stupid to work out that it was this janitor. They counted him as part of our group, so they thought he was missing from us. But there was no one missing from our group. So we had to line up according to our tables and beds, and they didn't realize that he was missing from the main camp. They were too dumb to work it out. Anyway, the prisoner had put on an SS uniform and crossed the line of sentries wearing it. Afterward, they noticed that he had disappeared.

We had to stand by the gate from ten in the morning, and the SS said, "Unless the prisoner is caught, you'll stand there until no one's left alive!" We had to stand there all night long, and for a second day and a third day. During the third night, the military police found him in a café in Berlin. If he had taken refuge someplace with acquaintances, we would all have died. He was found after two and a half days. They brought him into the camp, beat him, and gave him a cold shower. That was shortly before Christmas. Then they beat him again and gave him another cold shower. It wasn't until after they hanged him that, at last, we were allowed to fall out and return to our block. We were utterly exhausted. We had gotten no food, nothing to drink, and hadn't been able to answer the call of nature. We just passed water on the roll-call square, in front of the gate. Several men collapsed. I was pretty much on the point of collapse myself.

During this incident, the following thing happened: there was a political prisoner who was well disposed toward us. He was a master electrician, and he said, "If you Jehovah's Witnesses don't pray now, we're all finished." One of the older brothers in the faith began to pray loudly on the roll-call square. Afterward, we found out that it was at that moment that the escaped prisoner was found.

48. Were there any inmates in the concentration camp who dared to stage a revolt against the camp authorities?

RUDOLPH: Yes, some tried it, but it was delusional, it was senseless. The Communists wanted to persuade us to join in, but we firmly refused, of course. That was in Neuengamme, shortly before the end. They wanted to liberate the camp with a couple of pistols. And what would they have done then? The SS would have overrun the entire camp.

49. Did you think you would ever make it out alive?

RUDOLPH: No, we didn't expect that at all, we didn't expect that at all. It would have been delusional to expect it. But secretly we hoped. But we didn't expect it.

50. Were there any times when you gave up all hope? If so, why?

RUDOLPH: That's relative. You can say, "Maybe we'll get out." We hoped it might be possible. I once had a talk with Karl Junge one evening when I went from Neuengamme to Watenstedt. I said, "Karl, we don't know which of us will get out of here alive." Yet we felt that the business was coming to an end. We didn't have an inkling of whether we would survive, though. Sadly, he died in the *Cap Arcona* disaster, when the prisoners were sunk.

51. Did anyone commit suicide?

RUDOLPH: Yes, we did witness suicides. There were several prisoners who ran into the barbed wire and killed themselves. In Neuengamme, a so-called habitual criminal chopped his fingers off to avoid conscription into the Wehrmacht. I was looking for building material for the barrack. There were various types of barrack construction, and I had to find the right components for the type I was working on: they had been left in a jumble. It was frosty outside, and I was rummaging through the various components. All at once, I noticed some fingers on the ground, and I thought, "My fingers have dropped off because of the cold." I looked at my hands. My fingers were still all there. The fingers I saw lying there were the prisoner's. He was executed.

52. During the Holocaust, did you ever consider committing suicide out of sheer despair?

RUDOLPH: No. My faith meant that this was never an option, of course.

53. What thoughts, ideas, hopes, wishes, or religious convictions did you cling to?

RUDOLPH: The knowledge of the truth of God's word—that Jehovah God will make his kingdom reality. That was my hope. I clung to that, and it sustained me.

54. Did you lose your faith in God while you were in the camp?

RUDOLPH: No, my faith only grew stronger. It grew stronger because we encouraged each other. Even though we had no access to the Bible, we had it in our heads. I had enough knowledge of the truth and based my hope on that.

55. What role did your religion play in how you felt about what was going on? Why?

RUDOLPH: Religion was a great help to me, mainly because we saw that Bible prophesies were being fulfilled. That made us very enthusiastic. For us, the whole time in the concentration camp was a sign of the "time of the end." That's why our perception of the whole concentration camp period was different from the way other people may have perceived it. In Neuengamme, we even had a link to Brooklyn, the global headquarters of Jehovah's Witnesses. Some brothers in the faith worked for a company in Bergedorf. There, they were able to secretly send our reports to Brooklyn, and we received news from Brooklyn. One of our sisters in the faith was also involved. That was tremendously uplifting and encouraging for us.

56. Did you pray during your internment?

RUDOLPH: Yes, a lot. In the concentration camp, we also prayed together. I prayed a lot, especially during my internment in East Germany, in the "Roter Ochse" prison. I always prayed, "Lord Jehovah, give me strength so that I don't go mad in here, that I don't lose my mind, and give me the strength to make a good statement at the interrogation." And there is absolutely no doubt at all that Jehovah answered that prayer. I was able to give such wonderful testimony that the interrogators were astounded.

57. Did you ever consider changing your religion (or ideology)? Why?

RUDOLPH: No, because for me, it was the truth.

58. What was the date of your liberation from the camp?

RUDOLPH: Early May 1945.

59. How were you liberated from the camp, or how did you manage to get out of it?

RUDOLPH: The SS had orders to take us prisoners from Ravensbrück concentration camp to Lübeck and put us on the *Cap Arcona*. But the military police were looking for me as well. We had already been marching for a couple of days and had made camp in the open country by the Müritzsee [lake] in Mecklenburg. I just happened to be away from the group easing nature. Then the military police arrived to pick me up. We used to call them "guard dogs" because they had a chain around their necks with a metal tag saying "Military Police." They drove up on a Victoria motorcycle and sidecar. The prisoners said to them, "He's not here." When I came back to the group, I saw the two "guard dogs" driving away. So the prisoners protected me in that instance. That was just before the end of the war. After that, the SS fled because the Russian army was already in Mecklenburg, and we were then free.

So it was the end of the war that liberated us, as it were, but not the Russian army itself because it didn't come to where we were.

The interesting thing is that political prisoners and prisoners from other countries then went into the barns and slaughtered the cows. I was with several French prisoners, two Poles, and a German who had been a foreign legionnaire. But we didn't join in the slaughtering. The others then crossed the border over the river Elbe in Wittenberge and went to France. They wanted to take me with them and said, "Come with us, Richard, because the Russians will take over the government here! Then things will go badly with you!" I said, "No, I'd rather go to Silesia because if I go to France, I'll be seen as a troublesome German and not as a concentration camp internee. Here, I'll fall into the hands of the Russians, and over there into those of the French. Things will go just as badly with me in France as here in Germany." That's why I didn't go with them.

60. How were you treated by the people who liberated you?
RUDOLPH: Well, I wasn't really liberated by anyone. To begin with, we hid in the woods, near Jännersdorf in Mecklenburg. You see, we didn't know what was going on. All at once, three women came running toward us, and we knew they were women prisoners from Ravensbrück concentration camp. So we came out, and then a farmer came up whose horse had bolted. I caught hold of the horse and gave it back to the farmer. When he saw my striped clothing, he yelled in horror. We told him to boil some potatoes for us, at least. So then he took us to his wife, but she didn't boil any potatoes for us, because we were concentration camp prisoners. She was afraid to give us anything to eat because she thought

that the SS would come back. So the farmer himself boiled the potatoes and we ate them.

61. What was the first thing you did after you were liberated?

RUDOLPH: After we had eaten the potatoes in their skins at the farmer's house, we went to a house where farmhands were living. It was one day after liberation. We had heard that there were Silesian women there. There was indeed a Silesian woman from my home region there, though not from my home village. Then a Russian came in and wanted a woman. He took a small young girl. I said, "Stop, the child stays here!" The Russian took out his pistol, pointed it at my chest, and looked at me. I looked him in the eye and prayed, "Lord Jehovah, so far I have been protected by you. Please don't forsake me now!" When I was done, he removed his pistol and grabbed one of the older women. He took her out and had his way with her outside. There was nothing I could do about that, but at least I had torn the little girl from his grasp. You couldn't call these Russians "liberators."

Then the mayor, who was a displaced former Nazi, found out that we were there at the farmhands' house and invited us for a meal. He produced a large meal, food was prepared, and we ate with a knife and fork again for the first time. While we were eating, a Russian adjutant came in. He needed women for the commandant and took a little girl. I said, "The girl stays here; and if the commandant wants a woman, he should come here himself!" At that, the adjutant turned on his heel and left. The others—everyone at the table—were frightened; they were shaking from head to foot. Then they wanted me to be mayor of Jännersdorf. They would have appointed me mayor, but I said, "I won't be your mayor, I'm going back home to Silesia."

Following this incident, I started walking through the towns in the direction of Silesia. The French prisoners taught me some French phrases I should say to the Russians if they held me up. That worked very well in one town. I would put a cap on at an angle, and the Russian thought I was French. The next time, the Russians stopped me in Rathenow and asked, "You *nemets* (German)?" I said, "Yes." I had to go with them, and they put me in a prisoner of war camp. Now I was in a POW camp with German soldiers, who were divided up into groups. I went over and sat with one group and said, "You know, if Hitler hadn't made such a mess of things, we wouldn't be here now." They wanted to beat me up for that. In the distance, I saw a Russian commandant who spoke German. The Russians were afraid of uprisings. He saw what was unfolding and called me over. "What's going on?" I said that I was one of Jehovah's Witnesses and had been in a concentration camp and so on. He said, "Man, get out of here!" Evening was falling, so I went to a farm. The farmer was a Communist. He bragged about that. Those who had been Nazis before were suddenly all Communists. I wanted to spend the night in the hayloft, but he wouldn't let me, because he was afraid of the Communists, the Russians. The old farmer's wife brought me slices of cheese and locked me in the goose shed. So I slept in the goose shed. That was another experience on my journey home. I also went to see the mayor of Rathenow, and he gave me a little money. It was no use to me at all; I couldn't buy anything at all with it, because there wasn't anything to buy.

Then I arrived in Kleinmachnow, to the southwest of Berlin. It was a beautiful, sunny Saturday. I passed by a bakery, and all the women were there doing their shopping. A blond woman said to me, "Oh look, a poor private." I said, "A happy 'concentrateur.'" She was a businesswoman from Berlin. She had been driven out of Berlin by the bombing and now lived on a small plot of land near Kleinmachnow.

Then she said, "Listen, I have a little house. If you would like to rest there for a few days, be my guest." I said, "I would be glad to." The thought had already occurred to me that I would really like to have a good rest here. She took me to her plot of land. She had a little dog and a little house, and I slept there. But she couldn't cook. She brought some horsemeat and I made goulash with it. We also studied the Bible: Daniel chapters 10, 11, and 12. I spent two days there, but suddenly she started to make romantic advances. I said to myself, "You had better get out of here!" So I told her, I was leaving the next day, which I did, and she accompanied me. We said goodbye at the [canal] lock, and she was so happy. She thanked me and said, "I am so grateful to you that nothing happened between us. I can still look my husband in the eye as a faithful wife." I never saw her again.

62. Did you have any problems when you returned home? How did people in your home environment react to you?

RUDOLPH: I never reached my home, and never saw it again. It was now Polish.

63. Were you able to rejoin your family?

RUDOLPH: Not until much later, because my mother and my sister were also refugees.

64. Did you have any acquaintances, friends, or relatives in the camps? Did they survive their internment?

RUDOLPH: Yes, one of them survived, but he has long since died. That was Gustav Sterz who was arrested with me for smuggling literature. I was with him in Sachsenhausen, and he stayed there. He survived, and we met up in Berlin where he then lived.

65. What happened to your possessions?

RUDOLPH: I don't know. They were all divided up, they all vanished. I never saw any of it again. Everything was lost owing to the occupation by the Poles.

66. To what extent have you received compensation for your internment?

RUDOLPH: I have received several sums as compensation. I don't remember how much they were, but I did receive something in compensation.

67. How did you set about rebuilding your life?

RUDOLPH: The situation in East Germany was such that there weren't many opportunities for earning a livelihood. In 1946, I started preaching "full time," so I devoted most of my time to spreading the "good news" and was able to establish congregations in several places, such as Finsterwalde. This work gave me a lot of pleasure, of course.

68. How long did it take you to return to a "normal" life after the Holocaust?

RUDOLPH: I found my feet again very quickly and soon returned to a normal life.

69. What was your life like after the war?

RUDOLPH: I couldn't go back home, so I decided to visit Karl Junge, whom I had befriended in Neuengamme concentration camp. I thought he was still alive. But I didn't get to see him, because he had already died. Then I met his wife, Frieda, whom I married sixteen years later. As I said, from 1946 onward, I established congregations and visited them to lend them spiritual support. This went very well until 1950, when the Communists issued their ban in East Germany. The ban was issued just as I was cycling through a large wood from Burkersdorf to Ruhland. I was surrounded by members of the *Volkspolizei*, the East German police. They knew I would be taking that route. It was around midnight, and I was arrested in the middle of the woods. I was initially held in a tiny cell in the police station in Hoyerswerda, but later I was sent to Dresden. Conditions in Dresden were terrible. The cell was nice, and at first I thought, "I can live with this." But then the dogs started to bark. The dogs barked incessantly from evening to morning, for two and a half nights. At first, I thought it was only natural, but in reality, they had played a tape recording so that I didn't get any rest and couldn't sleep. That was really bad; you can't imagine how tough it was.

Then they played impersonations of the voices of my brothers in the faith to make me think they were in the prison too and were bad-mouthing each other. But I guessed that Brother Frost, Sister Unterdörfer, and Brother Wauer were in fact already safe, as indeed they were. Because I didn't believe that those three were in custody, they transferred me to the "Roter Ochse" prison in Halle an der Saale out of sheer resentment. There, I was in really deep trouble. To start with, the cell was filthy, the windows were boarded up, and the sanitary conditions were appalling. Every day, I was given potato peelings in hot water to eat. The potato peelings had the effect of clogging up the villi of the intestines so that I had no proper bowel movements anymore. Breakfast was a piece of bread, sometimes with a smearing of fat on it, and occasionally a spoonful of sugar. At any rate, in my extreme despair, I prayed very often that I wouldn't go crazy. After about ten or eleven weeks, a guard came and said, "Do you know why you're being treated this way?" I said, "Yes, I can imagine why." He said, "We want to prove the theory of evolution: that under certain conditions, human beings regress . . ." I interrupted him and said, "Your aim is to make human beings return to an apelike state under atrocious conditions." He said, "Yes!" and I replied, "I can quite believe that's the kind of thing you would try." Then he left me, and afterward, the expected interrogation took place.

The interrogation was held at night in the cellar. When I arrived, three guards were there. One of them said, "If you don't tell us what we want to know, you won't get out of here alive." I said, "I am not afraid of dying. I spent nine years in concentration camps and have lost all sense of fear." The guard then asked, "When was that? What were you in for?" I said, "Everywhere I went, I told people that since 1914, we have been in the 'time of the end' and that Jesus Christ has begun his reign." The guard said, "You'll have to prove it." I then quoted the book of Daniel, chapter 4, and proved that the 2,520 years, the seven periods of time, began in 607 BC and ended in 1914. I had just finished my explanation when the prison warden came in and called out, "Is this guy giving you any problems?" They said, "He was already in a concentration camp." The warden said, "What, that guy was already in a concentration camp?" He went out, returning a short time later with a man who had been in Neuengamme as a Communist and with whom we had studied the Bible. He was now employed there as a driver. When the driver saw me there, he was horrified and said to the first guards, "If you don't stop this nonsense, you're going to have to walk. I'm driving home now." So they had to call a halt, and I was naturally very pleased to have been able to bear such effective witness to the glorification of the name of Jehovah. Following that, I was put in a shared cell with two brothers in the faith, Seliger and Pfennig. Brother Pfennig removed the stuff from my rear. It was like resin. I had no bowel movements anymore. The potato peelings I was given to eat ruined my intestines.

Then came the so-called court hearing. The hearing was a joke. A large audience had been invited because it was to be a public hearing. They wanted to make us look completely ridiculous. The presiding judge asked, "Defendant, what is your opinion of Stalin?" I said, "I don't know the man personally, so I cannot allow myself to make a judgment." Then of course they all jumped up like jack-in-the-boxes. Then he asked me another question because I had said that Jehovah will bring to ruin those who are bringing the earth to ruin. He asked, "Defendant, who will bring the earth to ruin?" I said, "All those who talk of peace and do the opposite are bringing the earth to ruin." Well, that made them all jump up again. They escorted me out in chains and continued the trial without me. I was sentenced to fifteen years' imprisonment. In 1957, the sentence was reduced to ten years. I served the ten years; some in Torgau and some in Waldheim. I was released from Torgau. The guard who released me said, "If you ever talk about the beliefs of Jehovah's Witnesses again, you'll be sent back to prison. Our arm is very long." I thought to myself, "That long arm will soon be broken off." And sure enough, that's exactly what happened: the long arm was broken off, and when the Communist system collapsed and East Germany was dissolved, they had to disappear. So I was interned in East Germany from September 9, 1950, until September 21, 1960. The Nazis had claimed we were Communists, and the Communists said we were Nazis in disguise.

After my release, I first went to Gera because my mother was living there. I had to look for work, of course. I worked for Bau-Union Gera. Then one day, I resolved to marry Frieda Junge and escape to West Berlin. She had visited me regularly for many years while I was in prison, but she was already in the West, in Eberbach on the river Neckar. So I tried to escape, but the *Volkspolizei* caught me and brought me back again. I then had to

43. Richard Rudolph after his imprisonment in East Germany, 1960/61

report to the police. The police chief said, "You were trying to escape!" I said, "Why would anybody want to escape from here? How do you know [I wanted to escape]? With the prosperity we have here, can someone really want to escape?" And it really was like that. I had no complaints, I had enough to eat, and that was all I needed. I didn't need any music or any chocolate. I wouldn't have escaped for that: that was the truth. What I didn't tell them was that I wanted to go and join my fiancée.

After that, I prepared my escape more thoroughly. I discovered there was a train in Berlin—a direct line, which went from East Berlin to West Berlin without changing trains. My nephew, who was allowed to travel to West Berlin, accompanied me on my escape. In January 1961, we took the bus to Potsdam and then we continued to Berlin, where we saw the train already waiting. We quickly boarded the train and found a large compartment that was completely empty. My nephew sat in the furthest corner, I sat in the other. A whole load of policemen came into the compartment and saw my nephew sitting there. They went up to him. He did a fine job of holding them up so that they didn't even notice me at first. They asked him, "Where do you think you're going?" He replied, "To West Berlin. I want to have a good time." They said, "You can have a good time here." "Come on," he said, "there's nothing to do here." He kept them busy that way until the train stopped at the last station on East German [DDR] side. Then they saw me sitting there and came over. I held my finger over the name so that they only had a glimpse of my ID. Then the train started to pull out, and they had to get off. They could have dragged me out, but they didn't. So we were able to go to West Berlin, and we alighted there.

The first thing we did [there] was look for accommodations in a refugee camp, and then we were questioned. The Americans came to question us, and they didn't have a favorable opinion of Jehovah's Witnesses. They made pointed remarks, but had no option but to grant me refugee status. From there we flew to Hanover because there was thick fog in Frankfurt, and the plane couldn't land there. From Hanover, we went to Eberbach where I lived with Karl Junge's son until my wedding.

Frieda and I married on June 16, 1961. We lived near Heidelberg. Then my wife became very sick. She was restless and kept standing up and then falling down until she was black and blue. I moved into a rest home near Heidelberg with her. We were in the rest home until she died in 1993. I then lived in Burghausen and in Meersburg on Lake Constance, until I came to Husum where I met my present wife, Irmgard.

70. What is your life like today? Do you still often think back to those days?
RUDOLPH: Today, I'm married and live a normal life. The past sometimes comes back to me, in dreams at night, and when I talk as a witness of history.

71. What physical and mental scars do you carry from that time?
RUDOLPH: Above all, I have pains in my hands from hanging on the stake. But that only happens when my hands are hot. Then my hands

sometimes feel very hot and I'm in tremendous pain. When that happens, I can't hold anything and my hands are weak. If I'm holding a spoon, I have to make a great effort to keep ahold of it. When my hands are cold, they don't hurt so much. Everything that was a mental burden has disappeared thanks to what I know from the Bible.

72. Did you have any moral support to help your emotional and social recovery?

RUDOLPH: Through my marriage. With it, a completely normal life began, and I didn't think about that whole Holocaust business so much anymore. We didn't talk about it much, either.

73. Has your view of the world changed since that time?

RUDOLPH: No, my worldview has remained unchanged and has been substantiated.

74. Can you think of anything positive that you have gained from your experiences?

RUDOLPH: Yes, it was positive in the sense that our experiences showed us that we're living in the "time of the end," as the Apostle Paul says: "But mark this: there will be terrible times in the last days." And we have had to suffer the full force of these terrible times.

75. Have you ever been back to visit the concentration camp you were held in, and if so, what were your feelings?

RUDOLPH: I went to Neuengamme several times to visit Dr. Garbe. The camp no longer exists as it was then. Today there are only a few remnants—symbolic references and the like. That gives one less cause to think about the whole business.

76. Are you still in touch with your fellow internees from the concentration camps?

RUDOLPH: Not anymore. I don't know anyone who's still alive.

77. What did you tell your family about your internment in the concentration camp? How did your relatives react to what you told them?

RUDOLPH: In the immediate aftermath, we didn't talk about it at all. When we talk about it now, they are horrified and astounded.

78. Do you find it difficult to talk about those days?

RUDOLPH: I don't find it difficult; I've already held over thirty talks as a witness of history. Of course, those memories return every time. I experienced positive things too, such as SS men who were well disposed toward me. That redresses the balance in many ways.

79. Which moment from those days has remained most firmly etched in your memory?

RUDOLPH: I particularly remember the incident when they came to take me to be executed in Watenstedt, and the SS man Gustav Arndt said, "He's on a transport." After that, I got on very well with that SS man. I wrote to his mother in Hamburg, and the letter ended up in the hands of the police there. They wanted to know why I was interested in the SS man Gustav Arndt. So I wrote to them saying that he had helped me a lot and had practically saved my life. He initially fled to England, and when things had calmed down, he came back to Hamburg and established a chain of grocery stores, producing and selling lunches for workers in various districts. One day, the authorities became interested in him, and he had to report to the police. They asked, "Do you know the prisoner Richard Rudolph?" He said, "No." I mean, it was logical that he didn't remember the name. The police said, "He made a very favorable statement about you; he's one of Jehovah's Witnesses." "Oh, yes, I know him!" Then he came to visit me. Afterward, he lived near Heidelberg, and we visited each other quite a few times.

80. Did you ever see or meet Hitler?

RUDOLPH: No.

81. What was your opinion of Hitler in those days, and what is your opinion of him now?

RUDOLPH: Then, as now, I thought that he was a criminal. No more than that.

82. Hypothetically, if Adolf Hitler were still alive and you could have five minutes alone with him, what would you say or do?

RUDOLPH: Well, what could I say? If he were still alive, I wouldn't have anything to do with him and would ignore him. I wouldn't even speak to him.

83. After the war, did you ever meet any of the people who had tormented you?

RUDOLPH: No. I only met the "guard dogs" [military police] who wanted to arrest me at the end of the war. After liberation, I was near Finsterwalde and briefly worked for one of Jehovah's Witnesses. I mowed the meadow with his sons-in-law, and the two sons-in-law happened to have been among those "guard dogs." One of them later became one of Jehovah's Witnesses.

84. What do you think of the punishments the Nazis received after the war, in the Nuremberg trials, for example?

RUDOLPH: That they got their just deserts, but it's not my place to pass judgment.

85. Have you forgiven your persecutors?

RUDOLPH: Yes, I'm in a position to forgive, and if they've changed their attitude, they can even become my brothers in the faith.

86. What is your opinion of neo-Nazis?

RUDOLPH: They're delusional and have been lied to by former Nazis. They've been lied to about the Nazi era by people who made it out to be glorious.

87. What do you do to explain to people what exactly happened in the Holocaust?

RUDOLPH: In the talks I give from time to time as a witness of history, the subject is thoroughly dealt with.

88. From today's perspective, how can you explain that "normal people" were capable of such atrocities?

RUDOLPH: They allowed themselves to be led astray.

89. What exactly do you feel when you hear that there are still people who claim that the Holocaust never took place?

RUDOLPH: Well, those are stupid people who believe that kind of thing; there's no other way of describing them. Someone who believes that must be crazy.

90. What consequences did the proclamation of the "Nuremberg Laws" on September 15, 1935, have for you?

RUDOLPH: I saw these laws as a sign of terrible times to come. The laws were fashioned in such a way that everything that had to do with an international perspective was derided.

91. What are your personal memories of the "Night of Broken Glass" on November 9/10, 1938?

RUDOLPH: I heard about it in prison in Breslau. I was shocked by the horrendous atrocities that were committed. The Nazis didn't even regard them as atrocities: to them they were a glorious thing. But it was utterly deplorable.

92. What are your personal memories of the beginning of the war in 1939?

RUDOLPH: They're terrible memories, because we were immediately given a medical examination in Sachsenhausen concentration camp with the intention of forcing us to fight in the war. But because we rejected that out of principle, we knew what was in store for us.

93. Did you hear that the National Socialists had decided to implement the "final solution to the Jewish question"—the systematic extermination of Jews in Europe—at the Wannsee Conference on January 20, 1942? If so, when and how?

RUDOLPH: Well, we didn't have any newspapers. We couldn't read anything. We only saw what was going on. We felt the consequences. We didn't know what they had decided to do. It was dreadful. We knew that whenever the Nazis decided on something, they went ahead and did it. So they proceeded to kill masses of Jews in an appalling manner. Not just the men, but women and children, very young children even. That was the most disgusting thing the world has ever seen.

94. When you heard that World War II was over, what feelings did you have?

RUDOLPH: It was a happy circumstance, of course, because it meant freedom had come. However, it was not without a degree of uncertainty, because there was still time for many people to be killed.

95. Do you think that humankind has learned something from the Holocaust?

RUDOLPH: No, humankind hasn't learned anything.

96. Should the atrocities be forgotten and no longer talked about, as some people wish?

RUDOLPH: That's the wrong approach. They must be talked about so that the majority of the people wake up. But they still aren't waking up.

97. What plans do you still have for the future?

RUDOLPH: What plans should I have? My hope rests on the fulfillment of Jehovah's purpose, and then we shall see what the future holds.

98. How would you like to be remembered?

RUDOLPH: (*laughs*) As a sensible, good man. What else?

99. What else would you like to say to us? Which question was not asked?

RUDOLPH: It may be interesting that I had a fiancée before I was sent to prison in 1936. The lady ended our relationship while I was in the concentration camp. Later on, I met her again, and she broke down into floods of tears. But I forgave her because she had no way of knowing whether I would come out again alive.

100. After all you have been through, what advice can you give us young people?

RUDOLPH: I can only advise young people to take the principles of the Bible as their guide, specifically the concepts of love, peace, joy, long-suffering, kindness, goodness, faith, and self-control. Those are the fruits of the spirit. Anyone who brings forth these fruits of the spirit will live in peace with all humankind.

Appendix

Photo acknowledgments

Selective Bibliography

Brown, Daniel Patrick. *The Beautiful Beast: The Life & Crimes of SS-Aufseherin Irma Grese*. Ventura, CA: Golden West Historical Publications (2004).

Burger, Adolf. *The Devil's Workshop: A Memoir of the Nazi Counterfeiting Operation*. Barnsley: Frontline Books (2009).

Jakubowicz, Josef. *Auschwitz Is Also a City: A Survivor of the Shoah Tells His Story*. Nuremberg: Thiemo Graf Verlag (2005).

Liebster, Max. *Crucible of Terror: A Story of Survival Through the Nazi Storm*. New Orleans: Grammaton Press (2003).

Liebster, Simone Arnold. *Facing the Lion: Memoirs of a Young Girl in Nazi Europe*. New Orleans: Grammaton Press (2000).

Mair, Birgit. *Überlebensberichte von Josef Jakubowicz: Eine biografische Analyse*. Nuremberg: Birgit Mair (2006).

Manoschek, Walter (ed.). *Opfer der NS Militärjustiz: Urteilspraxis— Strafvollzug—Entschädigungspolitik in Österreich*. Vienna: Mandelbaum (2003).

—. *Der Fall Rechnitz: Das Massaker an Juden im März 1945*. Vienna: New Academic Press (2009).

Rammerstorfer, Bernhard. *Unbroken Will: The Extraordinary Courage of an Ordinary Man—The Story of Nazi Concentration Camp Survivor Leopold Engleitner, Born 1905*. Herzogsdorf: Bernhard Rammerstorfer (2009).

Zürcher, Franz. *Crusade Against Christianity: Modern-day Persecution of Christians, A Compendium of Documents*. Zurich/New York: Europa-Verlag (1938).

Acknowledgments

For scientific consultation on this project, I thank
Walter Manoschek, political scientist, Department of Government, University of Vienna, Austria

For proofreading and editing the English version and assistance beyond the call of duty, my very special thanks go to the following:
Brian Dorsey, proofreader
Frederic G. Fuss, proofreader and coeditor
Solange Fuss, proofreader and coeditor

I thank the following institutions for their support of this project:
Austrian Service Abroad, Austria
Center for Jewish Studies Shanghai, China
Illinois Holocaust Museum and Education Center, USA
International Tracing Service (ITS) Bad Arolsen, Germany
Jehovah's Witnesses in Germany
Ketani Association, Austria
Kreismuseum Wewelsburg, Germany
Los Angeles Museum of the Holocaust, Los Angeles, USA
Moringen Concentration Camp Memorial, Germany
Neuengamme Concentration Camp Memorial, Germany
Simon Wiesenthal Center, Los Angeles, USA
Sydney Jewish Museum, Australia
The South African Holocaust and Genocide Foundation, South Africa
United States Holocaust Memorial Museum, Washington, D.C., USA
Verein Lila Winkel, Austria
Yad Vashem, Israel

For their help with research relating to the questions, transcriptions, translations, and discussions of the interviews, etc., for this project, I thank the following:
Avril Alba, Australia
Marieta Alonso-Collada, Spain
Olimpia Aventaggiato, Switzerland
Sergio Aventaggiato, Switzerland
Mirta Bacigalupe, Argentina
Marie-Luise Balkenhol, United Kingdom
Natalia Basualdo, Argentina
Daniela Baumann, Namibia
Helmut Baumann, Namibia
Francesca Beligni, Italy

Anja Bell, Austria
Verena Bohr, Paraguay
Steve Boyle, Australia
Daniel Patrick Brown, USA
Robert Buckley, USA
Sonja Büttner, Germany
Hieronymus Cadonau, Switzerland
Sonia Cantu, USA
Ursula Child, England
Judith Cohen, USA
Cezar Constantinescu, Japan
(Austria)
Amanda Cooper, South Africa
Daniel Corondan, Romania
Daniele Cortesi, Italy
Renato Dapporto, Italy
Emmanuelle Declerck, France
Sara DiGrazia, USA
Elisabeth Dorfmayr, Austria
Brian Dorsey, Austria
Esther Dürnberger, Austria
Judith Ehrismann, Switzerland
Karin Fäs, Switzerland
Monika Fechner, Slovakia
Klara Firestone, USA
Eike Fischer, USA
Peter J. Fredlake, USA
Richard Freedman, South Africa
Stefan Fugger, Czech Republic
(Austria)
Marjorie Fulton, USA
Olga Gallego de Trigo, Paraguay
Clemens Gammer, China (Austria)
Alicia Garay, Argentina
Detlef Garbe, Germany
Horst Giesler, Australia
Rosemary Gon, South Africa
Luis Ángel González Ibán, Spain
Steve Green, Australia

Tove Grolitsch, Austria
A. Ferenc Gutai, USA
Beatriz A. Gutai, USA
Beate Hammond, Austria
Waltraud Herrmann, Canada
Christian Höllinger, Austria
Katrin Hofer, Austria
Renaldo Horvath, Austria
Irene Hubmann, Austria
Karl Hubmann, Austria
Juha Huida, Finland
Rosana Infante Villegas, Mexico
Ivana Jiříčková, Czech Republic
Kirsten John-Stucke, Germany
Evelyn Kapahnke, Slovakia
Gerson Kern, Austria
Uwe Klages, Germany
Wera Klages, Germany
Francesco Königsberger, Czech
Republic (Austria)
Tobias Krank, India
Ivelina Krastev, Austria
Hermann Kurahs, Austria
Conrad Lacom, Peru (Austria)
Marnie Landrigan, Australia
Sven Langhammer, Germany
Sabine Langrehr, Thailand
Jürgen Löfflad, France
Andreas Maislinger, Austria
Thomas Malessa, Germany
Rosa Gitta Martl, Austria
Liviana Masetti, Italy
Megan Mathews, USA
Ursula Mertins, Germany
Erwin Meyer, Brazil
Sandra Milakovich, USA
Jaime J. Monllor, USA
Birgitt Morris, Austria
Sabahudin Mujevic, Austria

Tina Nikolar-Lazzaro, Italy
Thomas Pölzl, Austria
Diethilde Porkert, USA
Eric Porkert, USA
Monika Porkert, USA
Dmitry Protsenko, Russian Federation
Jörn Puttkammer, Germany
Beate Rammerstorfer, Austria
Lea Chiara Rammerstorfer, Austria
Manfred Rammerstorfer, Austria
Ottilie Rammerstorfer, Austria
Uschi Regli, Switzerland
Jörg Reitmaier, Austria
Daniel Rozenga, Israel
Irmgard Rudolph, Germany
Stefan Sametinger, Austria
Michaela Schasching, Austria
Klaus Schedlberger, Austria
Harald Schober, Austria
Oliver Scholz, Germany
Fabian Schopper, USA (Austria)
Dietmar Sedlaczek, Germany
Boris Seidl, Austria
Manuel Seidl, Austria
Charlotte Shuck, USA
Markus Spindler, Russian Federation
Lillien Stevens, USA
Fabia Suter, Switzerland
Kelley H. Szany, USA
Bernd Thier, Germany
Gabriele Thier, Germany
Bernhard Trautwein, France (Austria)
Sirpa Turunen-Viljanmaa, Finland
Alexander Volkmann, China
Beatrix Wagner, Italy
Eva Maria Wallner, Austria
Martin Wallner, USA (Austria)
Rose Wanninger, Germany
Tamara Wassner, Israel

Matthew Webster, Canada
Martin Windischhofer, Austria
Max Wörnhard, Switzerland
Johannes Wrobel, Germany
Xu Xin, China
Hazima Zilic, Austria
Ulrike Zuschrott, Iran

Index

The Book "Unbroken Will"

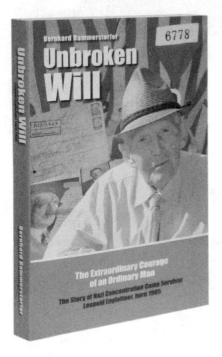

While Leopold Engleitner has been a contemporary of the outstanding watershed events of the twentieth century, from the sinking of the *Titanic* and World War I to the flight of space shuttles and the boon of the information age, there is more to his life than merely being an onlooker. He personally participated in events of historic moral and ethical importance, the significance of which draws us into his story.

This ordinary farmhand found the extraordinary courage to stand up for his conscience and refuse to serve in Hitler's army. He fearlessly rejected Nazism and did not even use the Nazi greeting "Heil Hitler!"

Suffering unspeakable cruelty in three concentration camps, he grew so thin that he weighed less than sixty-two pounds. Nothing and no one could break his will. Yet he could easily have had his freedom: all he had to do was sign a paper wherein he would have renounced his religious convictions as one of Jehovah's Witnesses. This he refused. It is remarkable that he never lost his optimism; in one concentration camp, he even bought a suitcase for the journey home, which seemed impossible he would ever make.

Despite constant rejection, Engleitner's unshakable faith in God helped him lead a full and happy life while never losing his zest for life. But the unexpected turnaround in his life was achieved thanks to an extraordinary friendship. As a result, though already far advanced in years, he has so far traveled over ninety-five thousand miles across Europe and the USA as an inspiring and convincing witness of history to ensure the past is not forgotten, and he has become a model of tolerance and peace for future generations.

Letters written by Engleitner during his internment and believed lost for nearly sixty years, original minutes of police and court proceedings, and reports from the concentration camps are combined with clear and detailed recollections of traumatic childhood incidents from one hundred years ago to constitute an impressive firsthand history. A brief biography of the German conscientious objector Joachim Escher provides further background information about those days.

"This book is a milestone in recording the horrors of National Socialism. It is essential reading, and I am delighted that the translation has already received such keen attention in the United States."
   —Dr. Heinz Fischer, president of the Federal Republic of Austria

"From a scientific point of view, this book is one of the most reliable biographies of a victim of National Socialism."
   —Prof. Walter Manoschek, political scientist, University of Vienna

354 pages, 158 illustrations

For further information and details of how to place orders:
www.rammerstorfer.cc or www.unbrokenwill.com

DVD "Unbroken Will"

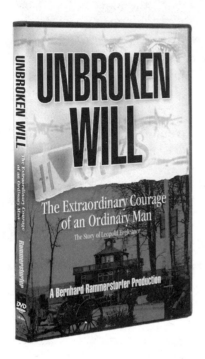

About the main feature:

As one of the world's oldest concentration camp survivors, the Austrian Leopold Engleitner, born 1905, returns to the places where it all happened and talks about his exciting life. This touching and impressive documentary recounts the experiences of this humble man, who, because he was a Bible Student (one of Jehovah's Witnesses) and objected to military service, had to endure the brutal machinery of the Hitler regime in three concentration camps. This film includes original film material from the years 1896 to 1945.

The DVD contains not only the full documentary (61 minutes) and an abridged version of it (27 minutes) but also five films (between 8 and 15 minutes each) showing events from 1999–2004 relating to Engleitner's awareness-raising as a survivor of Nazi persecution. It also features a quiz containing 20 questions and material for schools.

Written, produced, and directed by Bernhard Rammerstorfer
Total running time: 148 minutes
Languages and subtitles: English, German, Italian
Versions of the DVD are also available in German, Italian, and Spanish.
For full details, go to **www.rammerstorfer.cc**

Bonus materials include films of special events from Engleitner's lecture activities.

International awards and notable events:
—"Winner of the Golden Bear" at the 31st Festival of Nations from over 500 films from 37 countries and all continents, Ebensee, Austria.
—English version of *Unbroken Will* premiered at the Laemmle Theatre in Santa Monica, Los Angeles County, California, USA

For further information and details of how to place orders:
www.rammerstorfer.cc or www.unbrokenwill.com

DVD "UNBROKEN WILL Captivates the United States" Film of Leopold Engleitner's 2004 USA Tour

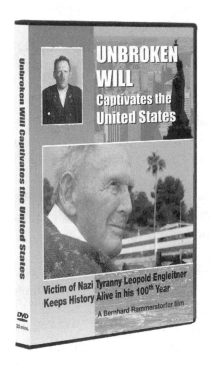

In his 100th year, the Austrian Leopold Engleitner embarks on an exciting journey that takes him clear across the United States. As one of the world's oldest concentration camp survivors, he captivates audiences in Washington, D.C., New York, and Los Angeles with his "unbroken will."

Leopold Engleitner, born 1905, refused to serve in the Nazi army because of his Bible-trained conscience as one of Jehovah's Witnesses and because of his belief in freedom, decency, and humanity. He was persecuted as a conscientious objector and tortured in three concentration camps. Through his courageous advocacy of peace and justice, this ordinary man is an outstanding example of adherence to one's conscience. Engleitner provides impressive proof that age is no barrier to reaching remarkable goals. And on Malibu beach, a long-held dream finally comes true.

Written, produced, and directed by Bernhard Rammerstorfer
Total running time: 33 minutes
Languages: English, German, Italian, Spanish

**For further information and details of how to place orders:
www.rammerstorfer.cc or www.unbrokenwill.com**

DVD "Unbroken Will USA Tour"
Film of Leopold Engleitner's 2006 USA Tour

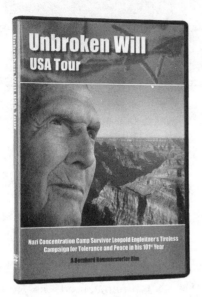

In 1945, Leopold Engleitner (born 1905), survivor of the Buchenwald, Niederhagen, and Ravensbrück concentration camps, was on the run from the Nazis. As one of Jehovah's Witnesses, his conscience would not allow him to serve in Hitler's army. Much later, Engleitner, already an old man and one of the world's oldest concentration camp survivors, began an amazing new career—giving presentations as an eyewitness who campaigns against forgetting the lessons of history.

In 2006, in his 101st year, he undertook a remarkable tour of lectures that took him clear across the United States. At universities and Holocaust memorial sites in Washington, D.C., New York, Chicago, San Francisco, and Los Angeles, he emphasized the vital importance of tolerance and humanity to ensuring peace. He encouraged his listeners to base their lives on just principles. And in Sequoia and Grand Canyon National Parks, dreams he had had since his youth came true.

Written, produced, and directed by Bernhard Rammerstorfer
Narrated by Frederic G. Fuss
Total running time: 50 minutes
Languages: English, German

For further information and details of how to place orders:
www.rammerstorfer.cc or www.unbrokenwill.com

DVD "LADDER in the LIONS' DEN"
Award Winning Documentary

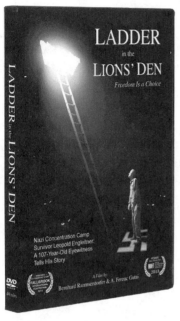

Why would a man faced with death in three Nazi concentration camps not sign a document granting him his freedom? This is the story of 107-year-old Leopold Engleitner. Given the choice between life and death, he found the courage to stand by his conscience. His refusal to join Hitler's army and to give the "Heil Hitler!" salute put him and thousands of other Jehovah's Witnesses in the crosshairs of the Third Reich.

As if receiving a "Ladder in the Lions' Den," he was given a way out. In exchange for his freedom, he was handed a document renouncing his faith and swearing allegiance to Hitler. He refused. After surviving Buchenwald, Niederhagen, and Ravensbrück concentration camps, he weighed less than sixty-two pounds, but his will remained unbroken.

Spotlighted by the perspective of others, such as Renée Firestone, a Jewish Auschwitz survivor, and Gottlieb Bernhardt (former SS bodyguard of Hitler), who himself faced a pivotal crisis of conscience, Leopold's story resonates with the power of conviction and hope.

If not for a chance meeting with Bernhard Rammerstorfer, Leopold would have disappeared into the shadowed subtext of history. Together, they traveled around the world promoting peace and tolerance. Their lectures took them to UCLA, Stanford, Harvard, Columbia, and Georgetown universities, the United States Holocaust Memorial Museum in Washington, D.C., the Los Angeles Museum of the Holocaust, and the Simon Wiesenthal Center, as well as other noted institutions throughout the United States, Europe, and the Russian Federation.

International awards and notable events:
— Winner: Best Documentary Short at the 2013 Fallbrook International Film Festival, Fallbrook, California, USA
— Winner: Best Short Documentary at the 2013 Rincón International Film Festival, Rincón, Puerto Rico, USA
— English version of Ladder in the Lions' Den premiered in 2012 at the Laemmle Theater in Encino, Los Angeles County, California, USA

Producer: Bernhard Rammerstorfer
Co-Producer: A. Ferenc Gutai
Directors: Bernhard Rammerstorfer and A. Ferenc Gutai
Script: Bernhard Rammerstorfer and A. Ferenc Gutai
Based on the book *Unbroken Will* by Bernhard Rammerstorfer
Narrator: Frederic G. Fuss
Voice of Leopold Engleitner: Gordon Piedesack
Total running time: 40 minutes
Languages: English, German

For further information and details of how to place orders: www.rammerstorfer.cc or www.unbrokenwill.com

DVD to Accompany the Book
"Taking the Stand: We Have More to Say"

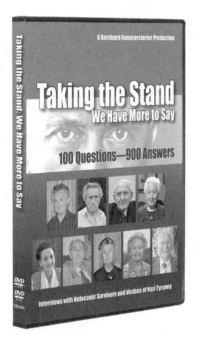

Nine Holocaust survivors and victims of Nazi tyranny have "taken the stand" to give their testimony as a legacy for future generations. They are from five different countries and were persecuted for reasons of ethnicity, politics/ideology, or religion. All in all, they were interned in fifty-four camps or institutions.

The catalog of questions, unique in the world, consists of 100 questions from 61 schools and universities in 30 countries on 6 continents. Those whose voices are heard in the film interviews range from an average housewife and an unskilled laborer to a fashion designer, from those who have been relatively silent to active Holocaust teachers and to survivors who have already been widely featured in the media and whose life stories have even been the subject of Oscar-winning films. Two of them have already passed their 100th birthdays.

The DVD contains not only a short film biography of each of the nine survivors, but also a selection of their most interesting answers lasting approximately 10-20 minutes each. Also included is material for educational projects and exercises about the Holocaust and the films. This makes the DVD eminently suitable for use in schools.

"Bernhard Rammerstorfer meticulously checked the historical accuracy of the interviewees' statements, discussed the answers several times with those concerned, and made additions where necessary."
—Prof. Walter Manoschek, political scientist, University of Vienna

Written, produced, and directed by Bernhard Rammerstorfer
Narrated by Frederic G. Fuss
Total running time: 128 minutes
Languages: English, German

For further information and details of how to place orders:
www.rammerstorfer.cc or www.TakingTheStand.net